ISSEI

Issei

JAPANESE IMMIGRANTS IN HAWAII

Yukiko Kimura

University of Hawaii Press · HONOLULU

97 96 95 94 93 92   5 4 3 2 1

Library of Congress Cataloging-in-Publication Data

Kimura, Yukiko, 1903–
    Issei : Japanese immigrants in Hawaii.

    Bibliography: p.
    Includes index.
    1. Japanese Americans—Hawaii—History. 2. Hawaii—
Emigration and immigration—History. I. Title.
DU624.7.J3K56   1988   996.9'004956   88–20623
ISBN 0–8248–1029–5

ISBN 0–8248–1481–9 (pbk)

Dedicated to

Robert L. Shivers, Chief of Hawaii Office of FBI

Lt. General Delos C. Emmons, Military Governor of Hawaii

Major General Kendall J. Fielder, Chief of Military Intelligence

Lt. Colonel Frank O. Blake, Military Intelligence

Oren E. Long, Superintendent of the Department of Public Instruction

Hung Wai Ching of the Morale Committee of Military Government

They kept Hawaii's interracial harmony intact during the war with Japan.

Contents

Acknowledgments

PROFESSOR Emeritus Yukuo Uyehara, former chairman of the Department of Asian Languages of the University of Hawaii, read the original manuscript. He was contemporary with many of the events described in this book. Dr. John J. Stephan, author and professor of modern Japanese history at the University of Hawaii, critically reviewed the manuscript. Dr. Albert H. Miyasato, former superintendent of Hawaii's public school system; former administrative assistant to Governor George Ariyoshi; educational advisor in Saudi Arabia for three and one-half years until late 1984, establishing public school system from grade school to high school; critically reviewed and appraised the manuscript.

Miss Agnes C. Conrad, State Archivist, and her staff at Public Archives, and the University of Hawaii librarians, especially in the Asian Collection and the Hawaiian-Pacific Collection, gave patient and expert help.

Mrs. Elizabeth Ann Larsen, librarian (retired in 1977), Mission House Museum, gave permission to copy and print the full text of the petition dated May 27, 1913, sent to President Woodrow Wilson, requesting a change in naturalization law of the United States, and the full text of Dr. Doremus Scudder's sermon on "Our Nation's Duty to Japan" delivered at Central Union Church on May 18, 1913. The petition was printed on the cover of the *Friend* of June, 1913, in which the sermon was printed.

The late Mr. Oren E. Long, then the Superintendent of the Department of Public Instruction, gave permission to quote his letter as well as the letter by the late Dr. Arthur L. Dean, then Chairman of Commissioners of Public Instruction, to All Principals and Teachers, giving them guidelines for their responsibilities during World War II.

Mr. Mitsuyuki Kido, then the executive secretary of Emergency

Service Committee, gave permission to quote various parts of *Cooperation of Racial Groups in Hawaii During the War* by Robert L. Shivers, pre-war and wartime Chief of Hawaii's Office of FBI, published by Emergency Service Committee in 1946, and *Report of the Emergency Service Committee* published in 1944.

Mr. Buck Buchwach, Executive Editor of *The Honolulu Advertiser,* gave permission to quote the full text of the statement by then Hawaii's delegate to Congress, Samuel W. King, published on March 23, 1941. Mr. John E. Simonds, Executive Editor of *Honolulu Star-Bulletin,* gave permission to quote the following articles, namely, the first address to the people of Hawaii by Lt. General Delos C. Emmons, published on December 22, 1941; Russ and Peg Apple's "Tales of Old Hawaii," published on May 15, 1977; Helen Oyakawa's "Coffee Picking Was Lots of Work," published on May 29, 1977; Ted T. Tsukiyama's "Varsity Victory Volunteers, Pearl Harbor Tragedy and Triumph," published on December 7, 1978.

University of Hawaii Press gave permission to quote the full text of Lt. General Delos C. Emmons' announcement for recruiting Nisei volunteers for combat in the European theater, printed in Gwenfread Allen's *Hawaii War Years: 1941–1945.*

The late Mr. Yasutarō Sōga gave permission to use freely the content of his book *Gojūnen no Hawaii Kaiko* (My memoir of fifty years in Hawaii).

The family of the late Mr. Matsujiro Otani gave the gift of his *Waga Hito to Narishi Ashiato: Hachijunen No Kaiko* (My memoir of the 80 years of my footsteps) and permission to use its contents.

The late Mr. Seinosuke Tsukiyama gave practical assistance in the author's study of the postwar social disorganization among the Issei, particularly by attending with the author the evening mass meetings of the Katta-gumi (Japan-Won-the-War-Group) in the Palama Area; his widow, Mrs. Yoshiko Tsukiyama, furnished the author with biographical materials of the Isseis, especially *Ko Okazaki Nihei-Oh Tsuito Kinenshi* (The memorial booklet honoring the late venerable Nihei Okazaki), an important document of pineapple enterprise among the Japanese.

Mr. Kiyoshi Ōkubo of the *Hilo Times* gave a gift of his *Hawaii-to Nihonjin Iminshi* (A history of Japanese immigrants on the Island of Hawaii).

The late Mr. Jinshichi Tokairin, the founder of Fukushima Kenjin-kai, gave gifts of Kanji Takahashi's *Fukushima Iminshi: Hawaii Kikansha no Maki* (A history of overseas emigration of Fukushimans: vol. on returned former emigrants to Hawaii) and Yakichi Watanabe's *Hawaii Zaiju Fukushima-Kenjin Ryakureki Shashincho* (The album of pictures and personal records of Fukushimans in Hawaii).

Mr. Toshio Tanji, the last Issei president of Fukushima Kenjin-kai in Honolulu, gave detailed information on Fukushimans, and two former Issei leaders made *Fukushima Isseiki* (The Century of Fukushima) available to the author.

The late Mr. Charlie S. offered his frank description of his reaction to the treatment accorded to Fukushimans on the plantations and gave his permission to quote his description of his unconventional radio show of the postwar years.

The late Dr. James Tengan and Mr. Seiyu Higa gave the gifts of *Raifu Gojunen Kinen Hawaii Okinawa Kenjin Shashincho* (The album of pictures of the Okinawans in commemoration of the 50th anniversary of the immigration of the Okinawans in Hawaii) edited by Takenobu Higa, and *Soritsu Sanjushunen Kinen Kaiho, Oahu Gushikawa Sonjin-kai* (Oahu Gushikawa Village Club's report commemorating its 30th anniversary), as well as generous information on Okinawans in Hawaii. The others who contributed to the author's study of the experiences of the Okinawans in Hawaii are: the late Dr. Shimpuku Gima, the first president of the United Okinawan Association; the late Mr. Ushisuke Taira; Mr. Ryokin Toyohira, editor of *Nippu Jiji* since 1922 and Chief Editor of *Hawaii Times* since 1945 until his retirement in 1974; Mr. Sadao Asato, Mr. Choki Kanetake, Mrs. Chiyeko Takushi, Mrs. Tsuruko Ohye, Mr. Shinsuke Nakamine, and Mr. Seiyei Wakukawa, former Chief Editor of *Hawaii Times* and author; Mr. Akira Sakima, former State House Representative; Mr. Steven Chinen; Mr. Takenobu Higa, author and journalist while on Hawaii; Mr. Thomas Taro Higa, author and a veteran of World War II; and Dr. Thomas H. Ige, Professor Emeritus of Business Economics of the University of Hawaii; Rev. Chiro Yosemori, Rev. Jikai Yamasato, and Rev. Chikai Yosemori of Jikoen.

On the other islands, the late Dr. Zenko Matayoshi gave his generous help, arranged meetings and interviews in Hilo and vicinity and introduced leaders and residents of the Okinawan communities in various areas of Hawaii; Mr. and Mrs. Shinyu

Gima and Mrs. Kame Nakamura of Maui enabled the author to participate in various activities in the Okinawan community; the leaders and members of the Okinawan communities on Kauai and residents of Lanai and Molokai were generous in their cooperation.

Bishop Yoshiaki Fujitani of Honpa Hongwanji Mission made available *Choshoin Ibunshu* (Collection of Writings of Choshoin, the late Bishop Yemyo Imamura).

Others who offered assistance include Mr. Rinji Hokkai Maeyama, a veteran journalist and author, who gave his personal observation and experiences of the early years; the late Dr. Tomizo Katsunuma, U.S. Immigration inspector from 1900 to 1924, gave information on the Issei, including picture brides; the late Mrs. Tokue Nishi, a staff member of International Institute; Mr. Yakichi Nakamura of Nakamura Hotel and Travel Agency gave information on Hiroshima dialect; the leaders of various Kenjin-kais (Prefectural Associations) gave their informations on their respective groups; and many others who contributed as interviewees and informants.

For the shortcomings, the author alone is responsible.

Introduction

THIS book is about the experiences of Japanese immigrants in Hawaii from 1885 through 1970. The Issei, the first generation, with whom this book is primarily concerned, all came to Hawaii before July 1, 1924, when the Japanese Exclusion Act became effective. The account of Issei contained herein is intended to be descriptive, self-explanatory, and readable for anyone interested in human nature and the social-historical circumstances that influenced the behavior of the immigrants both collectively and individually.

The volume is divided into four parts. Part I deals with the general background of the Japanese immigrants as contract laborers in the early years. With the annexation of Hawaii to the United States in 1898 and the enactment of the Organic Act by Congress in 1900, Hawaii's contract-labor immigration became invalid. This caused mass migration of Japanese plantation workers to the West Coast, resulting in increased anti-Japanese agitation. Finally, the Executive Order of 1907 prohibited migration of Japanese immigrants to the United States mainland by way of Hawaii, Mexico, and Canada.

From 1908 to June 30, 1924, the immigration of Japanese was restricted to close kin, which included "picture brides." With the Japanese Exclusion Act in 1924, however, Japanese immigration to the United States and its territories was stopped completely, except for nonquota immigrants.

As there were individual differences, there were also collective differences among the Japanese immigrants. Especially divisive were the provincial customs and dialects that had developed through the centuries of feudalism in Japan. When the immigrants came to Hawaii they met for the first time their fellow Japanese from the different regions of Japan. Because of difficulty in communicating and the strangeness of each others' customs, newly arrived prefectural groups met with open hostility from the old-timers of large prefectural groups.

Part II deals with the major occupations of the Issei. Two large-scale plantation strikes on Oahu, one in 1909 led by non-laborer intellectuals and one in 1920 organized and led by plantation workers themselves, provide interesting comparisons. The Japanese were also active in other fields, competing with other ethnic groups, but they monopolized the fishery industry. Commercial activities among the Japanese began primarily to serve the plantation laborers and their families. Later, when the number of city-dwellers increased, ingenious former plantation workers began small-scale commercial activities, while merchants from Japan engaged in large-scale importing and selling activities. Physicians comprised an important segment of the professional Issei. During the Hawaiian monarchy, many of them came to Hawaii as employees of the Immigration Bureau to serve as health inspectors-interpretors, some on the plantations.

Part III discusses the stabilizing influences on the Japanese community, such as family, religion, language schools, and other institutions and organizations.

Part IV looks at the position of the Issei in the two world wars. In World War I, Issei men and women participated in the American war effort fully and enthusiastically, and Issei men of military age were registered and many served in the U.S. Army. World War II, by contrast, threw the Issei into unprecedented agony and shame. They were eventually able to become full participants in the U.S. war efforts through the leadership of wartime policy makers with surpassing wisdom and absolute faith in American democracy. Their sons served with distinction in the U.S. Army in combat in Europe and in intelligence in the Pacific.

Definition of Terms

Issei, the first generation, are those Japanese immigrants who came to Hawaii before July 1, 1924. They were ineligible for naturalization, hence their legal status was one of alien. The terms *Issei, alien,* and *Japanese immigrant* are used synonymously.

Nisei, the second generation, are the Hawaii-born children of the Issei. They are American citizens by virtue of their birthright. The term *AJA,* an abbreviation of "American of Japanese ancestry," is used principally for those who served in the United States Armed Forces during World War II.

Kibei, "returned to America," are those Nisei who were sent to Japan in infancy or young childhood and spent their formative years there, receiving an education and being exposed to the social and cultural influences to which the people of Japan were subjected.

Although this book is about the Issei, the Nisei are included whenever they became crucial to the Issei's position and to their sense of security, such as during World War II.

Data Gathering

My earliest observations and contact with the Issei of Hawaii began in the years 1920–1923 in Yokohama, when, as a college student, I accompanied a secretary in charge of the YWCA's Emigration Department to the docks to see off and give advice to the young women, the so-called picture brides, who were sailing for Hawaii to marry their picture bridegrooms.

In 1930, I went to Hawaii as a delegate from Japan to attend the second Pan Pacific Women's Conference, sponsored by the Pan Pacific Women's Association of Hawaii, an international meeting of women representing the countries of the Pacific area. From mid-August to mid-October of that year, I visited plantation communities to observe the conditions of the Japanese immigrants. On Hawaii, my itinerary, carefully prepared by Mr. Kango Kawasaki, a lawyer and community leader, included overnight stays in the homes of plantation workers and meetings with them, meetings and discussions with language-school teachers, and a visit to the Rev. Shiro Sokabe's home for children of plantation workers in Honomuu. On Oahu, in addition to plantation communities, I visited other institutions that were involved with the immigrants' lives and met with several pioneer Nisei. My work was greatly facilitated by the help of people like Umematsu Watada of the Nuuanu YMCA; Professor Tasuku Harada of the University of Hawaii; Yasutarō Sōga, editor and publisher of the *Nippu Jiji;*

Mrs. Tsuru Kishimoto, the Japanese secretary of the Honolulu YWCA's International Institute; and Mrs. George Castle, then president of the Honolulu YWCA, who made my stay and study of the conditions of the Japanese immigrants possible.

Most of the data were gathered, however, after February 1938, when I joined the staff of the International Institute of the Honolulu YWCA to be in charge of the work among the Japanese, both the Issei and Nisei. In addition, I was assigned to make a series of studies of the problematic aspects of the Japanese community. The first was of Japanese barbershops and their barber-girls. Since there was no precedent for using women as barbers in Japan or in Hawaii, the larger community regarded this unconventional practice with disapproval. There were also complaints that the Japanese barbershops were undercutting the prevailing prices. Another study was of Japanese dressmakers, who drew similar criticism; the study revealed that they were using dressmaking students and could thus lower their prices. Through such studies and my continuous association with individuals and families as well as my participant observation both in the Japanese community and the larger community before, during, and after World War II, I gained intimate knowledge and understanding of the Japanese in Hawaii.

Other Sources of Data

Since this book concentrates on the Issei's experience as they saw it and from their own points of view, their own stories, including memoirs, are abundantly utilized. I also consulted works on Japanese immigrants, especially for historical data and for the early years of immigration, such as *The Japanese in Hawaii* and *The Peoples of Hawaii,* by Romanzo Adams, and *The Earliest Japanese Labor Immigration to Hawaii,* by Ralph S. Kuykendall, as well as his *Hawaiian Kingdom* (vols. 1–3). Books by Japanese authors include Ryūkichi Kihara's *Hawaii Nihonjinshi* (A history of Hawaii's Japanese), which is a comprehensive record of historical events among the Japanese immigrants, painstakingly researched; Keihō Yasutarō Sōga's *Gojūnen no Hawaii Kaiko* (My memoir of fifty years in Hawaii), recounting his personal experiences and observations from the time of his arrival in the last years of the nineteenth century, when he worked as a plantation store manager, through World War II, when he was the editor and publisher of vernacular newspapers; and *Ishoku no Hana Hiraku* (Blossoming of transplanted trees) and *Imin Hyakunen no Nenrin* (Annual rings of one hundred years of immigration), both by Kenpū Zenichi Kawazoe, an editor of *Nippu Jiji,* giving anecdotes about the Issei and the Japanese community. Other sources are given in the Bibliography.

Lastly, I have relied on my own extensive interviews and observations conducted over the past fifty years.

Part I
The Formation and Stabilization of the Issei Community

1

The Early Years of Japanese Immigration to Hawaii

THE first labor immigrants who came to work on the sugar plantations in Hawaii were recruited in the vicinity of Yedo (Tokyo) and Yokohama by a businessman, Eugene M. Van Reed, in the turbulent last years of the Tokugawa regime. One hundred forty-eight individuals, all nonfarmers, including six women and two teenagers, arrived in Hawaii in 1868, the first year of the Meiji Era of the Imperial government. Hence, they were called "Gannen Mono" (the People of the First Year). With no experience in hard plantation labor, which sometimes involved brutal treatment by mounted field overseers called *luna,* they complained to the Japanese government. Two officials, Kagemori Uyeno and his associate, were sent to Hawaii to investigate the situation. Soon after their departure, forty immigrants, including three women, one infant, and two shipwrecked men who had been in Hawaii since 1865, returned to Japan. When the three years of their contract expired in 1871, thirteen men returned to Japan while the remaining ninety individuals settled down in Hawaii. After this, there was no organized immigration of the Japanese for seventeen years. At the request of the Japanese government, United States Minister to Hawaii Henry A. Peirce and British Commissioner James H. Wodehouse looked after the interests of the Japanese immigrants. [1]

Despite the repeated requests for further Japanese immigration to Hawaii by the Hawaiian government, represented by such distinguished figures as King Kalakaua, who visited Japan in 1881 at the beginning of his celebrated world tour, and John Makini Kapena, sent to Japan in 1882 as Special Ambassador to negotiate Japanese immigration to Hawaii, the Japanese government continued to be reluctant about emigration of its subjects to Hawaii. However, by the time Colonel Curtis P. Iaukea went to Japan as

3

Special Envoy from Hawaii's foreign minister, Walter Murray Gibson, in December 1883, the Japanese government had become more disposed to consider the subject. After successful negotiations, Iaukea came back to Hawaii with Robert W. Irwin, Hawaiian consul in Tokyo, to prepare for resumption of Japanese immigration. As part of the preparations, they interviewed two Gannen Mono, who described their problems as the poor living conditions, the lack of understanding on the part of overseers and employers, the inadequate subsistence pay they received, and their inferior status compared to that of other ethnic groups.[2]

Contract Labor

The terms of the contract that resulted stipulated that the Hawaiian government was to pay the steerage passage of the laborers and their wives and children from Yokohama to Honolulu. During the course of the three-year contract they were to work twenty-six days a month and ten hours a day at field labor or twelve hours a day in the sugar mills. The hours of work were to include travel time from a designated point to the work site. The wages were $9 a month for males and $6 for females in addition to a subsistence allowance of $6 a month for males and $4 for women. Medical care, living quarters, and firewood for cooking were to be furnished free of charge. The Japanese government required the emigrants to save 25 percent of their gross wages, later reduced to 15 percent. The contract was to be signed by the emigrants and Robert W. Irwin prior to departure from Japan and confirmed by Charles T. Gulick, the president of the Board of Immigration, upon their arrival in Honolulu.[3]

The Japanese government approved the draft of the contract that Consul Irwin presented and gave him full cooperation through the prefectural governments and local offices of towns and villages, explaining the terms of the contract, application procedures, and conditions in Hawaii. The Japanese government made a special effort to recruit hardy farmers in the hardest-pressed, overpopulated rural areas of Hiroshima and Yamaguchi prefectures.[4] Instructions given to the contract emigrants by the governors of their respective prefectures emphasized working faithfully, saving, and returning home with money. The following excerpts from the official instructions of Miki Nabeshima, governor of Hiroshima Prefecture, issued on October 3, 1893, are typical of such documents:

> You, "Dekasegi emigrants," who are now leaving your most beloved parents, wives, and children behind, are going to cross 3,000 miles of ocean to that far-away foreign country with the sole purpose of earning and saving money in order to return home some day to live comfortably.
>
> If you should neglect your work and fail to observe the laws of the host country or, because of your greed, if you should join the ruffians to engage in bad activities, the money you will have earned will be gone right away, leaving you starving and with no prospect of salvation. It will be too late for regret after that happens. Therefore, I will mention the most important guidelines for you that you must remember day and night in order to be sure to return home with your wealth.
>
> Farewell, each of you. Take care of your health.
>
> 1. Remember that you are the subjects of the Japanese empire, and never disgrace your homeland with shameful acts.
>
> 2. In relation to your employer, always observe the contract, serve him faithfully, and never engage in thoughtless acts.
>
> 3. Think of your coworkers as your parents and siblings, help each other, and never quarrel with one another.
>
> 4. Since gambling is prohibited in Hawaii, never gamble.
>
> 5. Because drinking [alcoholic beverages] makes your mind loose, causes you to neglect your work, and leads you to delinquent acts, exercise self-control and never drink.
>
> 6. Always handle your money carefully, and in spending it or sending remittances home, consult immigration inspectors and follow their instructions. Never handle money carelessly.[5]

The first group of government-sponsored contract labor immigrants was made up of 945 individuals from the following prefectures: 420 from Yamaguchi; 222 from Hiroshima; 214 from Kanagawa; 37 from Okayama; 22 from Wakayama; 13 from Mie; 11 from Shizuoka; 5 from Shiga; and 1 from Miyagi. They sailed from Yokohama aboard the *City of Tokio* on January 20, 1885, arriving at Honolulu on February 8. They were accompanied by Consul Irwin and his wife; Jiro Nakamura, the first Japanese consul in Hawaii, and his wife; Viscount Tadafuji Torii, consular secretary; and Joji Nakayama who became chief inspector of the Japanese section of Hawaii's Bureau of Immigration.[6] At their arrival

King Kalakaua himself welcomed them, and the immigrants had the honor of presenting sumo and fencing matches before the king and the dignitaries of the kingdom.[7]

Contrary to their expectations, however, their living quarters were substandard and their working conditions subjected them to many indignities at the hands of ruthless overseers. Hardly a month had passed when a small-scale work stoppage occurred on one of the numerous plantations, beginning on Maui, where a Japanese laborer was brutally beaten. When the manager did not punish the luna who did the beating, the Japanese laborers went on strike. The strikers were judged guilty of disturbing the peace, however, and were fined $5 each plus $1 court charges.[8] The Japanese government dispatched Special Commissioner Katsunosuke Inouye to investigate the situation. He sailed aboard the S.S. *Yamashiro Maru,* which was bringing the second group of 983 contract immigrants from nine prefectures: 390 from Hiroshima; 270 from Kumamoto; 149 from Fukuoka; 74 from Shiga; 37 from Niigata; 33 from Wakayama; 12 from Kanagawa; 10 from Gunma; and 8 from Chiba. They arrived on June 17 of the same year.[9]

In order to protect the welfare and rights of the immigrants, the following points were stressed in the agreement reached by Inouye and Foreign Minister Gibson: the Hawaiian government must (1) assume guardianship of the Japanese immigrants; (2) increase the number of interpreters in order to reduce misunderstanding; (3) employ Japanese physicians for better medical services; (4) safeguard immigrants from acts of violence by overseers; and (5) Chief Inspector Nakayama must undertake all investigation and disposal of Japanese cases.[10] Subsequently, the striking Japanese laborers at Paia, Maui, were transferred to Paahau on Hawaii, and a third of those at Hamakuapoko Plantation, also on Maui, which also had a strike, decided to leave while the rest chose to remain in view of the decision of the manager to raise their wages and improve medical service and working conditions. Also, the Hawaiian government increased the number of Japanese inspector-interpreters and physicians.[11]

In spite of all such official remedial measures on the part of the Hawaiian government, the customary practices on the plantations did not change. Suffering indignities daily, the immigrants became increasingly rebellious. Many began to indulge in heavy drinking, gambling, and licentiousness, disregarding completely the regular savings and remittances that were required by the Japanese government. Consul Nakamura was recalled because of his inability to control the degeneration of the immigrants. To replace him, the Japanese government appointed one of its most brilliant diplomats, Consul General Tarō Andō, serving in Shanghai, by upgrading the consular status in Hawaii and making him a diplomatic minister. He arrived in Hawaii in February 1886. He toured the plantations, urging the immigrants to stop their wild living, but they paid no attention to him. Only with the dedicated cooperation of Rev. Kanichi Miyama of the Methodist Conference of San Francisco were orderly life and self-respect among the plantation laborers restored. Subsequently, the Japanese Mutual Aid Association and the Temperance Society, which contributed to the welfare of the Japanese immigrants, were founded through the joint efforts of Miyama and Andō.[12]

During the period of the Republic of Hawaii after the overthrow of the Hawaiian monarchy in 1893 and a year of a provisional government, the conditions on the sugar plantations changed little and the luna-labor troubles continued. *Hole-hole Bushi* (Songs of Cane Leaves), with its wailing tune, originally from the coastal region of Yamaguchi and Hiroshima prefectures or a rural area of Kumamoto Prefecture, had been sung among the contract laborers since the early years. Its verses were spontaneous expressions of their feelings about their daily experiences and reflected the harshness of their situation: "The luna found me lying in the field with a high fever and he beat me up [as a slacker]"; or "I woke up just when I was [in a dream] beating up the luna who was yelling at me"; or "Neither earthquake nor thunderstorm do I dread, but just to hear the luna's voice makes me shudder." To stay away from this kind of treatment some immigrants made themselves sick by drinking shoyu sauce. They were sent to work nevertheless. Sometimes, however, those who were really ill were forced to work and died as a result.[13] Yasutarō Sōga, at the time the manager of a plantation store on Oahu, described such a case:

> In those days [1896] one of my responsibilities was to be at the plantation office by 4:30 every morning to serve as an interpreter for the doctor and laborers. The laborers who didn't feel well and wanted to

stay away from work were examined by the doctor to determine whether they were sick enough to be excused from work. There were some who made themselves sick with a fast heartbeat by drinking shoyu sauce. At that time many new immigrants were plagued with high fever of unknown cause and every day two or three died in each camp [living quarters]. The plantation authorities seemed unconcerned about it, however. One day a laborer from Yamaguchi Prefecture who really had a high fever was forced to go to the field despite a strong protest from me as well as from the man himself. He died while working. That night several hundred Japanese went to the manager's house to protest such irresponsible treatment of the sick man. Hearing about the commotion, I rushed to the scene. It was such inhumane treatment that caused the death that I couldn't help reporting the incident to *Hawaii Shinpo,* which published the news.[14]

The contract laborers were tied to the plantations until the expiration of their three-year contracts. Many deserted the plantations, however, seeking freedom elsewhere. If they were caught by plantation police, they were flogged and imprisoned. Sōga recalled such an incident:

Watanabe was an amateur wrestler and a well-built young man. Hating to be treated like a horse and bull on the plantation, he tried to run away several times, but each time he was captured and imprisoned. One day he ran away and was captured again. This time he was put in a room of the plantation office, with all the windows and doors tightly closed, and the big manager himself, carrying a leather whip, entered the room. After a while Watanabe crawled out of the room, his shirt and Ahina pants torn to shreds and his back covered with blood. An issue could have been made of this, but in those days the manager had the power of life and death over the laborers, like a feudal lord, and the judges of the local court and policemen were all under him and no one could do anything about this incident. Several days later Watanabe disappeared again. According to the rumor he moved to Hawaii. The plantation did not pursue him any more.[15]

There were other causes for desertion, including accumulated gambling debts, debts to stores, or the attraction of higher wages and easier work in the coffee industry. Often deserters found such isolated areas as Waimanalo on Oahu or Kona on Hawaii a haven where they could start their lives anew with changed names. According to Secretary Wry Taylor of the Bureau of Immigration, who inspected fourteen plantations on Hawaii in 1898, there were 388 Japanese and 82 Chinese who deserted on that island alone during the first six months of that year. Desertion caused financial loss on the part of the immigration companies in Japan because they had to reimburse the commissions they had received from the plantations for the laborers they had supplied. For example, Kumamoto Immigration Company reported a loss of $3,700 due to desertion. The Japanese government, however, did allow the immigration companies to confiscate the money deposited by the immigrants in case of their desertion from the plantations before their contracts expired.[16]

Some plantation authorities treated their Japanese laborers with exceptional kindness, as the following examples show. The owner of Grove Farm on Kauai, George Wilcox, allowed the laborers to rest and smoke when they reached the end of a row of cane. When they deserted, Wilcox did not allow the luna to bring them back for punishment. He let them go. He never allowed whipping of laborers, and he fired a manager who knocked down a laborer in a rage when the latter accidentally set a fire in the cane field from cigarette smoking. Manshichi Tsunoda, who arrived in 1885, recalled that the laborers at Puunene Plantation on Maui were treated very leniently, and the lunas were very patient, individually showing those who were slow how to use the hoe. There were many such cases of kindness by the managers toward individual workers.[17]

Most of those who worked as domestic servants in private homes were treated kindly as members of the household, and it was not rare that their employers became the guardians of the children whom they left in Hawaii when they retired to Japan. These guardian-parents sent Nisei children through schools and colleges, attended their graduations, and continued to treat the latter as part of their families even after they had married.

Nonfarmers among Contract Labor Immigrants

As early as 1884, while recruiting was still in process, *Jiji Shinpo,* an influential Tokyo daily, reported that among the contract labor emigrants were some ambitious young men who were students. Consul General Andō also reported to the Japanese government that the composers of the letters protesting against the treatment of the immigrants on the plantations showed an intellectual caliber above that of the average peasant from Japan. The following are some of the nonfarmers who were among the first contract labor immigrants.[18]

Katsugoro Haida, born in 1863 in Hiroshima Prefecture, had studied for the Buddhist priesthood but later became interested in Western medicine and was studying to become a physician when the recruiting of laborers for Hawaii was announced by the government. While working as a contract laborer at Paia Plantation on Maui, he was a spokesman for the laborers. After leaving the plantation, he worked as a domestic servant and then went to San Francisco in 1887. He entered Cooper Medical College (which later became part of Stanford University) in 1894 and received his medical degree in 1898. He returned to Hawaii in 1902 to practice medicine.[19]

Saiji Kimura of Nagasaki had spent five years in Paris. His ability was recognized quickly in Hawaii and he was appointed to become an immigration inspector. After eight years of service he returned to Japan but eventually came back to Hawaii as a businessman. He helped to organize the Japanese Merchants' Association, made up of thirty-seven merchants who helped the victims of the Honolulu fire of 1900. It became the Japanese Chamber of Commerce in 1908. Kimura also built the Rice Refinery in Kakaako to polish the cheaper raw rice imported from Japan and thereby reduced the price of rice in Hawaii.[20]

Sasuke Yasumori of Toyama Prefecture was a travelling medicine salesman. Toyama is a mid-northern province of Japan that was known for the manufacture of medicine, and its travelling salesmen were found throughout Japan during the Tokugawa and Meiji eras. Yasumori and his brother went all the way to Shikoku, a southwestern island, selling medicine. When they stopped in Yokohama on their way home, they heard about the recruiting of emigrants to Hawaii. Yasumori joined the first contract emigrant group. After working on a plantation on Kauai, he moved to Honolulu in 1889 and opened a general merchandise store on Nuuanu Street. Three years later when it became legal to sell Japanese medicine, he obtained a license to do so. In those days most of Japan looked down upon labor emigration to Hawaii, considering it a relief measure for impoverished prefectures. Whenever

Yasumori visited Japan, however, he urged the governor of Toyama Prefecture to send emigrants to Hawaii, but the governor always refused his proposition, saying, "Toyama-ken is not that poor."[21]

Umekichi Asahina, the first Japanese dentist in Hawaii, was one of eleven from Shizuoka among the first group of contract immigrants. He worked on a cattle ranch on Niihau for several years before opening a dental clinic in Honolulu.[22]

In Japan, Toshiyuki Hirai had been a tax collector. While at Koloa Plantation, he was elected spokesman by two hundred Japanese laborers. His efforts on their behalf resulted in great improvement in their working conditions.[23]

Free Immigrants

There were also immigrants such as merchants, priests, ministers, physicians, newspaper correspondents, teachers, and students who were not under contract when they came to Hawaii. They paid their own travelling expenses and were classified as "Hi-Imin" (nonlabor immigrants). Their passports were stamped as such.

In March 1894, the legislature of the Provisional Government of Hawaii passed an act requiring all free Japanese immigrants to have $50 as proof that they could support themselves without becoming public charges while waiting for jobs. Contract laborers were required to carry with them written proof of their contracts from their employers. Yasutarō Sōga, a free immigrant, described the circumstances under which he came to Hawaii and his experiences on landing in Honolulu:

> Actually, I thought I would work for a couple of years in Hawaii to accumulate enough money for my education in America, never dreaming that I would spend the rest of my life in Hawaii. Born in Tokyo, I studied English at the English Language Institute run by Mr. Eastlake [an Englishman] and then I studied British law at Tokyo Law School. In my junior year I changed my plan to major in medical chemistry at the Tokyo School of Medical Chemistry. My eyesight became very poor because of continuous microscopic laboratory work, and I was obliged to stop my studies. After that, I worked in various stores.

I was twenty-three years old when I sailed from Yokohama on February 18, 1896, aboard the *China-go* with Mr. and Mrs. Takahashi. Mr. Takahashi was to become the chief editor of *Hawaii Shimpo,* a vernacular. We settled down in a corner of the steerage. Mr. Takahashi made an arrangement so that we could have better meals. We arrived at Honolulu on February 28. Hawaii at that time was the only independent republic of the Polynesian people in the Pacific under President Sanford B. Dole, after the overthrow of the monarchy a few years earlier.

In those days the immigrants from Japan were detained for health inspection for a certain period of time. So, we carried our baggage, walking on the long pier to the immigration quarantine quarter, the so-called "Senningoya" [a barracks for a thousand people]. It had tiers of rough board for beds and looked like a jail. Rice and beef, etc., were provided, which we cooked ourselves. If there was any case of contagious disease among us, our stay would be prolonged. So, we all hoped that nobody would become sick while there. On March 5 we were released. When I showed my 100 yen [$50] in a bundle of 100 one-yen bills to the customs officer, a mean-looking Japanese interpreter yelled at me furiously, saying, "Who in the world has time to count them in the middle of busy inspections" and threw the money at me. His rudeness made me very upset, but I kept silent to avoid further trouble. I borrowed that 100 yen from my dear friend. I carefully brought that bundle of 100 one-yen bills just the way he handed them to me.[24]

Each plantation had a store where the laborers bought commodities on credit, payable on their pay day, deducted from their wages. The new plantations that had no stores of their own asked established merchants in Honolulu to open stores for their laborers. Yasutarō Sōga became the manager of such a plantation store.

After eleven days in Honolulu, I was sent to Waianae to be in charge of the branch of Shiozawa store. I wore a shirt and Ahina pants just like a plantation laborer, receiving the same monthly wage of $12.50. My job included all the miscellaneous duties of the store from cleaning to transporting merchandise of all sizes and weights on a wheelbarrow from the railroad depot to the store's warehouse. Every day I worked very hard from 6:00 A.M. until 10:00 P.M. At night I did bookkeeping of the sales accounts of the rows and rows of five cents and ten cents, preparing a bill for each customer, to collect the money on the plantation pay day.

The plantation store was a miniature department store which had everything for household use including foodstuff, fabrics, Chinaware, kitchen utensils, hardware, ice boxes, medicine, liquor, toilet and laundry articles, stationery and writing materials, newspapers and magazines, etc. The main commodities were rice, sake, shoyu sauce, and miso. At that time we had two sales boys who made the rounds of the plantation camps to get orders and delivered the commodities twice a day.

The customers did not come to the store during the weekdays. However, on Saturday evenings and on Sundays they came to the store. Actually, the store was closed on Sunday, but they came in from the back door, not only to purchase goods, but to ask me to write letters on their behalf or to consult me on various personal problems. In fact, Saturdays and Sundays were the busiest days for me. My store was like a village office. Only late Sunday afternoon was I somewhat free.[25]

Those who intended to work on plantations also made efforts to come as free immigrants by borrowing money or selling or mortgaging their property to have enough money for passage and $50 to show at landing. In contrast to contract labor immigrants, whose passage from Yokohama to Hawaii was paid by the planters and had to be reimbursed in monthly installments, free immigrants received higher wages. In 1899 the monthly wage of contract laborers was $15.58 while that of free immigrant laborers was $18.84. According to the Board of Immigration, there were 10,527 contract laborers and 5,208 free laborers, in addition to 1,051 female laborers, who were wives of the workers, in Hawaii in 1898.[26]

Out-Migration of Plantation Laborers to the West Coast

In 1898 Hawaii became a territory of the United States and in 1900 Congress passed the Organic Act, making the laws and Constitution of the United States applicable to Hawaii, nullifying contract labor immigration. The sudden sense of freedom the immigrants experienced resulted in massive out-migration from the plantations. From 1900 to 1907, known as the period of free immigration, more than 68,300 Japanese came to Hawaii from Japan. Because they were no longer bound by contracts, and attracted by higher wages, the emancipated plantation laborers left the islands for the West Coast of the United States in large numbers. Agents for West Coast industries such as fishery operations, canneries, and agriculture actively recruited Japanese workers, offering a daily wage of $1.25 to $1.35 in contrast to the 69 cents they were getting in Hawaii. More than 35,000 left Hawaii, leaving the plantations with acute manpower shortages and the Japanese business circle, which lost a tremendous number of its customers, in utter confusion. To check this out-migration, the Hawaiian legislature passed an act in 1905 to charge each labor recruiter for U.S. mainland firms an annual fee of $500. Japanese Consul General Miki Saitō strongly urged the immigrants to stay in Hawaii, warning that hardships might await them on the mainland, but he was bitterly criticized by the immigrants as an appeaser for the capitalist sugar planters. Finally, the Japanese Merchants' Association petitioned the Japanese government to stop the migration of Japanese in Hawaii to the mainland, with no response. The Territorial government appealed to Congress for assistance in halting the out-migration.[27]

The case of the immigrants from Kanagawa Prefecture is an example of such mass migration to the West Coast. The Kanagawans were the third largest prefectural group in terms of the number of immigrants (214) who came to Hawaii aboard the *City of Tokio* in 1885. By 1907 all but a few had left for the West Coast. Hideo Naito, a restaurateur, recalled that his father, who was the head clerk of Fukuoka Hotel in Honolulu, helped all the Kanagawa-ken immigrants to go to the U.S. mainland with the intention of following them himself, but before he could leave migration of the Japanese to the mainland by way of Hawaii was prohibited by law.[28]

On the West Coast, the sudden increase in the Japanese population had intensified anti-Japanese feelings there. When the San Francisco School Board decided to have Japanese children attend a segregated school in Chinatown in 1906, causing diplomatic tension between the United States and Japan, the subsequent investigation by the Federal government found no justifiable reason for their segregation. President Theodore Roosevelt advised the San Francisco School Board to withdraw its ordinance, and, as compensation, further immigration of the Japanese by way of Hawaii, Canada, and Mexico was stopped in 1907 by executive order.[29]

In view of the increasing anti-Japanese agitation in California, Secretary of State Elihu U. Root and Ambassador Plenipotentiary Kogoro Takahira of Japan met in 1908 and reached the so-called Gentlemen's Agreement by which Japan took the initiative to restrict emigration by not issuing passports to prospective emigrants except the close kin and picture brides of those already in the United States and its territories. This period from 1908 to 1924 was called *Yobiyose Jidai,* the period of summoning kin. This restricted immigration continued until the persistent efforts of California senators and representatives, who dominated national legislative action concerning the Japanese in the United States, finally resulted in the enactment of the Japanese Exclusion Act by Congress on June 30, 1924. This act completely prohibited Japanese immigration to the United States and its territories. Exempted from this regulatory measure were nonquota immigrants such as government officials in diplomatic service, ministers and priests, college professors, language school teachers, international merchants, the wives of those in the foregoing categories and their children under eighteen years of age, bonafide students, and travellers for short visits of six months.[30]

There was some opposition to this measure in Hawaii. For example, after Congress passed the Japanese Exclusion bill, the Inter-Church Federation in Hawaii held a special meeting and cabled President Calvin Coolidge, urging him to veto the bill. The Honolulu Chamber of Commerce also cabled the president, protesting the Congressional action and urging that Japan be treated on an equal basis with other nations.[31]

Ineligibility of Japanese for Naturalization

Long before Hawaii became a territory of the United States, some Japanese had become citizens of their new homes. There were at least three Japanese, all rescued seamen, who were naturalized and became subjects of the Kingdom of Hawaii in the 1840s—one in 1844, another in 1845, and another in 1847.[32] In 1893, Heizaburo Inouye and Den Sugawara, both naturalized in the United States, came to Hawaii and made a speaking tour of the islands, urging the Japanese immigrants to become naturalized. As a result, Tamekichi Abe and Kenzaburo Ozawa applied for naturalization and became subjects of the Kingdom of Hawaii. Inouye and Sugawara must have returned to the United States, since they were never heard from again. When Hawaii became a territory of the United States, in 1898, the naturalization of Abe and Ozawa remained valid. They were treated like other subjects of Hawaii, who automatically became citizens of the United States. On the other hand, the American citizenship of Masakichi Suzuki, who had been naturalized in New York, and that of Jo Makino, whose father was English and mother was Japanese and who had been naturalized in Hawaii, was revoked on the grounds that they were ineligible for naturalization. According to the naturalization law promulgated in 1790, only free whites and Africans were eligible for naturalization.[33]

When the number of Orientals was small in the United States, a considerable number of Chinese and Japanese in various states were naturalized. Before 1905, approximately fifty Japanese were naturalized. Tomizō Katsunuma, formerly an immigration inspector in Hawaii, who was naturalized in Utah in 1895, was one of them. When the number of Japanese immigrants increased, the naturalization law was more strictly observed. As in the case of Katsunuma, the citizenship of those Japanese naturalized in the United States prior to 1905 was not revoked. Katsunuma voted in the territorial and municipal elections, exercising the rights and privileges of American citizenship. He remained a citizen until his death in 1950 at age eighty-seven.[34]

Inconsistencies in the definitions and interpretations of the naturalization law at times caused irreparable injustice to children of the few naturalized Americans of Japanese origin. The children of American citizens are automatically Americans, regardless of where they are born. Also, because of the principle of *jus soli,* the children of immigrants who were ineligible for naturalization were automatically American citizens, as long as they were born in the United States. If, however, the children happened to be born outside of the United States, for instance, in Japan while their immigrant parents were visiting there, they were classified as aliens even though they may have returned to the United States as infants. This latter definition was also used arbitrarily to determine the citizenship of infants born aboard Japanese or American ships when they arrived in Hawaii.

Kiyomi Suzuki, the daughter of naturalized citizen Tomizō Katsunuma, was born in Japan while her father was recruiting emigrants to Hawaii in Fukushima and other prefectures of northern Japan as a temporary agent of the Kumamoto Emigration Company. Her father's American citizenship automatically made her a citizen also. Suzuki and her parents returned to Hawaii in 1898. After graduating from McKinley High School in Honolulu, she attended Normal School to become a teacher. She taught at a public school as a trainee and then as a regular teacher from 1922 to 1923. Then, unexpectedly, she was discharged by the Board of Education for the reason that she had been born in Japan. She described her reactions and her wartime experiences as follows:

It was a terrible shock for me because I had thought of myself as an American all the time. My family, especially my father, was completely Americanized and brought us up as American citizens. All my brothers and sisters [two brothers and two sisters] attended Punahou School. That's why we all spoke good English at home. I never dreamed of becoming disqualified to be a teacher just because I was born in Japan. During the war I was classified as an enemy alien, even though I felt and acted completely American. I cried when Japan attacked Pearl Harbor and I felt angry about the fact that Kibei who had spent most of their formative years in Japan and who could hardly speak English were free citizens just because they had been born in Hawaii. Also, since my husband, a plantation engineer, was active in the community, an FBI agent came to our house to investigate him more than once during the war years. Our plantation [Ewa] manager always vouched for his integrity and loyalty. Finally, I told the FBI agent firmly, "Don't you ever come to this house again." He never came again. Anyway, I was busy during the war years as a volunteer worker in the Red Cross and other war service activities.

After the war when the McCarran Act made it possible for alien Japanese to acquire American citizenship by naturalization in 1952, I applied for naturalization. Then I was told that my application was unnecessary, since I was an American citizen since the day I was born because my father was an American citizen, having been naturalized in the State of Utah, and I was given a certificate of citizenship. I was appalled about the fact that I had to endure the unnecessary suffering and humiliation for so long because of the careless mistake of the Board of Education. But I calmed myself by telling myself that those were the years my children needed me at home most and I was able to take care of them full time. I wouldn't be able to do that if I were teaching.[35]

Just as the American public based its suspicions about the loyalty of Japanese immigrants on their ineligibility for naturalization, the Japanese immigrants themselves also suffered from the American legal restrictions that forced them to remain Japanese subjects, thereby legally tied to their old country and separated from their children, who were American citizens and belonged to the United States. Their keen desire to eliminate racial discrimination in the naturalization law was evident in the widespread interest among the Japanese immigrants in the test case of Takao Ozawa.

Takao Ozawa was born in Japan in 1875 and went to California at the age of nineteen. After graduating from Berkeley High School, he studied law at the University of California. He applied for naturalization in 1902, but his application was denied by the Alameida Court in California. Observing the hardships suffered by Japanese immigrants because of their racial ineligibility for naturalization, he devoted his time to investigating the problem. He came to Hawaii in 1906 and went to work for Theo H. Davies and Co. He spent most of his spare time in the Supreme Court Library in the Judiciary Building, examining the naturalization law of the United States. Being convinced that the Japanese were eligible for naturalization, he applied in 1914 at the United States District Court in Honolulu. On January 30, 1913, Judge Sanford Ballard Dole declared that Ozawa was qualified. His case was postponed, however, until March 25, 1916, when Judge Charles F. Clemens ruled that Ozawa was ineligible for naturalization because the Japanese were Mongolian by race, which was neither white nor black African. Ozawa took his case to the Circuit Court of Appeals at San Francisco in 1918 with D. L. Withington, the president of the Hawaii Bar Association, as his attorney. The Circuit Court subsequently suspended its decision and asked the Supreme Court of the United States for instructions. On November 13, 1922, the Supreme Court ruled that Ozawa was ineligible for naturalization because he was neither white nor black.[36]

There was always a portion of the white community in Hawaii that was apprehensive about the Japanese. As Yasutarō Sōga observed in the late 1890s, "The Japanese population in Hawaii was 24,407 of the total of 109,020. This tremendous increase was causing alarm among some Americans."[37] The other portion, however, which was more influential, made a number of attempts to eradicate legal discrimination against the Japanese and to integrate them into the mainstream of the community. The leaders of the Central Union Church—for example, particularly its pastor Doremus Scudder, Frank S. Scudder, superintendent of the Hawaiian Board of Mission's work among the Japanese, and its influential lay leader, William R. Castle, a senator in the territorial legislature—worked hard to eliminate racial discrimination in the naturalization law. They saw their work in terms of basic human justice and in promoting goodwill with the Asian nations. Their efforts climaxed on the occasion of the observance of Peace Sunday May 18, 1913. In a momentous sermon entitled "Our Nation's Duty to Japan," Doremus Scudder challenged the naturalization law of the United States for treating Asians as a subhuman species unworthy of American citizenship. It was the time when the California State Legislature was preparing to pass the Alien Land Law, aimed specifically at Japanese nationals, which limited the ownership of agricultural land to Americans only, disqualifying those ineligible for naturalization.

After the Peace Sunday service at Central Union Church, Senator Castle drew up a petition to President Woodrow Wilson, which was circulated among concerned citizens in Honolulu, requesting him to urge Congress to eliminate racial discrimination in the U.S. naturalization law. About a hundred individuals signed the petition before it was sent to Washington.[38] The full text of the petition was published on the cover of the June 13 issue of *The Friend:*

On American Citizenship.

To the Honorable Woodrow Wilson,
   President of the United States.
Sir:

The undersigned, citizens and residents of the Territory of Hawaii, respectfully make petition, and, for grounds therefor, represent as follows:

In Hawaii the relations between the races are more cordial, probably, than anywhere else in the world. Every person here is not only theoretically but actually equal before the law. Every one in the Territory understands this perfectly well, and it therefore affords an ease of mind that does not seem to exist in those parts of the world where there is not that equality. Of course the language barrier prevents close social intercourse, but this is perfectly well understood by our different nationalities and therefore no objection or feeling arises on that account.

Just at the present juncture of affairs in our country we feel that it would greatly help to adjust ill feeling and get rid of suspicion and soreness, provided the laws of the United States were so adjusted as to revert to the condition, which was regarded as ideal by our fathers, that America is a refuge for the oppressed of all nations and that citizenship might be acquired in the United States upon compliance with certain conditions, such as ability to understand the laws, customs and manners of that country, coupled with residence of a number of years, etc. The years of prior residence might well be increased, coupled with other requirements now set forth in the laws, and adding thereto such further requirements as may be necessary to more perfectly safeguard our institutions; but entirely abolishing any race distinction.

Your petitioners, therefore, respectfully pray that the influence of your administration may be thrown in favor of the enactment of such legislation in Congress as may be required to do away with race barriers to naturalization, even while it may increase and add other qualifications necessary to be met prior to admitting any person of any nationality to citizenship under our laws.

Respectfully submitted,

Dated, Honolulu, T. H., May 27, 1913.

The members of Hawaii's legislature were greatly disturbed over the impending Alien Land Law in California. The sponsors of this bill asserted that it was not only to stop Japanese expansion in agriculture but to drive the Japanese out of California eventually. President Wilson had tried to prevent the bill's passage by sending William Jennings Bryan to Sacramento to plead with the legislature and with Governor Hiram Johnson, but without success.[39] In articulating the concern of the Hawaii legislature, Archer Irwin, representative from the island of Hawaii, introduced House Resolution No. 137 at the regular session of the Seventh Legislature of the Territory of Hawaii on April 23, 1913. This bill pointed out that the Alien Land Law violated the treaty between Japan and the

United States and would imperil the friendly relations between the two countries. Hawaii would be most severely affected by that strained relationship. He urged the House to oppose its enactment by sending copies of his proposed resolution to the governor of California and to the president of the Senate and Speaker of the House in California. Irwin moved that the resolution be adopted, and David Malo Kupihea, representative from Oahu, seconded the motion. In the Senate, there was much debate about Hawaii's legislative body attempting to control the legislature of California. The resolution was tabled on the recommendation by the Judiciary Committee that as each state had the exclusive right to regulate its own internal affairs, it should be the federal government to intercede in case of any violation of the treaty between Japan and the United States.[40]

Another example of the injustice caused by racial ineligibility for naturalization was the act passed by Congress in 1922 establishing that American women who married alien men automatically lost their citizenship. This act caused much inconvenience and injustice to women throughout the United States, including Hawaii. Due to the strong pressure from such influential women's organizations as the National Association of Women Lawyers, the National League of Women Voters, the General Federation of Women's Clubs, the National Council of Jewish Women, and the Women's Bar Association of the District of Columbia, Congress passed in 1931 the Cable Act, which declared that no native-born American woman need forfeit her American citizenship by reason of her marriage to a foreign-born man unless she chose to do so by acquiring another nationality, and that if she had already forfeited American citizenship, she could regain it within ninety days. Many Hawaii-born women of Japanese ancestry who had married men of Japanese origin took advantage of this new act and regained their American citizenship.[41]

2

Prefectural Groups in Hawaii

DURING the period of government contract labor immigration, 1885 to 1893, the Japanese government made a special effort to recruit emigrants in the most overpopulated, impoverished areas of the country, such as the coastal counties of Hiroshima-ken and Yamaguchi-ken, the adjoining prefectures (ken) of the Sanyo area of Chūgoku Chiho or region.[1] By 1924, the total Japanese population in Hawaii had reached 125,368, including 58,721 aliens and 66,647 Hawaii-born citizens. Their prefectural backgrounds were: Hiroshima-ken, 30,534, or 24.3 percent of the total Hawaii Japanese population; Yamaguchi-ken, 25,878, or 20.6 percent; Kumamoto-ken, 19,551, or 15.7 percent; Okinawa-ken, 16,536, or 13.1 percent; and Fukuoka-ken, 4,936, or 4 percent. The other 15,514, or 12.4 percent, came from seventeen different prefectures.[2]

The two largest groups, Hiroshimans and Yamaguchins, were a formidable factor among the Japanese numerically, culturally, economically, and socially. Being from neighboring localities, the Hiroshimans and Yamaguchins had practically the same dialects and customs, with little local variation. In their early years in Hawaii they established the Hiroshima-Yamaguchi Joint Prefectural Association of Honolulu, with officers, directors, and auditors representing both prefectural groups.[3] When the Japanese refer to Chūgoku Chiho no hito (the people of Chūgoku region) they mean principally the Hiroshimans and Yamaguchins, and Chūgoku-ben refers to their dialects. Geographically, the Sanyo area includes Okayama-ken, the prefecture east of Hiroshima-ken, but only 37 Okayamans, in contrast to 612 Hiroshimans and 420 Yamaguchins, came to Hawaii in 1885. Their dialect is also different from those of Hiroshimans and Yamaguchins. In 1924 they numbered only 727, including their Hawaii-born children.[4]

Fukushimans began to arrive in July 1898, the time of Hawaii's annexation to the United States, and Okinawans started arriving a year and a half later, in January 1900. These two groups came to Hawaii in a new era. They began their lives in Hawaii on the sugar plantations, but since it was the period of free immigration, ambitious young men from both these newly arrived prefectural groups eagerly joined other Japanese plantation laborers in their mass out-migration to the West Coast as soon as they accumulated enough money. Many Fukushimans openly admitted that they regarded Hawaii as a stepping stone to the U.S. mainland. Originally, approximately 10,000 Fukushimans and 20,000 or more Okinawans came to Hawaii, but about one-third of the former[5] and an unknown number of the latter went to the mainland before 1908. There were 4,938 Fukushimans and their Hawaii-born children and 16,536 Okinawans and their Hawaii-born children in the islands in 1924, the former constituting 4 percent and the latter 13.1 percent of the total of 125,368 Japanese immigrants and their Hawaii-born children.[6] In other words, Okinawans were the fourth largest prefectural group, while Fukushimans were the seventh largest in the Japanese community.

The thirteen to fifteen years separating their arrival made a great difference in social and economic status between the old-timers and the newcomers. The first and foremost point of encounter was the language. Neither the Fukushimans nor the Okinawans spoke Chūgoku-ben, the prevailing Japanese dialect in Hawaii. Spontaneous communication between these two new prefectural groups and the old-timers was nonexistent. To avoid insult and ostracism the new prefectural groups invariably took the course of independence from the dominant earlier settlers. Such independence was reflected, for example, in the establishment of inns for immigrants from the same prefecture where they could speak their dialects freely. By 1923 there were three ryokans in Honolulu operated by Okinawans and one operated by a Fukushiman.[7] Thus, they followed different courses of collective adjustment despite the similar problems they encountered at the beginning.

Both these groups were at a disadvantage in comparison with the other prefectural groups, given their difficulties in communication and the fact that those who arrived earlier were well established on the plantations as well as in independent trades and agriculture outside the plantations. The Fukushimans and Okinawans were keenly aware of their position. They measured their success in terms of how close they were to the other Kenjins as well as to the Caucasians, who were regarded as the top of the social, economic, and political ladders in Hawaii.

Distribution of Prefectural Groups

During the early years of contract labor the sugar planters had a policy of sending immigrants from the same prefecture to the same plantation and assigning them to the same living quarters. According to Rinji Maeyama, a veteran journalist and author who lived on the island of Hawaii for twenty-two years, the first group of thirty-seven immigrants from Niigata-ken, his native prefecture, was sent to Wainaku Plantation near Hilo. Since they arrived on June 17, 1885, aboard the second ship, the *Yamashiro Maru,* their living quarters were called the "Nikai-Sen Camp" (second-ship camp).[8]

Soemon Nakamura of Mie-ken, Kinki Chiho, recalled that all of the fifteen immigrants from Ise who had arrived in 1885 were sent to Papaaloa Plantation on Hawaii. In landing at Laupahoehoe they were put in a large box and pulled up from the boat like cattle. Then, they were sent to the Kea Valley Camp. There were Portuguese and Chinese workers on the plantation, and they often competed with the Portuguese to see which side could finish first in planting a row of cane.[9]

Another reason for the concentration of the members of the same prefectural group on the same plantation was the fact that the immigrants tended to move to the plantations where their friends were after completing the contracts with the originally assigned plantations, as in the case of the Fukushimans who moved to Ewa and Waipahu plantations on Oahu and Puunene and Paia plantations on Maui.[10] In the case of very large prefectural groups such as the Hiroshimans, Yamaguchins, Kumamotons, Okinawans, and Fukuokans, they were found on practically all the plantations on all the islands of Hawaii.

Where there was a large number of immigrants from the same prefecture, their dialect predominated. Maeyama recalled that about 95 percent of the Japanese laborers on Kaupakuea Plantation on Hawaii were from Kumamoto-ken, and the Hiroshimans and Yamaguchins learned to speak the Kumamoto dialect for daily communication. That was the only plantation where the Kumamoto-ben was the prevailing language.[11]

Smaller prefectural groups were thrown together on the same plantation. For example, at Onomea Plantation on Hawaii there were immigrants from Miyagi-ken in northern Japan and from Kagoshima-ken, the southernmost prefecture of Kyushu Island. Maeyama recalled that, because the Kagoshima dialect was unintelligible to non-Kagoshimans and the "Zuuzuu-ben" Tōhoku dialect of Miyagians was impossible for non-Tōhoku people to understand, there were frequent disputes due to misunderstanding. His father, a salesman from Niigata-ken who was used to having customers speaking various dialects, often acted as a mediator between the two prefectural groups.[12]

Prefectural Associations

Prefectural associations called Kenjin-kai were organized by the immigrants for mutual aid in time of illness or death, as well as for various kinds of misfortune. Especially during the early years when most immigrants were single men, the Kenjin-kai provided collective assistance to those from the same ken. The large prefectural groups had numerous locality clubs organized by those from the same village, town, or county for mutual aid and fellowship. In most instances such locality clubs were formed before the prefectural associations were organized. Some Kenjin-kai were formed when a need arose; for instance, Etsuyu-Kai (Association of Friends from Echigo Province) was formed when the immigrants from Niigata-ken began to scatter across the island of Hawaii. The Niigata Kenjin-kai of Honolulu was organized in 1909 with 205 members. The origin of its formation was explained by Rinji Maeyama as follows:

> The Niigata Kenjin-kai of Honolulu was organized to collect donations from those from Niigata-ken to buy a set of new clothes for a man from our ken who committed murder and was sentenced to death. Those from Niigata-ken felt that he should at least wear respectable clothes to end his life. After that, when there were some sailors of Niigata-ken background on the Japanese naval training ships

which visited Honolulu, our Kenjin-kai gave a welcome party for
them.[13]

The Rev. Seido Umemura, a Buddhist priest of Kagoshima origin who served for fifty-two years on Hawaii and Oahu, recalled
the Kagoshima Kenjin-kai:

> The Kagoshimans used to have their Kenjin-kai, called "Hayato-
> kai." But nobody understood what "Hayato" meant. So, they added
> "Kagoshima" to "Hayato." The complete lack of records of the arrival
> of the first Kagoshiman immigrants was due to the fact that only those
> with meager education came to Hawaii. However, it is probable that
> they came during the period of free immigration from 1900 to 1907.
> Because no one in Hawaii understood the Kagoshima dialect, they
> learned to speak the prevailing language in Hawaii, namely, the Chū-
> goku-ben of Hiroshiman and Yamaguchin immigrants.[14]

Chukichi Furuyama, who came to Hawaii as a teenager, spoke
of the Miyagi Kenjin-kai:

> I don't know exactly how many came from Miyagi-ken. Maybe
> about 300 altogether. Most of them stayed in Hawaii because they did
> not make enough money to return to Japan. Our Kenjin-kai has a get-
> together twice a year, a New Year's party in February, and a picnic in
> summer. At such gatherings about 70 people including children gather.
> Most of the elderly members are Nisei. There are about 10 members
> who were born in Japan and came to Hawaii as children. Although
> they are called "Issei," they grew up with the Hawaii-born Nisei.
> Hawaii-born are not concerned with the prefectural background of
> their parents. When my eldest son was attending a university on the
> mainland, he was asked from which prefecture his parents came, but
> he did not know. . . .
> Since six years [1973] ago the prefectural government of Miyagi-
> ken has given one Hawaii-born student of Miyagian ancestry a schol-
> arship each year to study at the Tohoku University in Sendai and also
> to travel and observe Japan. This scholarship covers all expenses,
> including travelling and living. There are six of those students who
> have returned to Hawaii. Since they take care of our annual picnic and
> New Year's party, we old people do not have to work for these func-
> tions.[15]

There were so many immigrants from Hiroshima and Yamaguchi that they found it difficult to feel intimate even among them-

selves. While their locality clubs provided them mutual identification and assistance at the village and town levels, they tended to be rather impersonal and even competitive on the prefectural level. It was difficult organizing them into prefectural groups, as Isoto Dewa, at one time manager of Kuakini Japanese Hospital, related in 1935:

> There are too many Hiroshimans, about 30,000 in Hawaii. Because of such a large number, there is no way to organize even the Kenjin-kai. About ten years ago someone from Hiroshima Kaigai Kyokai [Hiroshima Overseas Association] came and formed its branch, but it disappeared eventually. Feeling that something must be done, some of us started the Hiroshima Kenjin Shinko-kai [Hiroshimans' Friendship Promotion Association].[16]

The Kenjin-kai provided the means not only for mutual assistance and aid when there was trouble but also social opportunities for people who shared the same dialects and sentiments. Although some Issei were never a part of any Kenjin-kai, because their prefectural groups were too small to organize, the Kenjin-kai was essentially an Issei experience. Even when Nisei joined their parents' Kenjin-kai, they did not share the memories of the prefecture or the needs that brought the immigrants together.

Regional Characteristics of Japanese Immigrants

The Japanese community during the early years was described as a jumble of people from various prefectures of various chihos (regions) with different dialects and customs, so that they did not trust each other, and, lacking group cooperation, there was no way of talking rationally to settle their differences and reach consensus.[17]

The Fukushimans, for example, exhibited many characteristics that might have won them admiration, but everywhere they went they were laughed at for their speech and treated as if they were stupid and unable to talk. The Tohoku dialects of northern Honshu, with their characteristic heavy pronunciation, sound to outsiders as if the Tohoku people had speech defects and were unable to pronounce certain words. The editor of *Fukushima Isseiki* (The

Century of Fukushima) described the Fukushimans as reserved
and not sociable, but kindhearted and sincere. He noted that they
were tenacious and never gave up what they planned to do, and
they showed endurance in hardship and undaunted spirit in failure. It would take a long time, however, for others to recognize
those qualities in them.[18]

In 1935, the *Osaka Mainichi Daily* sponsored a meeting in
Honolulu to discuss the characteristics of the various prefectural
groups in Hawaii. Yasutarō Sōga, who was present at the meeting,
said of the Japanese community: "They came from various regions
of Japan. Their respective regional characteristics are reflected in
the formation of a mini-Japan [in Hawaii] and, in general, even
their occupations differ by prefectures."[19] The comments of others
at the meeting echo Sōga's view of the immigrants.

Seitaro Ogata, a labor recruitment agent for the Hawaiian
Sugar Planters' Association (HSPA) described the characteristics of
his recruits as follows:

> As I explained the conditions of the plantations to them, the Chugo-
> kujins [Hiroshimans and Yamaguchins] were smart. They listened to
> me, saying "Yes, yes," without uttering anything rude to me. In con-
> trast, the Kyushujins [Kumamotons and Fukuokans] were short-tem-
> pered and uncontrollable. They became impatient easily, shouting,
> "Don't be so fussy. We don't want to hear about so much details."[20]

Both Kumamotons and Fukuokans boast of their short temper
and frankness as the mark of the Kyushuans' honesty and sincerity, and they are proud of their difference from the Chugokujins,
who talk smoothly even when they are offended. This so-called
"Kyushujin nature" was invariably reflected in their choice of
occupations. According to their spokesmen, Kumamotons and
Fukuokans had very little interest in trade, which requires patience
and smooth-talking to the customers. Commercial activities did
not suit their nature. Once they left plantation work, the Kyushuans shifted to quarrying, construction of roads, tunnels, and
other such work.[21] Citing their contributions in this area, Tomizō
Katsunuma wrote for his column in the *Nippu Jiji*, April 30, 1922:

> Hawaii's road construction, the construction of ditches, blasting of
> rocks, and building of stone walls, all of which were dangerous and
> rough, often inflicting serious injuries and even death, were the work

of the Japanese immigrants, especially those from Kyushu. Most of the stones used for curbs of more than 240 miles of the sidewalks in Honolulu were quarried by the Japanese. Many lost their lives or were crippled from such tasks.[22]

Kumamotons, according to Yukuo Uyehara, former chairman of the Department of Asian Languages at the University of Hawaii, were frank and did not know how to flatter. They also did not like being behind others when it came to making donations, even though they may not have had money. "So," observed Professor Uyehara, "smart donation solicitors would go first to those who make large donations and make a list of their names and amounts of money and then show it to the Kumamotons."[23]

The Wakayamans in Hawaii were mostly engaged in fishery and related industries. At one time, tuna fishing was the monopoly of the Wakayamans. It was a Wakayaman, Gorokichi Nakaji, who introduced tuna fishing to Hawaii. Shujiro Takimoto, principal of the Kapalama Japanese Language School, said of them:

> Generally speaking, the Wakayamans in Hawaii lack in cooperation among themselves. Knowing that below the thin wooden bottoms of their boats is the deep sea, often treacherous, and facing death any day, they lack the idea of economy and saving money for the future. Their wives have the same tendency. On the other hand, they do not like to be behind other people in donations. Because of such tendencies, they give more than they can afford and lose money.[24]

The Hiroshimans and Yamaguchins, hardworking and competitive, displayed a proclivity toward commercial activities. "In the financial area," noted Isoto Dewa, "most of those [immigrants] engaged in business in Honolulu are Hiroshimans, and in terms of wealth it is considerable." In describing the Yamaguchins, Manzuchi Hashimoto, a store manager in Honolulu, said:

> I was born on the "emigration" island of Oshima County of Yamaguchi-ken. In our county overseas emigration was taken for granted, and it was the custom for young people to go abroad to work and make money. Since so many emigrated abroad, even the grade school children know where America is or where Hawaii is. . . . We don't have conspicuously successful people like the Hiroshimans, but we are hard workers. Gradually, we are following the Hiroshimans in the commercial field.[25]

The Language Problem

The area of perpetual confrontation among the settlers was the language. In general, the use of standard Japanese at home and outside the home was limited to educated people, most of whom were in occupations other than plantation labor. They were classified by the Japanese government as "Hi-Imin" (nonlabor emigrants). Although the immigrants eagerly sent their children to the Japanese language schools to learn standard Japanese, for daily conversation at home and among friends they used their respective regional dialects, mostly of the rural variety. Because an overwhelmingly large number of immigrants came from Hiroshima-ken and Yamaguchi-ken, their dialects, Chūgoku-ben, became the prevailing Japanese language in Hawaii. Those who spoke non-Chūgoku-ben were not readily accepted and were often ridiculed. The Tohoku dialects of northern Honshu were referred to by the derogatory nickname "Zuuzuu-ben," an onomatopoeic name for what the Tohoku dialect supposedly sounded like to non-Tohoku ears—"Zuu-zuu-zuu-zuu."

Many of the immigrants who did not speak the Chūgoku-ben when they came to Hawaii eventually learned to do so, as did Umeno Goto, widow of Methodist minister Chinpei Goto. She recalled their experiences:

> My husband came to Hawaii with his parents from Iwate-ken when he was eleven years old as free immigrants. On the boat transporting the immigrants to the island of Hawaii, their fellow passengers called them "Tohoku Tojin" [Tohoku Chinese]. Young Chinpei's immediate reaction was that these Chūgoku immigrants were so ignorant that they did not even know the real Japanese language. He barely refrained from shouting at them. For him the Tohoku-ben was the only Japanese language he knew. When we were on Maui [1921–1927], because I spoke the standard Japanese, some women felt uncomfortable and stopped coming to our church. So I tried hard to learn to speak the Chūgoku-ben. It became so natural to me that it was hard for me to speak the standard Japanese when we had visitors from Japan.[26]

"The people used to notice my Tohoku-ben and asked me where I came from," commented Miyagian Chukichi Furuyama. "But now, because most of my friends and acquaintances are of Hiroshima and Yamaguchi background, I talk the way they do."[27]

The Miyagians never suffered outright insult collectively from the dominant prefectural groups in spite of their "Zuuzuu-ben" because of their small number. There were also very small groups of immigrants from other Tohoku prefectures who were absorbed in the established community of predominantly Chugokuans.

The children of non-Chūgoku immigrants were also subjected to ostracism because of their dialects. An elderly Nisei who spent his early years on a plantation on Maui remembered that "As a kid I spoke the dialect of my parents, Kumamoto-ben. The other kids made fun of me and often bullied me, saying 'Shigoh shiteyaru' [to punish by force in Chūgoku-ben]. I was called 'Hoito' [greedy in Chūgoku-ben] by the other children. They used to say 'Hidarui' [hungry in Chūgoku-ben]. I don't know the meaning of that word even now."[28]

"I came to Hawaii from Wakayama-ken in 1923 to join my parents when I was thirteen years old," recalled an elderly housewife.

> Since I could not understand what the other young people were saying I was terribly lonesome. They teased me constantly, called me "Japan bobura," and "You Okinawan! You speak Okinawan!" They did not understand either my dialect [Kansai-ben] or Okinawa-ben. But I could not talk back because I could not speak their dialect.
>
> In those days all the children and young people who joined their parents after they finished elementary school [sixth to eighth grades] in Japan were teased by the other children and called "Japan bobura" [idiots from Japan], because they could not understand English or Chūgoku-ben.[29]

Rinji Maeyama, from Niigata-ken, recounted his experiences as follows:

> When my father and mother came to Hawaii they left me with my grandparents. My grandfather died when I was eleven years old and my grandmother died when I was twelve years old. So my parents called me to Hawaii. Right away I started to attend the first grade class of the public school. Naturally, I was bigger than the six-year-old first graders. But, since I did not know a word of English, I was called "Japan big bobura," which meant that I was physically big with an empty head. "Bobura" is Chūgoku dialect for "pumpkin."[30]

Chūgoku-ben, and its intonation and pronunciation, became in time common usage among the Japanese immigrants and their children in Hawaii. Words that were peculiar to Chūgoku-ben became part of Hawaii's standard Japanese language or "Hawaii no Hyojun Nihongo," as it was described by the late Hoover Tateishe, a veteran broadcaster on Honolulu's KZOO Japanese language radio station, in explaining the meaning of words and expressions to his listeners. Words like "bobura," "iriko," "hoito," "bakatare," "hidarui," "kotsuru," "Chorinbo," and "Inugami" and the short reflexive "no" at the end of a word or a sentence were originally Chūgoku-ben.[31]

Thus, the Issei community was not a homogenous society but a conglomeration of people from various regions of Japan with different dialects and different customs that emerged through centuries of feudalism. To the outside world they were "Japanese" but within the Japanese community they were identified by their respective ken.

3

Immigrants from Fukushima-ken

Tōhoku Chiho, the northernmost region of Honshu, politically neglected and with a cold climate, was regarded as poor and backward. Since it was not overcrowded, however, no special effort was made by the Japanese government to recruit overseas emigrants in Tōhoku Chiho. In 1898 when Tomizō Katsunuma, a veterinarian, stopped in Hawaii on his way to Japan after a prolonged sojourn in the United States, he was asked by the Kumamoto Emigration Company to recruit emigrants in the Tōhoku region. As a result of his campaign, the first group of a hundred or so Fukushima immigrants, accompanied by Dr. Katsunuma and his family, arrived in Hawaii on July 26, 1898.[1] After the devastating famine in Fukushima-ken in 1905, the number of immigrants increased to 1,512 in 1906. Of the 10,000 or so Fukushimans who came to Hawaii originally, about one-third of them went to the West Coast while another third returned to their homeland before World War II.[2]

Practically all of the Fukushiman immigrants were owners of farm lands, and their purpose in emigrating was to accumulate money, return to their homeland, and rebuild and expand their agricultural enterprises. They were not impoverished people, even though they became poor temporarily because of the famine. Yakichi Watanabe, who served as principal of the Makawao Japanese Language School on Maui and who was also president of the Japanese Language Education Association of that island, said that "since the large majority of [Fukushiman] immigrants had property at home, they had no intention of permanent residence in Hawaii. Therefore, without exception those who worked hard, endured hardship, and saved enough money returned home and became the object of envy as successful returnees from Hawaii. In contrast, those who had to remain in Hawaii spent all their energy bringing up their many children and educating them by working hard. . . ."[3]

Fukushimans as Plantation Laborers

Fukushimans were sent to various plantations on Oahu, including Kahuku and other northern areas of the island, but a large number of them were assigned to Ewa Plantation. Unlike the contract laborers of early years who had to cook their meals in their crowded sleeping quarters, the workers now ate at mess halls operated by ex-plantation laborers called "Big Cooks." The single men were served a simple breakfast and supper, and each man was furnished with a package of rice with soybean paste called miso for lunch. They were charged about $8 a month each.

> [The] meals were extremely poor, with thin Miso soup with noodles in addition to rice. But this noodle soup was the most popular dish of our supper, and everyone tried hard to scoop as much of the noodle at the bottom of the pot as possible, some trying four or five times to scoop it, with those waiting for their turn shouting "Hurry up! Hurry up!" For lunch we had rice and soybean paste, but once a week we had rice with a slice of salted salmon or a boiled egg. Some suffered malnutrition and lost their eyesight or died.[4]

The working and living conditions on the plantations had not improved much since the contract-labor years, however. The workers were crowded together into "camps," as their living quarters were called, as many as eight of them sharing one room in a crude shack built with rough boards whitewashed with cement. "The whole setting gave us the illusion of being in a prison cell," said Masajiro Suzuki. "At night mosquitos kept us awake and other poisonous insects such as scorpions and centipedes came into our room and stung us. Indeed, it was a miserable life."[5]

In general, Fukushimans seemed to choose heavy labor such as clearing land, digging up the roots of trees, construction of roads and railroads, and "hapaiko," loading cut sugar cane onto rail cars. Rising at 5:00 A.M., they worked twelve hours a day or longer in order to earn the extra "incentive" pay that was given on the basis of the tonnage of cane loaded onto the rail cars. Often they made this work a competitive game to see who could load the most. Minokichi Goto recalled that hapaiko was indescribably hard, but since the laborers could earn twice as much because of the incentive pay, it was an attractive job, and he advised those who were healthy to try it at least once. He himself was nick-named "Hapaiko Goto" because of his specialization in this heavy labor.[6]

The Fukushimans had a special liking for working the land. The editor of *Fukushima Isseiki* wrote that "they performed physi-cal labor silently, breathing pure, fresh air and the smell of dirt."[7] The goal was to save money and return home, as Tsuruji Umetsu did. One of the few Fukushimans who worked on the island of Hawaii, Umetsu, after finishing his contract at Ewa Plantation, moved first to Maui and then to Olaa Plantation on Hawaii. He went to work for a lumber company, earning $3 a day as a wood-cutter. In those days the wage for a plantation worker was $1 a day. Being in an isolated place, with no social expenses, he was able to save, and his savings increased every day. In 1921, ten years after his arrival in Hawaii, he sent for his wife and four chil-dren to join him. Eventually the entire family returned to Fukushi-ma and became the operators of a successful pear orchard.[8]

Even on the plantations, the Fukushimans, as newcomers from northern Japan in an established community of people predomi-nantly from the western prefectures of Japan, suffered from an "inferiority complex," according to the founder of the Fukushima Kenjin-kai, Jinshichi Tōkairin.

> Because we Fukushimans came recently we were behind such pre-fectural groups as Yamaguchins, Hiroshimans, Kumamotons, and Wakayamans economically and socially. Those who were engaged in commercial activities in Honolulu were mainly those from such prefec-tures, and on the plantations, lunas and others in prestigious positions were those of the other prefectures who came to Hawaii earlier.[9]

There were exceptions to this pattern, however. Nihei Okazaki was appointed to be a luna (overseer) and also the supervisor of construction for an irrigation system. Later he was one of the founders of an all-Japanese pineapple company, and he became an authority on pineapple cultivation in Hawaii and Taiwan. "In the middle of our suffering from inferiority complex," wrote Jinshichi

Tōkairin, "Nihei Okazaki distinguished himself as an exceptionally able man among the other prefectural groups . . . and made us feel proud."[10]

The Fukushiman Community Emerges

Many ambitious men left the plantations after their six-month contracts were over to start independent businesses. One of the first such individuals was Otoji Okazaki, a member of the first contingent of Fukushiman immigrants, who were taken to Kahuku Plantation on Oahu's north shore by boat as soon as they reached Hawaii in 1898. He moved to Honolulu and worked as a cook at the Okumura Student Dormitory for a while and then he learned tailoring and opened a tailor shop on Hotel Street in 1902. His store became a gathering place for Fukushimans whenever they came to Honolulu.[11]

By 1909 about 165 Fukushimans were in nonagricultural businesses; they were working as tailors, barbers, store proprietors and clerks, cooks or servants for Caucasian families, the YMCA, and restaurants.[12] Many became independent farmers also, raising vegetables and fruits, including pineapple. Those who chose to continue plantation work eventually gravitated to Ewa and Waipahu plantations on Oahu and Puunene, Paia, and Keahua plantations on Maui. The old-timers asserted, "We Fukushimans want to live peacefully as a group."[13]

Nihei Okazaki, mentioned above, came to Hawaii in 1906 at the age of twenty-three. He began as a regular field laborer, using his spare time to study English. Among several thousand plantation workers, he was the only graduate of *chugaku* (11th grade), and he excelled in reading, writing, and speaking and came to be respected as an intellectual. He attended McKinley High School as an auditor and studied English.[14] He was described as a "broad-shouldered, genial young man . . . with unusual ability and a sharp mind."[15]

His ability was soon recognized by the plantation management and he was made a luna and later supervisor of the hazardous construction of the Helemano irrigation system in central Oahu that brought water from the Koolau Mountains onto the plains. This project involved excavating and connecting dangerously steep ridges, often resulting in fatalities among the workers. Only because of Nihei's compassionate leadership and genial personality, which inspired the men under him, was the irrigation system finally completed.[16]

Nihei could not ignore any situation in which others were in danger or threatened. When he noticed that a woman from his prefecture was being persistently harassed by a notorious gang leader, Nihei told him to stop. Angered by this interference, the troublemaker went to Nihei's lodgings, shouting, "I have come to kill you!" Nihei took off his shirt and sat on the floor, saying, "You, idiot. I have gone through bullets on the battlefields [in the Russo-Japanese War], so I am not afraid of losing my one or two lives. If you dare to kill me, try," and he stared at the man with piercing eyes. Astounded by this unusual show of courage, the gangster meekly expressed his admiration for Nihei and never bothered the woman again.[17]

In 1908, Nihei was invited by Dr. Gensho Hasegawa, a physician originally from Chiba-ken, to be the executive vice-president of the all-Japanese joint-stock pineapple company he was forming in Kipapa on Oahu. The venture was named the Waipio Pineapple Company, but the Japanese called it "Hyakunin Compa" [One Hundred Men's Company]. Unfortunately, it ended in bankruptcy because of the poor crop. Dr. Hasegawa gave up the enterprise, but Nihei continued to devote his time and energy to pineapple cultivation. He succeeded in organizing another joint-stock company called the Washington Pineapple Company by leasing 138 acres of land on the leeward side of Oahu with investments chiefly from Fukushimans. Although the crop was successful this time, the Caucasian-owned canning factories refused to buy pineapples from the Japanese growers. The Washington Pineapple Company ended up dumping 13,000 tons of pineapple in the valley and losing an estimated $32,500.[18]

Undaunted by repeated failure, Nihei Okazaki never gave up his efforts to improve the quality of pineapple cultivation. He took special courses at the University of Hawaii and made tours of pineapple plantations on Molokai, Lanai, and Maui and other South Pacific islands. He became known as an expert on pineapple, and in 1924 he was invited by Japanese pineapple concerns to advise and supervise the pineapple industry in Taiwan, where he made a tremendous contribution.[19]

One who became a leader of the Fukushiman community was Jinshichi Tōkairin, who arrived in 1907. After working for six years on Ewa Plantation and another six years on Waipahu Plantation, he and his family moved to Honolulu. In 1920 he bought a Japanese inn or *ryokan* from a man from Miyagi-ken, another Tōhoku prefecture, and named it Tōhoku Ryokan to cater to those from northern Japan as well as those from Niigata-ken. Niigata-ken is the adjoining prefecture to Fukushima-ken and the Niigatans speak a dialect of similar intonation and pronunciation. In the early days the Tōhoku immigrants had stayed at ryokans operated by Hiroshimans, Yamaguchins, Kumamotons, and other western Japanese, but Fukushimans and other Tōhoku people felt more comfortable having an inn operated by one of their own where their dialects were freely used and understood. Without much capital Tōkairin and his wife had to work very hard to operate their hotel. At first they had no cooks or servants or clerks to assist them. But they were successful, and later they acquired Nuuanu Onsen, an exclusive Japanese teahouse and restaurant, to help its owner, who was in financial trouble. This restaurant as well as Tōhoku Ryokan were closed during World War II. After the war, their second son started Tōhoku Travel Service at his father's old hotel while his daughter and son-in-law continued to operate Nuuanu Onsen restaurant.[20]

Distinguished Fukushimans in Hawaii

Fukushimans in Hawaii did not lack in individual distinction. Dr. Saburo Hayashi studied at Aomori Medical College before emigrating to the United States. After graduating from San Francisco Medical College, he moved to Hawaii where he was joined by his wife Matsu in 1895. They lived in Holualoa in North Kona on the island of Hawaii for more than forty years serving Japanese immigrants of all prefectural backgrounds from the North to South Kona area. Physician, educator, and community leader, Dr. Hayashi was a champion of justice and a fighter for the rights of the defenseless. He criticized severely those who took advantage of poor people. He began to publish a vernacular *Kona Hankyō* (Echo of Kona) in 1897 and continued it until 1941. In 1898, Dr. Hayashi was the main force in founding the Japanese school in

Holualoa that was independent of religious affiliation, Buddhist or Christian, for the children of the immigrants who had no school to attend in those days. Five men were elected from among the parents of the children to serve on the Education Committee, which was to be responsible for the operation of the school, and Mrs. Hayashi taught until Sukezo Takeda was secured by this committee as a teacher.[21]

Minkei Ouchi left Japan for Canada in 1905 and later studied elementary education in the United States for three years. On the recommendation of Ryusaku Tsunoda, who was then principal of the middle school of Fort Gakuin of Honpa Hongwanji Buddhist Mission in Honolulu and later became a professor of Japanese history, literature, and language at Columbia University, he came to Hawaii in 1909 to be principal of the mission's elementary school. In the early years there were perpetual competition and conflict between independent Japanese language schools and Buddhist-sponsored language schools. To eliminate such troubles, Ouchi helped organize the Japanese Education Association as a means to make a unified effort to provide effective language instruction. As its executive director, he edited a new textbook suitable for Hawaii-born children with Dr. Yaichi Haga of Japan as his advisor.[22] He thus made an invaluable contribution to language teaching for children who knew only the dialects of their parents.

In 1909 there were altogether eight Japanese language school teachers of Fukushiman background in Hawaii, including two principals. Later, two more Fukushimans joined their ranks; in 1914, Yakichi Watanabe came to Hawaii with his wife and founded a language school on Maui, and in 1915 Shichiro Watanabe arrived and founded a language school in Honolulu. Shichiro Watanabe also taught at the University of Hawaii as an instructor. Parents who spoke only their own dialects were anxious to have their children attend language schools to learn standard Japanese, regardless of the prefectural backgrounds of the principals or teachers.

Dr. Tokuei Takahashi, a surgeon, came to Hawaii in 1918 after practicing in Japan and Mexico. He was in private practice, using the facilities of the Kuakini Japanese Hospital. In 1921 he and his family went to Europe and stayed on at Oxford, England, where he did research in cancer surgery. After returning to Hawaii in 1930, Dr. Takahashi joined the surgical staff of Queen's Hospital in Honolulu as a cancer specialist, the first Japanese doctor to become a member of the hospital's professional staff.[23]

Citizen Katsunuma

Tomizō Katsunuma was born in Miharu in Fukushima Prefecture in 1863, the third son of a samurai family. After graduating from the prefectural boys' middle school, he attended the Foreign Language College in Sendai and later taught English at the boys' middle school in his hometown. Soon he was awarded a scholarship to study at the College of Veterinary Science of Tokyo for four years. He and an elder brother travelled to the United States in 1889, his brother proceeding to the east to observe the electrical industry while Katsunuma remained in Utah and Idaho studying veterinary science along with agriculture, English, and theology. While in Utah, he became a Mormon and a naturalized American citizen. He also served in the National Guard there. His brother returned to Japan after a year, but Katsunuma's eldest brother came to the United States and together they toured the country, studying the dairy industry and animal husbandry. Katsunuma returned to Japan in 1898 and recruited emigrants from Fukushima and other northeastern prefectures as a temporary agent of the Kumamoto Emigration Company.

Soon after his return to Hawaii Katsunuma became an inspector for the Immigration Service and served in that capacity until the end of Japanese immigration to the United States on June 30, 1924. When the last shipload of picture brides arrived that day Katsunuma lined them up and shouted, "Banzai for picture brides" (Long live picture brides) three times.[24] No Japanese who arrived in that period, regardless of his or her prefectural background, landed in Hawaii without being inspected and advised by Katsunuma. He was known for his sharp wit and was widely respected by the Japanese. Many, including those who came as picture brides, consulted him on their personal problems.[25]

Katsunuma participated in many community organizations. He was a director of the Japanese Benevolent Association; he served on the Prince Fushimi Scholarship Committee for Nisei education; and he was a member of the Rotary Club of Honolulu. He was also vice-president of the vernacular newspaper *Nippu Jiji*. Chief editor Yasutarō Sōga described Dr. Katsunuma as follows:

> The editorial staff called him "Rōhkō" [Venerable Elder], but in the community he was known as "Dr. Parties" because he was present at practically all the parties and receptions, including those at the governor's mansion and at the Japanese Consulate as well as small private parties. . . . Dr. Katsunuma never used chopsticks, even at the parties where Japanese food was served. At the Japanese Ryōtei style restaurants, it was customary that the waitresses brought knives and forks as soon as they saw Dr. Katsunuma. He had a wide circle of friends and acquaintances among Caucasians, Chinese, Hawaiians, Portuguese, as well as Japanese. He mingled with them with natural friendliness regardless of race, religion, social status, education, or age. When I happened to walk with him on the streets of Honolulu, he stopped so often to talk to them that when their conversations became prolonged, I felt impatient. He also loved to study and write articles for the newspaper.[26]

Editor Kempū Kawazoe recalled that it was his custom to bring his weekly article every Saturday morning to the *Nippu Jiji* office. As soon as the article appeared in the paper, he would call up his friends for criticism, asking, "What do you think of today's article?" If they answered, "There are places where the meaning is not clear," Katsunuma would say, "My wife said so too," and laugh heartily. His pen name was "Laughing Horse," a reference to his veterinary practice. His favorite stunt at parties was imitating a horse's whinnying, saying it was a laughing horse. When he bought the old Japanese Consulate building in 1907 and moved it to Metcalf Street for his residence, he named it "Basho-an" (Laughing Horse's hermitage).[27]

Among the many episodes about Dr. Katsunuma was his April Fool's Day story, which he wrote about on April 2, 1922:

> On April Fool's Day, I had a forced day off. So I decided to peddle the sweet potatoes which grew abundantly in the Basho-an vegetable garden. I borrowed a truck and a driver from the Asahi Store and went to Komeya Hotel first and asked Mrs. Komeya if she wanted sweet potatoes. She said instantly, "I will buy 30 lbs." Deeply impressed, I gave her an extra 10 lbs. of potatoes. Otaru San of Yamashiro Hotel bought some gladly. When I stopped in front of Onomichiya Hotel,

passersby and housewives in the neighborhood bought the potatoes eagerly, some saying, "Is this for a donation to Mid-Pacific Institute in Manoa? Keep the change."

After that, I went to the kitchen of the consul general's residence. Three maids came out and said, "We are not sure if the consul general and his family would want to eat potatoes. When you come next time bring some other vegetables." Next I went to the kitchen of Vice-Consul Naito's residence and shouted, "Do you want potatoes?" Mrs. Naito came out and said, "Oh, thank you for the potatoes. I still have some that your wife gave me." I excused myself and went to the kitchen doors of the Nakanos, the Takiyamas, and the Nishiguchis of the consular staff. They all thanked me for the large quantity of beautiful potatoes, taking them for granted as free gifts. Thus, I left the Consulate compound with no gain. On the way home I stopped at Dr. Negoro's but the result was the same as at the Consulate. Next I knocked at the door of the Kyōraku-kan. The housewife there willingly bought all of the remaining potatoes. I learned that trading is not an easy job. I made up my mind never again to engage in unfamiliar trading.[28]

Dr. Katsunuma was always critical of the expression of excessive modesty in Japanese speech, including the way Mrs. Katsunuma referred to her cooking. He wrote:

Whenever we invite guests my wife is apt to say, "Please come for luncheon on such and such day at such and such time. We have nothing, but please come, etc." the term "nothing" is the customary expression to say that it may not suit your taste. So when my wife was planning a luncheon for a group of ladies, I did the telephoning on her behalf and said "This coming Sunday, February 5, there will be a large gathering of ladies at our house. We are going to offer you a luncheon with plenty of good things to eat. Be sure to come by 12:30. You can bring your children, too. We are looking forward to seeing you." That was the way I invited them. Sixty-eight ladies including the consul general's wife came.[29]

Dr. Katsunuma was unconventional, unpretentious, and had an open and direct way of doing things. Japanese residents of Hawaii, rural and urban, accepted him with affection and respect because of these characteristics.

Relations with Other Kenjins

Despite their subordinate position as newcomers among the larger, dominant prefectural groups, the Fukushimans collectively enjoyed a positive self-concept. One reason for this was the level of education most Fukushimans were exposed to before coming to Hawaii:

> Compared with immigrants from western Japan, Fukushiman immigrants had a somewhat higher educational background. In rural communities in Fukushima-ken young men continued their education after finishing the compulsory education by attending evening schools, especially during the slack season in winter. We studied world history, modern history, and various other subjects. For this reason, some of the Fukushiman immigrants could even recite what they learned, for instance, about historical events, as if they were singing familiar songs. In contrast, those from western prefectures worked in the fields during the winter and missed the educational opportunities of the youthful years.[30]

Fukushimans were often called upon to participate in activities in the larger Japanese community because of their superior educational backgrounds. An Issei leader of the Fukushima Kenjin-kai recalled that in spite of his Zuuzuu-ben he was often asked to make a congratulatory speech at wedding parties on behalf of all the guests, who were mostly Hiroshimans and Yamaguchins. He was a member of the Board of Trustees of a Japanese language school. "The chairman of the Board was usually a Hiroshiman or Yamaguchin, because he had money, which the school needed. I was usually a recording secretary, because they knew I kept the minutes of the meetings scrupulously."[31]

There was nevertheless animosity between Fukushimans and members of non-Tōhoku prefectural groups that was often expressed in terms of language. The average Fukushiman was regarded as a Tōhoku immigrant with queer, unintelligible speech. One Issei leader recalled that he had a standard response to derogatory remarks about his speech. "I am a mixed blood of Ainu-Japanese background. My tongue is three inches shorter than yours. So, I can't lie or flatter with smooth-talking as you do. What mixed blood are you? Korean-Japanese?"[32]

Far more outspoken was a well-known figure, Charlie S., for his public denunciation over the radio of those from the western prefectures who became the leaders of Japanese organizations. Charlie S. came to Hawaii in 1924 to join his elder brother, and together they developed a successful gravel business in Mokapu on Oahu before World War II. His brother was respected among the Fukushimans for his quiet personality and various service activities. In contrast, Charlie S. was a nonconformist, disregarding conventional politeness. He began his radio show soon after World War II. He always opened the program by saying, "If you don't like my show, just turn off the radio and go to sleep." He described the experiences that led him to start a radio program:

> In those days the Japanese community was dominated by Hiroshimans and Yamaguchins, and the language used as the Japanese language in Hawaii was actually their dialects and not real Japanese. But we Fukushimans were insulted because they could not understand what we were saying. When Okinawans came they were also insulted because they could not understand the Okinawan dialects. There were many Fukushimans on Ewa Plantation and I used to visit my friends there. I noticed that both Fukushimans and Okinawans were looked down upon and living in inferior housing. Such discrimination made me indignant. The old-timers also looked down upon those whom they called "Chorinbo." That's Hiroshima-Yamaguchi dialect for "Eta." Hideyoshi Toyotomi, who invaded Korea [in 1597], brought back some Koreans and had them settle in western Japan. Naturally, their descendants are in that region. But why should they ostracize "Chorinbo"? They themselves may very well be "Chorinbo." Anyway, they were arrogant and meddlesome, and even when they were superficially nice to you, they were haughty, especially if they became officers or directors of important Japanese organizations.[33]

Because of the insults to Fukushimans Charlie S. witnessed, he started what he called his "Zuuzuu-ben Warukuchi Hōsō" (Zuuzuu Dialect Derogatory-Remark Show), over KPOA in 1946. He contracted with the radio station and paid by the month for a one-hour show. Later when KPOA raised the price, he moved the program to other stations, the last one KTRG. The show continued until that station went off the air in 1970.

> At first I had my show every night, but later I had it once a week. Also, the time of my show was changed from 7:00 P.M. to 9:00 P.M. at

the request of my listeners. My show kept me very busy, gathering information, tape-recording the interviews, etc. Then, I had to write the script. No arrogant, self-righteous leader in the Japanese community escaped from my abusive attacks. They were all mad at me, but at the same time they did not miss my show in order to know whom I was attacking and what I was saying about him. If they were in the middle of a party, they would stop whatever they were doing and listen to my program. Finally, these prominent members of the Japanese organization complained to the manager of KTRG about my show, and they sued me. I told them that I was willing to go to court to contest it. They sure gave me a bad time. They dropped the matter, however, for fear that the news might hurt the reputation of the Japanese community. The Japanese vernacular papers denounced me harshly. So, I attacked their editors for being the tools of big shots in the Japanese community."[34]

In the meantime Charlie S. had an unusual experience that resulted in a change in the course of his life.

I had never paid any attention to Ogamisama [the Dancing Goddess]. One day when I went to the airport to meet my friend from Japan, I saw a crowd of Japanese chanting and dancing. I wondered who these crazy people were. When my friend came down from the plane, he told me that the Dancing Goddess was on the same plane and that these people must be her converts to welcome her.

When I saw her, I walked straight to her and said, "You crazy old woman! What in the world are you doing in Hawaii?" She retorted, "You stupid! I know all your weakness and faults." So, I challenged her, saying, "My religion is Zuuzuu-ben Sect. I have a one-hour radio show. Let's have a debate over the radio and see which side can denounce the other side more maliciously. The defeated side will completely surrender to the winning side and become the victor's follower." I heard afterward that her followers in Honolulu urged her not to accept my challenge, but that she insisted on appearing on my show, telling them that she might use me later. That was in 1960. . . .

To my surprise, she knew that I had stomach cancer. I had it for about ten years. When I had the attack, it was real agony, but much of the time it was dormant. I believed that as long as I took care of my general health, I could carry on my usual activities. So, my stubborn nature kept me going. In our radio debate the first thing Ogamisama said was, "Charlie, you have stomach cancer. You have only two more years to live, but I will let you live twenty more years." In every argument she had the upper hand, and finally, I was obliged to surrender to her. Her followers in Honolulu never accepted me in their group. So, I denounced them, especially the leaders, on my radio show. Even now I have no connection with them. I am alone as Ogamisama's convert and her witness of my new faith. Every year I make a pilgrimage to the headquarters in Tabuse of Yamaguchi-ken.

I have never joined the Fukushima Prefectural Association because, once it was organized, it had a political structure like other groups. I don't like that. In fact, I stay away from the Japanese community. My close friends are Chinese, Portuguese, Hawaiians, and some of the other Caucasians.[35]

Although Charlie's bizarre attacks on the dominant prefectural groups over the radio were meant to be punishment for the insults Fukushima immigrants suffered, the other Fukushimans had no connection with his broadcasting adventures and did not quite approve of his tactics. He acted as an individual, and he was never a spokesman for the Fukushiman community as a whole.

Returnees from Hawaii

Approximately 3,000 of the Fukushiman immigrants returned to their homeland before World War II as financially successful people. Practically all of them bought additional farmlands for orchards to raise apples, peaches, and pears or to grow mulberry trees for silkworms for their sericulture industry. Some who had tenant farmers, however, were stripped of their lands in the post-war redistribution of farmlands during the American occupation of Japan. Those who had worked in Hawaii as cooks or bakers for Caucasian families or restaurants were able to recover from their losses by selling American-style cakes and bread or serving American-style foods at restaurants they opened.[36]

In 1956–1957 Kanji Takahashi, a former Japanese language school principal on Maui who returned to Fukushima with his family in 1933, launched a survey of the survivors. He found out that there were 233 individuals, including 22 widows. These returnees had brought with them some of their children born in Hawaii while leaving behind their older children, including those born in Japan. While practically all of the returnees had married Fukushima-born spouses or Hawaii-born men and women of Fukushiman parentage, a few married spouses of Niigata background. Niigata being the adjoining prefecture to Fukushima, Niigatan spouses had no difficulty in adjusting themselves in Fukushima where the language and other cultural practices were similar, and their relatives were congenial and visited each other as intimate kin.[37]

For mutual assistance and to renew fellowship among the returnees from Hawaii during the disorganization of the postwar period, the Hawaii-kai (Hawaii Association) was formed in 1948 under the leadership of Nihei Okazaki.[38] The subsequent closing of the Hawaii-kai vividly reflected the passage of time for the returnees, as explained by Toshio Tanji, the former president of Fukushima Kenjin-kai in Honolulu.

> The Hawaii-kai in Fukushima was closed in 1978 after thirty years of existence because of the fact that the few remaining members were all ninety years old or older and unable to carry on the business of the association. For the past thirty years the Fukushima Kenjin-kai of Honolulu, Aiea, Maui, and Hawaii together regularly sent donations to the Hawaii-kai in Fukushima because they sent us their Kaiho [News Magazine of the Association] four times every year. When we received a letter about the closing of their association, we wrote them a letter of appreciation.[39]

Those Who Stayed

While many successful Fukushimans returned to their homeland, those who remained in Hawaii also made quiet and steady advancement as their Hawaii-born children grew up to be responsible members of the larger American community. In 1957–1958 the number of surviving Fukushiman pioneers was altogether 448, including 38 widows, ranging in age from 52 to 83 years. In August 1957, 237 of them—65 in Honolulu, 75 in rural Oahu, and 97 on Maui—who had lived in Hawaii for 50 years or longer were honored by Governor Sakuma Otake of Fukushima-ken and each was give a wooden sake mug.[40]

On June 10, 1978, the Fukushima Kenjin-kai commemorated the 80th anniversary of the arrival of the first Fukushiman immigrants to Hawaii with a memorial service of the deceased pioneers at the Nuuanu Soto Mission (Zen Sect Buddhism) in Honolulu. Practically all of the Fukushimans were Zen Buddhists except those who were converted to Christianity. Governor Isao Matsudaira came to Hawaii as the chief speaker for the memorial services in Honolulu and on Maui. About a hundred Issei and some Nisei participated in the service in Honolulu.[41]

The Fukushima Kenjin-kai, which was organized in 1921, was closed during World War II, but in 1949 it resumed its meetings. Toshio Tanji, the last Issei president of the Kenjin-kai, who came to Hawaii in 1917 at the age of fifteen to join his father, in 1980 described the present and future status of the Fukushima Prefectural Association:

> We have about 300 members of whom about 60 are Nisei. Most of the Issei members came to Hawaii as teen-agers or small children, and their ages now range from late 70 to late 80 years. From this year [1980] the officers of our association are Nisei. They are all successful businessmen. Once a year, in summer, we have a Kenjin-kai picnic in Ala Moana Park. Since it is an annual affair, it is something we all look forward to and our families including children join. We have generous donations from our members. So, we make it substantial with prizes. Also, our New Year's Party is very popular and everybody looks forward to it. We have it at Kanraku Ryōtei, which is in a convenient location. For the sake of elderly members we have our New Year's Party at noon.
>
> As the leadership of the Kenjin-kai has been transferred to Nisei, the records of the organization will be in English. At any rate, some of us Issei got together at Tendai-shu Temple every week and made video-tapes by discussing some of the events and experiences of Fukushiman immigrants. We have finished this project now. These video-tapes will be kept at Bishop Museum and will be available for posterity.[42]

The Fukushiman immigrants overcame the handicap of being late arrivals and the problems posed for them by their dialect and established themselves in various fields in the Japanese community of Hawaii. The Issei Fukushimans did not expect their Hawaii-born children to be their successors as Fukushimans, but as members of the larger community.

4

Immigrants from Okinawa-ken

THE Okinawans were the last large-scale prefectural group of Japanese immigrants to come to Hawaii. Okinawan immigration was initiated by Kyūzō Tōyama, a brilliant educator in Okinawa and Tokyo and a leader of the civil rights movement in Okinawa, which was organized to protest the policies of the dictatorial governor Shigeru Narabara, a Kagoshiman appointed by the central government in Tokyo who, among other offenses, had indefinitely postponed the local election of prefectural legislators.[1] While in Tokyo, Tōyama came across an advertisement recruiting emigrants to Hawaii. This prompted him to think that overseas emigration might be the only positive solution to the problems of an increasing population and inevitable food shortages in the island prefecture. At the same time it was a way to liberate Okinawans from the oppressive political domination of high-ranking officials of non-Okinawan origin. Returning to Okinawa, Tōyama concentrated on promotional work for emigration to Hawaii among the people, and he succeeded in getting the approval of Governor Narabara, who at the beginning firmly opposed Tōyama's proposition.[2]

Thirty men of various occupational backgrounds, ranging in age from twenty-one to thirty-five years, from cities and rural communities, were selected. With Kuhachiro Uyehara, a thirty-two-year-old school teacher from Itoman, as the leader, they sailed from Naha on December 5, 1899, aboard the S.S. *Satsuma Maru* and reached Osaka on December 13. Three men failed to pass the preliminary physical examination in Osaka and Yokohama, and twenty-seven Okinawan men sailed from Yokohama aboard the S.S. *City of China* along with 641 emigrants from other prefectures, arriving at Honolulu on January 8, 1900. Another Okina-

49

wan failed the physical examination in Honolulu and had to return home. After a week at the Immigration Quarantine Station, twenty-six Okinawans were admitted entry. On the same day all of them were sent to Ewa Plantation on Oahu, as had been arranged by the agent of the immigration company in charge and agreed to by the immigrants before their departure.[3]

Soon these men found the life on the plantation extremely hard. Cutting sugarcane and loading it on rail cars for ten hours a day was rigorous enough, but harder to endure was the humiliating experience of being closely supervised by a mounted overseer who had a whip in his hand, shouting, "Go ahead, go ahead." For these young men, charged with the pioneer spirit and highly conscious of their role in helping to solve the population problem of their homeland, their situation was more than they could endure. Chinzen Kinjo from Naha was the first Okinawan, in fact, the only Japanese immigrant, who dared to challenge the brutal luna singlehanded with karate. He recalled his daring encounter:

> There was no one who wasn't whipped. Once when this luna whipped me by taking me for someone else, I was really mad and all the anger which had hitherto been suppressed in me exploded and I challenged him with karate. Since this luna was a big man, a six-footer, it wasn't easy for me. But, finally, I threw him to the ground. . . . There was a big crowd surrounding us, some waving cane knives, shouting, "Kinjo, go ahead, go ahead!" The others shouted "Beat him up! Finish him!" I was at the point of jumping at him, risking my whole life in that one blow. Just at that moment, Big Luna [superior overseer] came and calmed me down, saying, "Wait, wait. I will fix everything all right." Thus, the incident ended short of serious consequences. We wanted revenge even to the point of committing murder. You can understand how brutally the laborers of early years were treated.[4]

Because of the labor conditions, the immigrants decided among themselves to appeal to the governor of Okinawa and the immigration company to cancel their contracts with the plantation. Since the immigration companies acted only as employment agencies for the immigrants, they were under no obligation to help them return home. For this they would have had to save or borrow money. Before their plan was carried out, however, Congress passed the Organic Act, which made the laws and Constitution of the United States applicable to Hawaii, thus making contract labor immigration in Hawaii invalid. It was three months after their arrival. Many of the Okinawans moved to other plantations while some remained at Ewa under improved conditions.[5]

Back in Okinawa, without any news of the first emigrants to Hawaii, rumors about their fate were rampant. Deeply concerned, Tōyama asked his younger colleague in the civil rights movement, Shinsuke Taira, who was studying in Tokyo, to proceed to Hawaii to find out what happened. Taira arrived in Hawaii in June 1901. By then most of the first group were scattered, some having moved to the other islands while three, including Matasuke Tōyama, Kyuzō's younger brother, had gone to San Francisco. There were eight or nine Okinawans still working on Ewa Plantation from whom Taira got detailed information on their experiences in Hawaii. Then he went to Aiea Plantation where Kuhachiro Uyehara, the leader of the group, was working. Taira stayed at his lodging for several days and got detailed information on what had happened to the first group since their departure from Naha.[6]

In the meantime, six of the group returned to Okinawa, and, although their reports were mainly of hardship at the beginning, they began to build tile-roofed houses, which were rare in the rural villages, or bought farmlands. These visible signs of success helped Tōyama's emigration campaign. With rigorous plantation work in mind, Tōyama concentrated his efforts to recruit emigrants from among the hardy farmers in Kin, his native village. Forty-five men responded. For their travel and incidental expenses, Tōyama managed to borrow 5,000 yen from generous individuals as well as moneylenders. He also organized the "Kyodai-kai" (Brotherhood Association) to receive the money sent in installments by the emigrants out of their earnings in Hawaii to pay their debts.[7]

The Second Group

Tōyama himself led the second group, forty-five men who left Okinawa in March 1903. In Kobe and Yokohama, while undergoing medical examinations and attending to the business matters of emigration, practically all of them suffered from the severe cold of the early spring weather, being used to the warm March weather of Okinawa. Tōyama was also infuriated by the outrageously high brokerage charges the Okinawans had to pay the emigration companies and innkeepers. These men, all farmers who spoke nonstandard Japanese and wore the Okinawa-style short kimono, must have seemed like country bumpkins, and the emigration company officials, innkeepers, and others took advantage of them. Finally, thirty-five Okinawans, accompanied by Tōyama, reached Hawaii on April 4, 1903, followed by four in May and one in July, a total of forty men altogether. Hence, the second Okinawan arrivals were called "Shijunin-gumi" (Forty-men company).[8]

Tōyama and the group were immediately assigned to Honokaa Plantation on the island of Hawaii. It had been nicknamed "Oni Kochi" (Devil's Plantation) because of its extremely hard labor conditions and it had a perpetual labor shortage. Tōyama, however, was soon incapacitated with fever, and he asked Shinsuke Taira, who happened to be in Hilo, to take over the responsibility of the group. Tōyama inspected various plantations in the Hilo vicinity and after three months on Hawaii, he moved to Oahu to inspect plantations there. In the meantime, Taira had reached Honokaa and found most of the second group sick due to the lack of drinking water. They decided to move to the Hilo area and work on Piihonua and Olaa plantations. Because of the continuous rainy weather, however, the men suffered from ill health. Finally, they moved to Ewa Plantation on Oahu. They found the conditions at Ewa excellent and regained their health.[9]

Tōyama and Taira helped the men to adjust to life in Hawaii, and every Saturday evening the workers gathered at Honouliuli in Ewa to hear their two leaders' inspiring talks reminding them that they were pioneers in Okinawa's overseas emigration, stressing that industry, thrift, and unity among them would save their homeland from poverty and stimulate further emigration to Hawaii. Realizing that they were handicapped because of their dialect, which was unintelligible to the immigrants from other prefectures, these two leaders helped them to improve their standard Japanese by having them engage in debate and discussion.[10]

As the success of the second group resulted in increased interest in emigration to Hawaii, numerous emigration companies in Japan began to recruit emigrants in Okinawa. Tōyama was called back after six months in Hawaii to prevent exploitation by such companies. He subsequently affiliated himself with Teikoku Shokumin Goshigaisha (Imperial Overseas Emigration Company, Ltd.) and opened an office in Naha to promote overseas emigration of Okinawans. Taira left Hawaii for the West Coast of the United States in the meantime. After the departure of their two leaders, the forty men worked doggedly on the plantation, earning overtime pay to be able to send a large portion of their monthly earnings to the Kyodai-kai in Okinawa. They repaid all their debts in two and a half years.[11]

In Okinawa the enthusiasm for emigration to Hawaii picked up momentum; there were more than 260 young men in the third group, who arrived in Hawaii in 1904, followed by 1,200 in 1905. In 1906 the number increased to nearly 4,500, and in 1907 about 2,500 came. The Okinawan immigrants constituted about one-fifth of the total Japanese immigration of more than 44,000 during this period of free immigration.[12] An unknown number of ambitious Okinawans joined those from other prefectures in the mass exodus to the West Coast during this period. From August 1907 until the end of June 1924, the *Yobiyose Jidai* period, families and close kin, including picture brides, joined the earlier arrivals, although some returned to Okinawa. In 1924, the year Japanese immigration was terminated, the total number of Okinawans and their Hawaii-born children was 16,536. Thus, despite their late arrival, they became the fourth largest prefectural group in Hawaii, following the Hiroshimans, Yamaguchins, and Kumamotons.

Okinawans on Plantations

Okinawans performed the same rigorous tasks on the plantations as the other prefectural immigrants. Issei members of the Okinawa Kenjin-kai described their arrival and early years of plantation life at a meeting in 1960. "It was in the 40th year of Meiji [1907]," said Kasaku Yonashiro, "that twelve of us headed for Hawaii, left our native village Haneji-son to walk for 50 to 60 miles to Naha, carrying our baggage on our shoulders. Thus began our journey to hell. At Naha Harbor we were loaded like cargo on a small crude boat. After three days we arrived at Kobe where we stayed in the big hall of a low-class inn infested with swarms of bedbugs."

The group made the crossing aboard the *Nihon Maru,* a huge

steamship. After they arrived at Honolulu and passed the health inspection at the Immigration Service, they all scattered.

"I was among those assigned to go to the Island of Hawaii," recalled Kasaku Yonashiro. "Again on a cargo boat, we arrived outside of Hilo Harbor. As our ship, taking advantage of the swelling of the waves, rose close to another small boat, two huge men threw each of us down to that small boat, which took us to the pier. This time the operation was reversed. We were thrown to the pier where we were caught by a man waiting to catch us." He went on to describe living and working conditions at the plantation:

> Our camp [living quarters] was five wooden shelters built of rough boards, where more than 100 immigrants were living, washing clothes, or cooking. The cooking place was outside of the shelter, protected from the rain and wind by empty bags for curtains, and inside the bag curtains was an amusing sight with the rows of more than a hundred empty kerosene cans used as cooking stoves.
>
> At 5:30 in the morning we marched in a single line to the cane fields, each carrying his lunch. The luna, the watchdog of hell, mounted on a horse, followed us so closely that those at the rear were almost trampled and some were forced to step aside to avoid being trampled. Except for thirty minutes for lunch, there was no time to rest until 4:00 P.M. If anyone resting was caught by the Watchdog, even if it was a minute before four o'clock, the closing time, he would be told, "You go home. You Pau." [You have no pay for that day.] Anyone who was declared "Pau" would be beaten half to death by the Big Luna [superior overseer] unless he ran away to another plantation during the night. That was the first chapter of hell's slavery law. Since the Big Luna was an uneducated upstart, he was indeed dangerous and disastrous to the immigrants inside the kingdom of the capitalists who were out of reach of the police.
>
> The wage during the early years of immigration was 69 cents per day, working 10 hours. It left us very little to save and our original dream of returning home after three years in Hawaii disappeared. Due to lack of sanitation and inferior food, many suffered from beriberi and other diseases. While there was a plantation hospital, a token facility, the immigrants did not want to go there because of the bad reputation it had. There was a Japanese hospital of a *naichi* doctor [non-Okinawan doctor] in Hilo, but unless one could pay cash for treatment, he was not admitted for hospitalization. So, it was good-for-nothing as far as we immigrants were concerned. For those who

were sick and wanted to return to their homeland, their friends went around to various plantations to collect donations ranging from 25 cents to 50 cents each, to enable them to pay for their return passage. There were also some successful ones who returned to their homes with $300 to $400.[13]

The Okinawans also encountered insults and discrimination from the dominant prefectural groups, who had different dialects and customs. Despite such handicaps, those who continued to work on the plantations gradually rose to higher-status jobs with minor responsibilities. Some Okinawans became labor contractors for various plantations, travelling between the islands, recruiting laborers. Those who worked for the same plantations for thirty to forty years or longer had a substantial pension and social security benefits. Many Okinawans also started cultivating pineapples or sugarcane on leased lands, selling the crops to the companies on a contract basis. At times such independent growers suffered a great loss when the market prices were low. Okinawans were good truck farmers, raising vegetables and fruits, and active in whole-sale businesses for the distribution of their produce.

Hog-Raising, the Okinawans' Foremost Contribution to Hawaii

The Okinawans made more contributions in the hog industry in Hawaii than any other national or ethnic group. For this remark-able distinction, however, they were looked down upon by their fellow Japanese immigrants as being engaged in the business of raising "filthy animals," and their children were tormented by the children of the other Kenjin who shouted, "Okinawa-ken-ken Buta Kau-kau" (Okinawa Prefecture, Pig-raiser, Pig-eater). "Kau" in Japanese means to keep animals or birds for pets, such as "inu o kau" (to have a dog as a pet). ("Kaukau," a term commonly used in Hawaii for "food" or "to eat," is a corruption of a Chinese word, probably Cantonese.)

The hog industry developed principally on Oahu because of the large market and greater availability of feed in the form of garbage collected from the kitchens of hotels, restaurants, mess halls of the armed forces as well as private homes. The first Okinawan hog farmer appeared in 1910 in Moiliili, but later he acquired land in Kaneohe to do truck farming. In 1915 there were 75 Japanese hog farmers on Oahu: 30 (41 percent) Yamaguchins, 26 (36 percent) Kumamotons, 15 (18 percent) Hiroshimans, 3 (4 percent) Okinawans, and 1 Fukuokan. By 1930, the number of Japanese hog farmers had increased to 243. Of these, 119 (49 percent) were Okinawans, almost one-half of the total Japanese hog farmers on Oahu, followed by 34 (14 percent) Kumamotons, 29 (12 percent) Yamaguchins, 22 (9 percent) Hiroshimans, and 39 (16 percent) others.[14] The increase of Okinawan hog farmers was conspicuous in comparison to that of the other prefectural groups.

According to the U.S. Census of 1930, there were 469 commercial hog farmers on Oahu who owned 25 or more hogs and derived their main income from hog-raising. This meant that the Okinawans constituted 25 percent of the commercial hog farmers on Oahu. In 1940 there were 246 Japanese hog farmers, showing little increase from ten years earlier. By prefectural background, however, the number of Okinawans had increased to 153 or 62 percent of the total, while those of the other prefectural backgrounds decreased: 28 (11 percent) Kumamotons, 23 (9 percent) Hiroshimans, 22 (9 percent) Yamaguchins, 20 (8 percent) others.[15] There were 349 commercial hog farmers on Oahu in 1940, which meant that the Okinawans constituted 44 percent of Oahu's commercial hog farmers.

The main reason for the increase of Okinawans in the industry was their positive conception of hog-raising. They considered hog-raising an integral part of agriculture; hog farmers were respected as business entrepreneurs, and they took pride in being hog farmers. Moreover, to Okinawans pigs were not only a precious commodity; the Okinawans had warm sentiments about them, because traditionally farmers in Okinawa kept pigs and from childhood they had the same tender feelings toward pigs that they would toward other pets. Kiman Kaneshiro, who operated a large-scale piggery with more than 1,300 animals on eight acres of land in Koko Head, described the piggery as a maternity-pediatrics hospital with hog farmers as doctors, nurses, and midwives, watching the health of the piglets from the time of their birth, using preventive measures to protect them from disease, taking care of their daily food, and cleaning them and their pens. He explained that despite the endless hard work day and night, hog farmers got great pleasure from watching the piglets grow and giving them loving care.[16] Also, pork was a delicacy in Okinawa and indispensable for official banquets. Fortunately in Hawaii, since all the ethnic groups that constituted the larger community were their customers, the Okinawans developed hog-raising without much difficulty.

Kaneshiro also spoke of the background of his hog business:

> After I left the plantation, I bought 12 pigs and began hog-raising in Moiliili. By the time I had 60 pigs, hog-raising was prohibited in the city. So, we moved to Waialae. During the war hog farmers and their adult children were frozen to hog-raising as part of the essential food production. We got all of the feed from the garbage of the army. After the war when our hogs increased to 400 we moved our piggery here where our large-scale piggery developed. Every day two truckfuls of leftover food and garbage are brought in and recooked in the large cooking facility for our feed. Since hog raising is essentially a family business, as long as we have good facilities, three people can do six people's work.[17]

Kaneshiro's son was the manager of the piggery while his third and fourth sons worked as assistants and his wife and other members of his family worked in various capacities.

Another large-scale hog farmer, Taru Chinen, who operated a piggery with more than 2,000 hogs in Koko Head, described the background of his enterprise:

> With a low wage of one dollar a day for ten hours of hard labor, I realized that there was no future in plantation work. So, after four years, I moved to Honolulu to start hog-raising. I bought 30 pigs and started a piggery in Moiliili. We operated it for six years. Then, suddenly all our pigs died of disease. I had no money even to buy adequate food for our children. They suffered malnutrition. We moved to Waialae, and I borrowed money and bought 400 pigs. Again, all of our pigs died. Fortunately, however, my insurance matured and I got $1,400. With it I bought 100 pigs. Since then everything has worked all right. After the war I moved our piggery to its present place. At present I have more than 2,000 pigs on the six acres of leased land. The characteristic nature of the Okinawans is that even in the darkest day of hardship they never lose sight of their ultimate goal and never give up their determination to succeed.[18]

Postwar Land Development and Closing of Hog Farms

In 1955 there were 226 commercial hog farmers on Oahu. Of these, the Okinawans numbered 153 or 68 percent of the total. Compared with them, those from other prefectures numbered 51, or 25 percent, and the remaining 9 percent were Chinese, Filipinos, and others. That Okinawans were the dominant factor in the hog industry was evident in the fact that all of the 16 hog farmers on Oahu who owned from 700 to more than 2,000 hogs were Okinawans, 7 of them having 1,000 or more hogs. Of 46 farmers who owned 300 to 699 hogs, 38 (83 percent) were Okinawans, the rest being other Japanese, Chinese, and others. Of 149 who owned 25 to 299 hogs, 97 (65 percent) were Okinawans, 36 (24 percent) were other Japanese, the rest being Chinese, Filipinos, and others.

In 1955 the Planning Department of the City and County of Honolulu ordered the removal of all the piggeries in the Kamehameha IV and Kalihi areas within one year. Of 31 Okinawan hog farmers, a large majority moved to Waianae, while some moved to Koko Head and other rural areas. The Bishop Estate's Land Management Division required the removal of all the piggeries in the Waialae and Kahala areas between 1949 and 1959. A large majority involving 110 farmers moved to the Koko Head and Blow Hole areas where they operated large-scale piggeries, each with 300 to over 2,000 hogs. When the Okinawans were at the peak of success in their hog enterprise, they were again required to move elsewhere because of the Hawaii Kai housing project being developed by the Kaiser Land Development Co., which leased the Koko Head–Blow Hole area from the Bishop Estate. As a result, by 1966 all of the 53 farmers in the Koko Head area closed their piggeries. Among them 5 moved to Waianae to continue hog-raising while 4 retired. The remaining 44 changed their occupations. All of the 37 hog farmers in the Blow Hole area either moved to other rural areas or changed their occupations. The State's Department of Agriculture had urged these hog farmers to move to Maui to reestablish their piggeries, but none accepted this proposal, considering it impracticable. Since then, Waianae has become the largest hog-raising area on Oahu, with forty-five piggeries, about 25 percent of the total number of commercial hog farmers on Oahu, raising 65 percent of the hogs in Hawaii. About 30 of these hog farmers are Okinawans, owning several hundred to more than 1,000 hogs. Socially and economically, the Okinawans are the most influential prefectural group among the Japanese in Waianae.[19]

Restaurants

Another field in which Okinawans were prominent was restaurants. In 1935 at the meeting sponsored by the Osaka *Mainichi Daily,* Tetsuo Tōyama, publisher and editor of *Jitsugyo no Hawaii* (Industry of Hawaii), stated that 70 to 80 percent of the restaurants and cafes in Honolulu were operated by Okinawans.[20] This trend not only continued, but it developed into large-scale sophisticated enterprises. The proprietors usually started as dishwashers or kitchen helpers in a restaurant, gradually becoming cooks, and when they had learned sufficiently, they started their own restaurants. Since the Okinawan diet included meat, both pork and beef, the American-style restaurant business was a natural occupational field for them. Okinawan restaurants began to thrive during World War II when a large number of Armed Forces personnel became their customers during leaves.

Makari Goya, a successful entrepreneur in the laundry business on Liliha Street, explained the success of Okinawans in various businesses:

> The Okinawans work hard. Also, they help each other. For instance, if someone with ability desires to start a business and if it is a sound business, his friends get together and help him financially to get started. That was the way all the successful businesses among the Okinawans began. There is less conflict among the Okinawans. If there is any troublesome individual, we leave him alone.
>
> The characteristics of the Okinawans are speculation, persistence, and hard work. The other Kenjins do not mind economizing and saving by producing small yields. The Okinawans tend to like a large-scale enterprise. Another trait of the Okinawans is that they are persistent. No matter how hard the work is, they don't give up. They are determined to succeed.[21]

Other Business Enterprises

The following are examples of some of the other business ventures Issei Okinawans started and succeeded in during their early years in Hawaii. These accounts are all taken from interviews with the pioneers in their later years.

My pal C. and I were thinking of starting a business together. So we went to Hilo and stayed at a hotel. While there we heard that someone in Pepeekeo wanted to sell a butcher shop. We persuaded O., and three of us together bought that butcher shop for $300. That was in 1908. We bought two legs of meat in Hilo and brought them by buggy and sold them to the families in the camp every day.[22] We had to sell all the meat on the same day. Otherwise, the meat would be spoiled. When each of us earned $300 a year, C. returned to Okinawa. He had his wife and children there. Three years later when my other partner returned to Okinawa, I was left alone and could not operate a butcher shop by myself. So I started my stage coach business. I used a buggy for the first two years. Then, I started a "Teiki Bus" (Scheduled Bus) between Hilo and Pepeekeo for 25 cents a trip. I operated this bus service for thirty years, using five buses with five employees. At the outbreak of World War II I had to sell my business, because no driver's licenses were issued to aliens during the war. I married my wife when I started my "Teiki Bus" business at the age of thirty years. I am using my spacious land for such businesses as timber, cattle ranch, dairy, etc. [Interview with Kana Onaga in Honokaa in 1960]

I came to Hawaii in 1906 when I was 19. I went to Kohala Plantation and worked in the canefields until 1919. Then, I worked in the mill. I was the only Okinawan there. I was young and energetic, so my boss liked me very much. My wife came in 1918 as a picture bride when she was eighteen years old. I have eleven children altogether. Most of them are in professional jobs. Among them are a dentist, a medical technician, a scientist working for a Ph.D. at X University, school teachers, etc. My sixth son attended a confectionary school on the West Coast and when he came back he worked at a bakery in Honolulu. When he proposed to start our bakery in Hilo in 1950 I was hesitant, because I knew that it would require quite a sum of capital to buy equipment. I told him to wait for a while, but he insisted that we should start it soon and the money needed should be borrowed from a bank. Well, my life insurance was not mature yet, but we got the money from it. Also, we made use of all my wife's and daughters' savings. The manager of X bank was very pessimistic about our prospective bakery and discouraged my son when he asked him for a loan. But the manager of the other bank loaned him the needed amount of money. Well, once we started our bakery, it became very popular. At that time a few bakeries in this town [Hilo] had to close their business, but ours kept us very busy. Besides my ten employees my sons-in-law help me in the bakery. For Thanksgiving we make more than 3,000 pumpkin pies. At Christmas time we make more than 1,500 cakes. At such times we really work twenty-four hours a day. [Interview with Zensho Taira of Robert's Bakery in Hilo in 1960]

For five years we raised cattle. My wife looked after the cattle while I worked on the plantation. Then we sold our cattle business to a Chinese and we moved to Waipoli and started to cultivate rice. It was during World War I, and we had a very good harvest each year. Then suddenly our rice began to have worms and never grew. It was a complete failure. We lost about $3,000. We used to buy goods on credit, but since we couldn't pay, the stores demanded we pay in cash. Since we had no money, we couldn't buy anything. Our children had no clothes, no food. We had only one pound of "Iriko" and we ate it for one month, stretching it as long as possible. But I realized that we were not giving nourishment to our children. I thought if we gave them milk, we would not need to give them other foods for nourishment. So, I borrowed $100 and bought one milk cow. My wife took care of it. She sold one quart of milk a day for a month and got $3. Thus the money from the sale of milk was accumulated and enabled us to buy another cow. We bought one cow for $40 to $50. After twelve years we moved to Kapaa in 1931. I bought 300 acres of land in four different places as pastures. Now we have 200 cows, producing over 500 gallons of milk every day. Our regular customers include the schools, hotels, restaurants, hospitals in the Kapaa, Lihue, and Hanamaulu areas.

We Okinawans have a characteristic of not giving up. It was this characteristic that helped me to rise when I lost. I never inherited any fortune. Only thing I had was a healthy body. So, if I lost, it didn't bother me much. I just made up my mind to rise again. [Interview with Ryoju Sokei of Sokei Dairy of Kauai in 1960]

Okinawan Women

Okinawan women were known for their hard work, business ability, and ingenuity. In the early days, most Issei women had a so-called "side business" to supplement the family income, such as raising chickens and selling eggs, raising hogs, manufacturing and selling tofu, raising vegetables and fruits, or doing laundry for bachelors, while their husbands worked full time on the plantations or in their independent businesses. Mrs. Shinyu Gima, the wife of a retired plantation worker who had a painting shop in Puunene, Maui, represents such hard-working, ingenuous Okinawan housewives.

> For fifteen years I made tofu [soybean curd]. Every morning I got up at two o'clock to start making it. I also raised hogs. My two older sons helped me. Every morning, before they went to school, they went to town to collect garbage for our pigs. In the afternoon I washed clothes of single men in the camp. I also learned dressmaking. I had many, many customers. I also taught dressmaking to young girls. Their mothers appreciated it very much, because their daughters could make dresses for the whole family. My husband was working on the plantation. I wanted to make enough money to send our children to school. We have ten children. The youngest one (the only daughter) will be a freshman at the University of Hawaii. When they were small, I was very, very busy. But I loved them all and enjoyed raising them.[23]

Mrs. Gima was a good cook, and both she and her husband loved to invite their friends and visitors to their home. The Ryukyu Music Club, a group of *jamisen* players of which Mr. Gima was a member, often practiced at their house.

Okinawan women were often their husbands' business partners. An outstanding example of such women was Mrs. Kame Nakamura. She and her husband Josho Nakamura planned and operated together many business ventures until they finally founded Nakamura Mortuary in Wailuku, Maui. Mrs. Nakamura recalled their experiences:

My husband wanted to be independent, so he left the plantation in Lahaina. We opened a store to sell soft drinks. He also started a taxi service. We spent about $5,000, but it was a failure. My husband had two Filipino drivers working for him. He had to pay their wages, so I asked him to teach me driving so that I could help him in his business. But he refused, saying that a woman would not be a safe driver. I insisted on learning to drive, however, and in 1925 I got a license. I think I was the first woman taxi driver on Maui. We relieved our two employed drivers and both my husband and I drove. We worked very hard, sleeping only about two hours a day. We made $300.

About that time our "Tanomoshi" was due, so we got the money and built a house and started a cheap hotel, charging 50 cents a night per person. We served coffee and eggs for breakfast. Later we served lunch also. We had learned more about business by then. We charged 50 cents a night for a single bed, 75 cents for a three-quarter-sized bed, and a dollar for a double bed. We included sushi and manju to sell in our store, but they did not sell well. Later we borrowed $2,000 and opened a gasoline service station. I kept the accounts for our business. I was better in that than my husband, and I was a pretty good manager of our business.

In 1928 my husband and I started a mortuary, which was most needed among the Japanese. There was a Caucasian mortuary on Maui, but the Japanese had a crude way of bathing the body, putting it in the rough wooden coffin provided by the plantation and carrying it to the common cemetery and burying it. We employed a Portuguese who was a licensed mortician. My husband and I took care of all the aspects of our business. Often I had to drive alone a long distance to a hospital or a home after midnight to bring the body to our mortuary. Fifteen years ago, our son who had graduated from a morticians' school in California took over our mortuary.[24]

Mrs. Umeno Goto, a former minister in charge of the Japanese-speaking congregation of Lahaina Methodist Church, said of Mrs. Nakamura, who was eighty-seven years old in 1980:

Mrs. Nakamura is an unusual person with a brilliant mind and ability and a big heart. The members of the church respect her and the church leaders listen to her opinions and advice. Often she was the one who spurred the crucial decision-making. She is still active in the church, and as usual she takes care of many people. The only thing she does not do is driving. She used to teach driving to the wives of the ministers of the church. She taught me driving also so that I did not need to depend on the members of the church for my pastoral calls.[25]

Prejudice and Discrimination against the Immigrants from Okinawa

The most unbearable experience of the Okinawan immigrants was the treatment accorded them by the immigrants who had established themselves as the old-timers in the Japanese community. Being the last prefectural group to emigrate on a large scale, the Okinawans remained targets of ostracism and discrimination until after World War II when they and their children began to emerge as prominent figures in the economic as well as in the political, educational, and professional fields. After Japan annexed Korea in 1910, many Yamaguchins and Hiroshimans went to Korea to earn money as "Dekasegi" laborers. The term "dekasegi" means "making money away from the homeland," usually a reference to overseas emigration. In order to distinguish themselves from the native Koreans, they called themselves "Naichijin" ("the people of Japan homeland"). When the Okinawans came to Hawaii, other Japanese began to use the same term to distinguish themselves from the Okinawans, whom they viewed as an inferior group. Yasutaro Sōga recorded his observation of and reaction to such "anti-other" practices:

> The Japanese are most sensitive to being treated with discrimination. In spite of such dislike of discrimination for themselves, it is a shocking and indeed terrible contradiction that they are extremely "Haita-teki" [anti-others] in feeling and behavior. Moreover, they instill their mistaken idea of "anti-others" in their children, who are growing up in a completely different environment in Hawaii.
>
> Not long after my arrival in 1896 I heard of some people being called "Chorinbo." I thought it was a Hawaiian word for some of their people. But later I found out that the word was a dialect of the emigration prefectures (Hiroshima-Yamaguchi prefectures) of Japan for the Suiheisha [formerly called "Eta," outcastes]. In Japan, due to the old conventions, such discrimination against one group may be conceivable, but in Hawaii, far away across the Pacific Ocean, such an evil custom should have been done away with completely. There have been several instances of a tragic end for marriages between young people because of objections from their Issei parents.
>
> Similarly the so-called Naichijin's prejudice and discrimination against the people from Okinawa-ken is based on a mistaken idea of anti-others due to ignorance. Some time ago in a vicinity of Waipahu

Plantation I asked a Japanese worker how many Japanese there were. It shocked me when he answered that there were so many Japanese and so many Okinawans.[26]

Ushisuke Taira, one of the pioneer leaders of the Okinawan community, described his experiences in the early years:

> While waiting for my visa to go to the mainland to study in 1908, I stayed at Komeya Hotel [in Honolulu]. I helped them to send the immigrants to various plantations. The agents in charge called those from Okinawa-ken "Okinawa" instead of their names. They did not know I was an Okinawan. Anyway, I told them, "Stop calling them 'Okinawa' as if they were not Japanese." No one called those from the other prefectures by their ken name. The immigrants from Chugoku region, chiefly Hiroshimans and Yamaguchins who made up a large portion of the Japanese population, noticed the very different dialects and customs of the Okinawans from theirs and began to treat us as inferior outsiders. They were ignorant with very little schooling and had no idea of where Okinawa-ken was. I came back from the mainland in 1914. I made a tour of Hawaii and visited all the plantations and found out that the word "Okinawa" was used more and the Okinawans were treated as a distinct group from the other Japanese. Since the other Kenjins referred to those from Okinawa-ken as "Okinawa," the lunas, who were mostly Portuguese and other non-Japanese, called us "Okinawa" and regarded us as a separate group.[27]

Harry S. Uehara, a pioneer restaurateur and successful businessman, also ascribed the prejudice and discrimination against the Okinawans to ignorance and lack of communication due to different dialects:

> On the way to Hawaii, there were many immigrants from the other prefectures on the same boat. When I told them that I came from Okinawa, they didn't even know where Okinawa was. They had no knowledge of geography. They asked me if the Okinawans spoke Japanese. So, I told them that the Okinawans had the same education as those of the other prefectures, and that the Okinawans would call the people like them "baka" [idiot]. It was true that the early immigrants from Okinawa didn't have much education, so they did not speak the standard Japanese. For this reason, they couldn't communicate freely with the people from other prefectures. That was one reason why the Okinawans were treated as if they were non-Japanese. The other Ken-

jins treated the Okinawans as they would the Koreans and the Chinese and looked down upon us.[28]

Dr. Henry S. Gima, the first president of the United Okinawan Association, explained in 1956:

> I came to Hawaii forty years ago to join my parents after I finished the compulsory education [6th grade] in Okinawa. Since the educational system was established in Okinawa ten years later than in other prefectures of Japan, a large number of Okinawan immigrants of early years did not go to school. My father never went to school. His younger brother did, however. Since they could not speak the standard Japanese, the people from the other prefectures felt that the Okinawans were inferior.[29]

Even when Okinawans spoke standard Japanese, there was at times a semantic difficulty. For example, an elderly Issei recalled his experience on board the ship coming over to Hawaii. When the immigrants, who had a custom of celebrating New Year's Day by eating mochi (rice cake), asked him how the Okinawans celebrated New Year's Day, he answered, "We kill pigs." It was a figurative description referring to the sumptuous feast of which pork was the main dish. Without knowing the real meaning, the passengers from other kens shouted to each other as if they were shocked, saying, "They kill pigs to celebrate the New Year's Day in Okinawa!"

Another example is the tattoo on the back of the fingers of Okinawan women, which were for decorative purposes or a status symbol of married women. For the women of other prefectures, however, it appeared unfeminine. The Okinawan women were unable to explain their custom because they could not speak the prevailing Japanese language (Chūgoku-ben) in Hawaii.

Not all of the other prefectural groups treated Okinawans as an inferior outgroup, however. In the early years on the plantations, the Okinawans received practical advice from their Kumamoton or Fukuokan friends.[30] A leading Kumamoton who lived in a plantation community on Maui until his early twenties recalled his experience and observations:

> Most of those on S Plantation were Hiroshimans and Yamaguchins. There were also a large number of Okinawans, but they were looked

down upon as an inferior class of people. I mingled with the Okinawans freely. They were my closest friends, and we invited each other to our homes. Once they trust you, they remain your life-long friends. They are very sincere and hard workers. Since they were discriminated against as if they were inferior by the other Kenjins, they had strong unity and cooperation among themselves and worked hard to prove that they were superior. Look at them now [1980]! They are superior to all the other prefectural groups in Hawaii in every field of business and profession![31]

A Nisei widow recalled her parents' attitude toward the Okinawans:

My father was from Kumamoto-ken and my mother was from Fukuoka-ken, both from Kyushu. We lived in Moiliili, the so-called Japanese town. I was born and grew up there. Kumamotons and Fukuokans are well-known for their independence and straightforwardness as well as their hot temper, unfit for commercial activities, but my father operated a small neighborhood store. Our neighbors were Hiroshimans, Yamaguchins, and Okinawans. Our closest neighbor was the Nakasones. The Hiroshimans and Yamaguchins looked down upon the Okinawans and didn't associate with the latter. I don't know why even now. But my parents mingled with the Okinawans, and when the Okinawans had a picnic they were invited. They went every year. I remember my father speaking of Okinawan music and "Jamisen." Most of the Okinawans in Moiliili were hog farmers. There was the Okinawa camp where they operated their hog farms. My father had a chicken farm near there. The hog farms of the other Kenjins were in the vicinity of the quarry. Since my father was the chairman of the Board of Trustees of the Japanese Language School in Moiliili, he was responsible to collect donations for it every year. He asked the other people to collect donations from the other Kenjins, but he always went to the Okinawa camp himself since he knew them very well.[32]

An elderly Nisei, aged 71 years in 1980, of Kumamoto parentage recalled his experience with the Okinawans as follows:

My parents came from Kumamoto-ken. They worked on the plantation in the vicinity of Pearl City. Our family was poor like most Japanese immigrants. I was the eldest and there were three below me, so I had to stay at home and take care of them while my parents were

working. Obasan [the lady] next door often brought us kids something she prepared for lunch. She was very kind to us. I never went to
school beyond the fifth grade. I also started to work to earn money to
help the family income when I was fourteen years old. I don't remember that the Okinawans were ever looked down upon by the other Japanese. My family was the only non-Okinawans in our neighborhood.
All the others were Okinawans. They were very nice to us. I have four
children, and one of my sons married a daughter of an Okinawan
family.[33]

The Okinawans themselves also asserted that neither the Kumamotons nor the Fukuokans ever treated them as an inferior group.
Mrs. Kame Shimabuku recalled that Kumamotons gave donations
for fund-raising for the building of the Okinawan Women's Association in Naha in 1958. Paul Agena, a well-known Waikiki restaurateur, began his long career at the Honolulu Cafe, which was
owned by Yakichi Watanabe of Fukuoka-ken. In 1937 when
Agena had been working for two years, his boss decided to return
to Japan. Someone offered Watanabe cash to buy his business, but
Watanabe wanted Agena and another employee, Sonei Higa, to
take over his cafe. These young employees had to borrow money
from the bank, and Watanabe accompanied them to the bank to
vouch for them. He told them to pay half then and the remaining
half when they made a profit. Higa and Agena worked doggedly
to make this venture a success. Watanabe chose them to succeed
him because of their trustworthiness and ability. Their Okinawan
background had no relevance to his choice.[34]

The people from Tōhoku Chihō, such as Fukushimans, had no
prejudice against the Okinawans. Since they themselves were ridiculed because of their speech, they were sympathetic toward the
Okinawans. Many Okinawans recalled that they were treated
kindly by the Fukushimans on Ewa Plantation. Immigrants from
the prefectures of Kinki Chihō were numerically small and mostly
in trade, so that they were independent of the prejudice that prevailed in the plantation communities. The only large-scale immigration from Kinki Chihō was that of Wakayama-ken. In Hawaii,
the Wakayamans were mostly engaged in the fishery industry and,
as noted earlier, monopolized deep-sea fishing in Hawaii until
World War II. Being away from the plantations occupationally and
residentially, they were not influenced by the dominant prefectural
groups. Temperamentally, they were daring seafarers, and their

habits were different. The president of the Wakayama Kenjin-kai in 1980 and an active member of the United Japanese Society in Honolulu recalled his reaction to the prejudice and discrimination against the Okinawans:

> I was shocked to find the Okinawans being treated as if they were an inferior foreign group by the other Kenjins. In Japan I never came across anyone who thought the Okinawans were not Japanese. Okinawa-ken was one of the prefectures of Japan and all the school children knew it. When I was a student of the Merchant Marine College there were students from Okinawa. My best friend was from Okinawa, and I was invited to his home in Okinawa during the vacation. Also, for our navigation training we went to Okinawa, and we stopped at Naha in our overseas navigation training. So I saw Okinawa personally and experienced intimately the warmth, sincerity, and honesty of the Okinawans, and I always admired them and felt close to them.
>
> The Okinawans never give up if they think they are right. I noticed this characteristic in my Okinawan friends. They argue until they find out that their points of view are wrong. That's because they are honest.
>
> It was ridiculous that the immigrants from the other prefectures opposed the marriage of their children to the children of the Okinawans. That they came to Hawaii fifteen years earlier than the Okinawans and had achieved more does not justify their mean treatment and discrimination against the Okinawans. There must be some psychological reasons like chronic disease in their persecution of the Okinawans. I wish someone would make a special study of the psychology of those who persecuted the Okinawans.[35]

When Sadao Asato and his friend (both Okinawans) started the Mutual Finance Co., Ltd., in 1935, they consulted Totaro Matsui, a leading financier and banker from Shiga-ken in Kinki Chihō who was Asato's advisor and life-long business associate from the time that the latter began to work in 1925 as the accountant in the Pacific Bank of which Matsui was the manager. In 1947, when the Commercial Finance, Ltd., was founded by fifteen businessmen, Matsui became its president and Asato its vice-president. This company was still thriving in 1980. Asato resigned from the Pacific Bank in 1937 after twelve years and opened an office as an agent of Sun Life of Canada Life Insurance Co. Asato became a director of three other well-known insurance companies as well as the Central Pacific Bank. He was active as an officer or director of the Honolulu Japanese Chamber of Commerce, Kuakini Medical Center, Kuakini Old People's Home, and the Economic Study group. Thus Asato overcame the prejudice against Okinawans and became a well-known and successful businessman in the Japanese community as a whole.

There were also enlightened individuals from the Hiroshima-ken and Yamaguchi-ken who had no prejudice against the Okinawans. Sadao Asato's first job was as the bookkeeper for S. Nekomoto Contractor in 1922, whose president, Shinichi Nekomoto, was of Hiroshima origin. Asato stated that Nekomoto was a man of consequence.

Hiroshiman Katsuichi Miho, the former principal of the Japanese language school in Wailuku, Maui, was another example. Steven Chinen, one of the leaders of the Okinawan community, recalled his student days at Miho's school, where he was treated very kindly. Miho's daughter Fumie Miho was an outspoken critic of Hiroshimans' prejudice against the Okinawans, and his son Katsuro Miho, a well-known attorney, was the best man at Chinen's wedding. Chinen worked as a medical technician at Kuakini Hospital until he retired in 1966, when he went to Okinawa to help in establishing the Central Hospital. His experience at Kuakini with the other members of the staff and physicians was one of close association, and whenever there was a gathering at the residence of Dr. Iga Mori, chief physician of the hospital, Chinen's presence was taken for granted. Chinen was one of those who claim that they have never experienced prejudice or discrimination from non-Okinawans.

A Nisei housewife of Hiroshiman parentage who grew up in the plantation community explained how she learned to prepare pork and cook Okinawan dishes:

> My father was a plantation carpenter, employed by the plantation (Waipahu), so he went to all the houses of the plantation employees to do repair work. Whenever he went to the homes of the Okinawans he was invited to a lunch of a delicious Okinawan dish. The Okinawans were very thoughtful people. Because he liked it, he would always ask them about the recipe and how to prepare it. When he came home he cooked it the way he learned, so I learned Okinawan cooking from my father.

It was true that the Okinawans were looked down upon on the plantation by the other Kenjins. The children acquired the prejudice against the Okinawans from their Issei parents. They heard their parents making derogatory remarks about the Okinawans in their own homes.[36]

Thomas Taro Higa, a Nisei of Okinawan parentage, learned standard Japanese from Giichi Sasaki, of Yamaguchi-ken origin, who was the principal of the Japanese language school in Kahaluu, Oahu, by visiting him in the evening; he was too busy helping his parents on the farm to attend the language school in the afternoon. By engaging in conversation with his teacher on various subjects he learned the Japanese language thoroughly and, in addition, they became close friends.

During World War II practically all the Japanese language school principals were interned along with the other leaders of the Japanese community. Higa visited his teacher on his first leave from the 100th Battalion then training at Camp McCoy, Wisconsin, travelling two days by train to Alexandria, Louisiana, to reach Livingston Internment Camp. After spending a day with his former teacher, Higa was arrested at the Alexandria Railway Station by the authorities on suspicion of being a Japanese spy. They had never seen an Oriental wearing the United States Army uniform. He showed his military identification, but for naught. He was put in jail. In the meantime, the army authorities contacted Camp McCoy to check. Shortly after midnight he was awakened by a knock at the door of his cell, and an Army officer apologized for the mistake and he was released to catch the next train.

Higa compared this experience with a similar incident while he was a student in Tokyo in 1940. Because he went to the American Embassy frequently to consult on his passport and other matters, he was suspected of being an American spy, jailed by the Japanese gendarmes, and beaten mercilessly by four of them. Utterly disgusted by such treatment, he returned to Hawaii in a hurry. Until he was drafted in the U.S. Army in July 1941, he was the president of the Kahaluu Young Men's Association and actively prepared the young men of the windward rural area for crisis by inviting the older Nisei leaders in Honolulu to come to speak to his group.

Higa was wounded twice in the European theater and sent back to the United States for hospitalization. When he recovered well enough, he was assigned by the army at the request of the Japanese

American Citizens' League, the mainland Nisei organization, to make a tour of the Relocation Centers to tell the worried and despondent Issei parents how the bravery and sacrifices of their sons helped to defeat the Germans and bring about the Allies' victory. After he finished his mission, he had a similar assignment in Hawaii, visiting the Japanese communities on all islands. When the battle of Okinawa began in April 1945, Higa was assigned to Okinawa on the recommendation by Col. Kendall Fielder, chief of G2, who believed that Higa's ability to speak both the Okinawan dialect and Japanese fluently would be invaluable. His task was not to fight but to urge those hiding in caves to come out and surrender, assuring them that the U.S. Army would give them protection instead of hurting them. Many obeyed and were saved. The war with Japan ended in August, and Higa returned to Hawaii with the other GIs on September 15 and was subsequently discharged from the army. On the basis of his intimate knowledge of the destruction of Okinawa, relief work for Okinawa began in Hawaii. Higa made documentary films of Okinawans in South America as well as in Hawaii. His book *Imin wa Ikiru* [Immigrants are living] was published in Tokyo in 1974.[37]

Like her husband, Taro Higa's wife experienced no insults or discrimination from other Japanese in Hawaii:

> I was born and grew up in Lihue, Kauai. All my friends were of non-Okinawan parentage. Since our marriage, we have lived on this windward side of Oahu all the time. We have had no experience of discrimination by those of the other prefectural backgrounds. Our children were all married to those of non-Okinawan parentage. We are getting along fine.[38]

Paul Agena's experiences were similar. "It is fifty years since I returned to Hawaii in 1929, but I have never been insulted personally by those from the other prefectures on account of my being of the Okinawan parentage. Rather, there were many of those of the other prefectures who helped me in my good fortune."[39]

Mrs. Shimpuku Gima, who grew up in Wailuku, Maui, and attended high school there, did not recall any instance of prejudice or discrimination:

> My classmates were Nisei of all prefectural backgrounds as well as those of other ethnic groups. They were all very nice to me. This year

[1980] I attended the fiftieth anniversary of our class' graduation and we had a wonderful reunion. They were so glad that I managed to attend it. I married soon after my graduation and my husband and I moved to Honolulu almost immediately. My husband never experienced discrimination either, but his younger brother did. When he and his sweetheart of Yamaguchi-ken background planned to marry, her mother objected, saying that it was not the boy himself, but it was because his parents were Okinawans.[40]

In cosmopolitan Hilo and Waianae in rural Oahu there was apparently no discrimination against Okinawans. All Japanese mingled freely and participated in community affairs. Jinsei Kaneshiro, a successful businessman, described Hilo in the early 1920s:

> There was practically no prefectural consciousness among the Japanese in Hilo. We also associated with other ethnic people with the same feeling. During the summer when schoolchildren were on vacation, every prefectural group and ethnic group had a picnic in Onekahakaha Beach Park. So the Japanese and other ethnic people all got together and spent all day happily. Especially when the Okinawans had a picnic, everybody who happened to be in the vicinity joined and spent all day, having a good time. The undeniable attraction was the kalua pig [a whole pig carefully prepared and baked underground the Hawaiian way] the Okinawans served at their picnic. In those days the Okinawans were known for hog-raising. In addition, the Okinawans were well known for their samisen music and folk dancing. There was a pavilion with an excellent stage in Onekahakaha Park. There we played samisen and danced and enjoyed the whole day. That's why so many came and joined us. . . . [After the war] when the relief work for Okinawa was announced, all the Japanese [of all prefectures] and even non-Japanese such as the Portuguese, Hawaiians, and other Orientals volunteered to help. Their kindness deeply touched me. Even while I am writing this [in 1980] I can see the faces of those who helped us. . . .[41]

In Waianae, according to long-time residents, there has never been discrimination against the Okinawans by the other Japanese.[42] This assertion was made by elders of the Japanese community such as Shigeo Murata, a Nisei of Hiroshiman parentage who lived in Waianae for more than seventy years, and Fushun Teruya from Okinawa who moved there from Maui in 1949 to start raising hogs on twenty acres of land he bought from the former plantation, which had closed. When some of the members of the Waianae Hongwanji left the temple after a disagreement in the early 1960s and started Waianae Doshi-kai, both those who remained members of the temple and those who joined the Doshi-kai included Okinawans, Yamaguchins, Hiroshimans, Fukushimans, Niigatans, and other Kenjins. Doshi-kai has its building on its own grounds, which the prefectural groups use during the Bon season in summer. The Okinawan Bon Dance is the most prominent, followed by the Fukushima Bon Dance and the Iwakuni Bon Dance of the Yamaguchins. All the Kenjins participate in dancing the folk dances of their respective kens.

The Minority Group within the Japanese Community

Regardless of individual cases of freedom from insult and discrimination, the Okinawans were collectively looked down upon by the so-called "Naichijin," principally those from Chūgoku Chihō who along with their children comprised nearly half of the total Japanese population in Hawaii. Being the newest arrivals with a dialect very different from the prevailing Chūgoku dialects, the Okinawans became the major target of ridicule and ostracism. The epithets and invective that had been used against non-Chūgoku immigrants were all replaced by the single word "Okinawa."

The dominant prefectural immigrants treated the Okinawans as an inferior outgroup, although the Okinawans themselves never thought that they were inferior. During the early years there were many skirmishes on the plantations, as described in the following statement.

> I was seventeen years old. The others were twenty-two or twenty-three years old. We were all young men. We had a luna to oversee us, but we couldn't understand the English he spoke. But worse than that was the way the other Kenjins treated us. They treated us as if we were not human. Our Japanese didn't sound like their Japanese, so they constantly made fun of us. They never called us by our names, but always by "Oi, Okinawa" [Hey, Okinawa]. When we were loading the cut canes on the freight train, they would pull them down. It delayed

our work. We had to reload them. The work was called "hapaiko," the hardest job. There were constant fights between the Okinawans and the "Naichijins." In such fights we Okinawans were always stronger. We knew how to use our fists and we always won.[43]

There were other forms of humiliation to which the Okinawans were subjected:

> Because of the discriminatory treatment of the Okinawans by the other Kenjins, even the Portuguese, Hawaiians, and Haole lunas treated us Okinawans separately from the other Japanese. On the plantation in Lahaina the laborers were grouped together by national groups for housing. The Japanese housing area was divided into two sections, Okinawans and Naichijins.
>
> We had a German boss. If he saw an untidy Japanese, he would call him, "Hey, Okinawa," assuming that such a person ought to be an Okinawan. Thus everybody, even Haoles, regarded the Okinawans as inferior to other Kenjins.[44]

Sadao Asato, although he had good relations with other Kenjins like Totaro Matsui, encountered discrimination from other sources.

> Wishing to enter the insurance business, I called on Mr. Malcolm Macintyre, the manager of Canada Life Insurance Co. The first questions he asked me were, "Are you from Tokyo? Are you from Kyoto? Are you a Hiroshiman? Are you a Yamaguchin?" When I said, "I am an Okinawan," he said, "Then, you are not eligible," and rejected my application. So I told him, "Okinawa Prefecture is part of Japan and the Okinawans are genuine Japanese and not of an inferior race," and I explained that there were many outstanding individuals of Okinawan background in Japan mainland as well as in Okinawa, and that if he doubted my explanation, he could check it with Japanese Consul General Chosuke Yada. Mr. Macintyre understood what I said very well and accepted me right away and gave me a written statement of my employment. That was the beginning of my long career in the life insurance business.[45]

The prejudice against Okinawans extended to the next generation. The children of non-Okinawan immigrants sometimes mistreated their Okinawan classmates. As the following statement reveals, they learned such behavior from their parents.

When my children were small they attended the Japanese school in Waialae. I used to be the treasurer of that school. My children were called "Okinawa! Okinawa!" and constantly ostracized by the children of the other prefectural parentage. My children had a hard time. I used to ask the principal of that school to stop his students from ostracizing my children. Undoubtedly, the other children were merely repeating what their parents and other adults were saying and doing.[46]

The experiences of mistreatment of young people of Okinawan parentage before World War II, particularly during the early years, were described as follows:

The other children stoned me on my way to school, calling me "Okinawa! Okinawa!" They tormented us of Okinawan parentage in every way they could until I myself came to believe that being Okinawan was something to be ashamed of and the Okinawans were really inferior to the other Japanese. I was sad and ashamed of myself and of my parents and of the other Okinawans. It was the Haole teachers at the public school who changed my total outlook. They asked me such questions, "Why do you look so sad always?" I answered, "Because I am an Okinawan. The people call me Okinawan and insult me." Then, they would ask me, "What's wrong with your being an Okinawan? Have you done anything wrong? Have you hurt anyone?" Then I answered, "No. I haven't." Then they would ask me, "Have your parents done anything wrong?" I answered, "No. Not that I know of, except that they came from Okinawa prefecture." The teachers asserted, "There is nothing for you to be ashamed of. You have no reason to look so unhappy." Then I would say, "But I am poor. My clothes are not pretty." Then they told me, "It is not the clothes you wear. It is the way you hold yourself that makes you look sad and unhappy." As you see, it was my Haole teachers who restored in me confidence and self-respect.[47]

It was 1910. About 40 students from rural Oahu and the neighbor islands lived in the dormitory of the Japanese school of Honpa Hongwanji Mission. We studied Japanese language every morning before going to public school which began at 9:00 A.M. and lasted until 2:30 P.M. We studied Japanese after we returned from the public school. One day a classmate of mine called me "Okinawa" with an insulting tone. Being very angry, I struck him with my fist and broke his front tooth. Mr. Komatsu who was in charge of our dormitory called me. When I explained how it happened, he said, "I don't blame you for getting angry, but you must not resort to violence." The case was settled then.[48]

I came to Hawaii with my father when I was eleven years old. The plantation policeman told me that I must attend school. . . . When I came to Honolulu I stayed at the dormitory of Hawaii Chūgaku (Japanese High School of Honpa Hongwanji Mission) and started to attend the public school immediately. I also passed the test and was admitted to the third year of Hawaii Chūgaku. The principal and other teachers were excellent and very nice to me and I was very happy. However, in those days [1914] there was strong prejudice against the Okinawans and I was looked down upon and often tormented by the other students. For example, when I was taking a hot bath, one of my classmates showered cold water on me. One evening a group of students covered me with four "futon" [thick quilts] that almost choked me. One day when another classmate repeatedly called me "Okinawa! Okinawa!" with intention to provoke me, I beat him up in the adjacent banana patch. Next day his friend T called on me and avenged him. For such constant ordeals I began to hate school and returned to Kekaha Plantation on Kauai and worked in the cane fields, although I never gave up my desire to study.[49]

I always carried a dictionary in my pocket, and during the lunch hour I studied English by myself. Later, for two years I worked for Dr. Ryoon Uyesato as his assistant and interpreter. Having saved some money, I came to Honolulu again. This time I lived at the dormitory of the Episcopal Church supervised by the late Rev. Taiji Fukao, and I attended the English School of the Episcopal Church for two years. Miss Shafer and the Rev. Fukao were our teachers. I also attended the Japanese language school of Hawaii Chūgaku, graduating from it in 1920. I also worked part-time as a school boy at the Japanese consul general's residence. I attended the School of Accounting, graduating from it in 1922, and became the bookkeeper for S. Nekomoto Contractor.[50]

Some children of Okinawan parentage who lived in the same neighborhood with those of the other prefectural backgrounds were not aware that the term "Okinawa" was directed only to those from Okinawa-ken and their children.

Since we were the only Okinawan family in this neighborhood, our children were brought up with the children of other Kenjins. They had no experience of discrimination. When the other Kenjins made fun of the Okinawans our children did the same thing without knowing the meaning. They thought the word "Okinawa" meant a bad thing for anybody.

It was about 1933 or 1934 when my daughter was attending Fort Gakuen Japanese language school. One day there was a quarrel among the students and one of the girls called her "You, Okinawa!" Then, the other girls joined in calling my daughter "Okinawa, Okinawa." When she came home, she told me about the incident. So I showed her the map of the Japanese archipelago with Okinawa at the southernmost end of Japan. I explained to her that, being far away from the main islands of Japan, the Okinawan dialects and culture were different from those of the other prefectures and ignorant people treat the Okinawans as non-Japanese or inferior. This explanation helped her. Nevertheless, the insult from her classmates hurt her feelings very much.[51]

In the plantation communities where both the Okinawans and the so-called "Naichi" prefectural immigrants were predominant, group fights took place between their children, who engaged in vindictive name-calling. They used such terms as "Ohkii Nawa" ("Big Rope," because of the sound similar to Okinawa) and "Nai Chi" ("No Blood," because of the same sound). Also, the sing-song type of insult "Okinawa-ken-ken Buta Kau-kau" (Okinawa Prefecture, Hog-raiser, Hog-eater) was common because the Okinawans were known for their hog-raising. A Nisei leader of the Okinawan women's group recalled such group fights in her school years on Hawaii:

> We always fought back. In those days many Okinawans raised hogs, so the children of "Naichi" Kenjins insulted us and made derogatory remarks. We wouldn't stand such insults. The fights took place always on the road on our way to and from the Japanese language school which we attended after public school hours. The fights were mostly verbal exchanges of biting words, although at times we became more belligerent. We tried not to fight in the school. But sometimes when fights broke out in the school, our principal, Mr. Shinoda, mediated. He was always fair and we respected him a lot. We never fought in the public school, maybe because of the punishment for such fights, or because there were children of other nationalities.[52]

Eventually, outright attacks and insults were replaced by more subtle discrimination such as exclusion in housing or differential treatment of Okinawan customers, as the following statements reveal.

My father came from Oshima County of Yamaguchi-ken. He never worked on the plantation. His parents were well-off. They had a sake winery. During the early years my father was very busy, writing letters for those who came from the villages of his old county Oshima-gun, because they had little education and could not write letters to their homes. My father owned several rental housing units in McCully for the Japanese, except the Okinawans. The tenants objected to having the Okinawans in the same housing units. They said that the Okinawans were dirty. At any rate, my father planned to have eventually only those from his own village, especially his brother and other close kin, to live in his rental units.[53]

I used to buy a lot of things at a nearby store. One day when I said that I was an Okinawan, the proprietor marked my name on his list of his regular customers. I told him right there, if he was going to sell me inferior goods or charge me higher price than his other customers, I would stop buying from his store. That was the end of my being his customer.[54]

Help from Religious Leaders

The Okinawan immigrants in Hawaii were both Buddhists and Christians and were active in churches of both faiths. Basically, Christians of Okinawan background joined the church of their choice regardless of the minister's prefectural background, and many became active lay leaders and the backbone of their respective churches.

In Christian churches there was no discrimination, and the membership and congregation were made up of people of various prefectural origins. The first Okinawan minister in Hawaii, who trained in Tokyo and served in Okinawa, was the Rev. Seikan Higa, who arrived with his family in 1921. He opened a small preaching center in Palama in Honolulu. His challenging message drew serious-minded young people of all prefectural backgrounds to hear him and to attend the prayer meetings and discussion meetings in the evenings. When the membership increased to sixty or so, they founded Reimei Church independently of the Mission

Board (Methodist). Renting an old building belonging to the Palama Settlement, they used the third floor as the student dormitory, the second floor as the residence of the minister and his family, and the hall and rooms on the first floor for church gatherings as well as for service activities such as employment counselling and consultation on other personal and social problems. Able lay leaders of his church assisted in these service activities. Rev. Higa also visited all the other islands, invited by churches as a guest preacher. He also served on Hawaii for several years as the principal of Japanese language schools, first in Piihonua and later in Honokaa. Since both were poor plantation communities, he obtained the assistance of an agricultural specialist from Hilo to help each household to raise chickens, sell eggs, or raise hogs to increase the family income.

After the war Rev. Higa returned to Honolulu and eventually resumed his ministry in the Wesley United Methodist Church. After his retirement in 1972, he continued his active life in writing and speaking and participating in worthwhile groups. He was the most forceful, eloquent preacher among the Issei ministers. With his magnificent physique, unusual for a Japanese, handsome features, and resounding voice, he carried his fearless message of challenge far and wide on all the islands of Hawaii. He was outspoken about social injustice and openly attacked the social system which perpetuated it. He was often confronted by another outspoken leader of Okinawan background who held somewhat conservative viewpoints, Tetsuo Tōyama, a well-known publisher of prewar days, who after the war worked hard to help the children of Okinawa. Tōyama was foremost a promoter of naturalization for the Issei Japanese.

On Oahu, because of the prejudice of other prefectural groups, many Okinawans who were Buddhist did not go to the Hongwanji temples. Therefore, when the Jikoen Buddhist temple was founded in Honolulu by the Rev. Chiro Yosemori, a Honpa Hongwanji priest, and the Okinawan lay Buddhists in 1938, it became their religious center as well as a place for social and cultural activities. After Rev. Yosemori returned to Japan in 1940, the Rev. Jikai Yamasato succeeded him as the chief priest and gave dedicated service and leadership to his parishioners until his retirement in 1981. Rev. Chikai Yosemori succeeded Rev. Yamasato. According to Rev. Yosemori, Okinawans were not pious Buddhists while in

Okinawa. Buddhism was introduced to Okinawa from China in the late thirteenth century, but it touched only the ruling class. The only Buddhist temple in Okinawa is Sogenji in Naha where the kings were enshrined. Ancestor worship was the indigenous religion of Okinawa. Rev. Yosemori added that he was never conscious of his Okinawan background until he came to Hawaii. Another well-known Buddhist priest of Okinawan origin was the Rev. Houn Tamayose of the McCully Higashi Hongwanji temple. He came to Hawaii in 1920 and served in Makaweli on Kauai for three years before moving to Honolulu. He served at the Higashi Hongwanji temple in downtown Honolulu before being assigned to the temple in McCully in 1936. Since his temple was for all Japanese of the Higashi Hongwanji Sect, he had those of other prefectures among his parishioners. He was among the most learned and influential leaders in the Okinawan community. In the postwar years, by way of radio and publication, he tried to explain the historical relationships of the Okinawans and those from the main islands of Japan.

Non-Okinawan religious leaders, both Christian and Buddhist, were helpful to the Okinawans in Hawaii. The widow of the Rev. Chimpei Goto of Kaneohe Methodist Church recalled the various efforts made by her husband to help the Okinawans.

When we came to Windward Oahu in 1927, most Okinawans lived in Kahaluu. They were small farmers, raising vegetables, taro, bananas, papayas, and other fruits. During the Depression when they could not sell their produce because their customers were poor, these farmers suffered very much. The other Kenjin farmers were also very poor. But they looked down upon the Okinawans, and they created an indescribably unpleasant atmosphere when the Okinawans were around even though they did not hurt the latter physically. The children of the other Kenjins inherited the attitude of their parents and tormented the children of Okinawan parentage. So when the Okinawan children came to our church we told them that there was nothing to be ashamed of their Okinawan background and that they were just as good as the children of other prefectural backgrounds. We were deeply concerned about the effects of the persecution on the Okinawan children if it continued, so my husband organized the baseball teams of the young people of various churches of windward Oahu, and had interarea tournaments. Actually, there was nothing for the rural youths in the way of recreation in those days. So baseball gave them a healthy outlet for their energy and let them mingle with each other regardless of their parents' prefectural backgrounds. They enjoyed it so much that they continued it even after they became adults.

Just before World War II, the government-owned land in the Kahaluu area became available for sale to the farmers for a very low price to be paid in forty years with very little interest. My husband urged these small farmers to buy the land, since the land would become very valuable later. Some farmers criticized him as "Seifu no Inu" [government's tool] to sell unworthy lands to poor farmers. Those who believed my husband's words were mostly Okinawans. During the war, since they were raising food for the armed forces as well as for the civilians, they were frozen to their jobs. Anyway, they made money, and instead of waiting for forty years, they paid for their lands in a short while. After the war many of them sold part of their lands and made money. At any rate, those who have money in Kahaluu are Okinawans.[55]

On Kauai the Jodo Sect Buddhist temple in Kapaa absorbed most of the Buddhist Okinawans while the Honpa Hongwanji temple was attended by Buddhists from other prefectures. The priests of both temples indicated that in later years there was no prejudice against the Okinawans but that the separation was established during the early years when there was prejudice.[56] The non-Okinawan priest of the Jodo temple, the Rev. Shoyu Kitajima, identified himself intimately with his Okinawan parishioners and participated in their social and cultural activities. He described his part as follows:

I came to Hawaii in 1932 and served at X temple on Hawaii which had many Okinawans among its congregation. I came to Kauai in 1938. I like the Okinawans very much and participate in their social activities. I even learned some of their folk dances. On New Year's Day they visit each other as they do in Okinawa, carrying their sansin [jamisen] to play and sing and have a good time. I go with them, visiting one home after another. I also officiate at "Senkotsu" [bone-washing ceremony]. As you know, the Okinawans have a strong concern over their deceased family members. Their religion is deeply tied with ancestor worship. Even if they don't attend the regular Buddhist services often, they attend the memorial services without fail. They build a similar type of grave as in Okinawa with a large hall-like interior. Some have "Senkotsu" even now, usually on Tanabata Day in July. They exhume the body of a deceased kin three to seven years after the first burial. They must get a permit from the County Office. The ceremony is to exhume the body from the grave and the closest of kin do the washing of the bones with gasoline and then put them in a new earthenware pot, placing the skull on the top and sealing it for permanent burial.[57]

Okinawans joined the Hongwanji temples or other Buddhist temples in their local communities on Hawaii, Maui, Molokai, and Lanai, and many of them became influential lay leaders of their respective temples, reflecting the general absence of anti-Okinawan prejudice. On Maui, where Buddhist Okinawans belong to the Hongwanji temple, they also had an exclusively Okinawan Buddhist temple of Rinzai-Zen Sect in Puunene, founded by the Rev. Nanshin Okamoto in the 1930s, who was succeeded by the Rev. Kiyoshi Oshiro. The temple is a religious-cultural center for the Okinawans. During the Bon season in August the Okinawans all over Maui gather there for ceremonies and Bon dancing.[58]

Okinawan Social Organization

How to cope with the prejudice and discrimination was a constant problem for the Okinawans. The major concern of the Issei mothers was to bring up their children without their losing self-respect and pride in their Okinawan background. The following statement reflects the feelings of a large number of the Issei parents:

> While the Naichijins continued their haughty attitude toward the Okinawans, we did not want to be bothered with such people. We kept our mouths shut and did not make an open protest. But in our hearts we were determined to prove that we were superior to them. One of such efforts was our determination to educate our children, and we did all we could to achieve this goal, even by reducing our meals to twice a day instead of three times a day.[59]

To overcome their handicaps, collective efforts were made among the young adults. They formed groups and organizations aimed at self-improvement. One such group was the Deigo-kai, organized at the YWCA in 1933 for young women of Okinawan parentage under the leadership of Chiyeko Takushi, a pioneer businesswoman in the field of insurance in Hawaii. Uruma Young

Men's Association was another group that aimed at improving their situation. Sadao Asato described the feelings of these young people.

> Those who were students sixty years ago [1920] and who are now the backbone of the Okinawan community were saturated with the desire to acquire knowledge. Whenever there was a chance, we got together to exchange our new knowledge and points of view and to discuss how to improve ourselves. According to some psychologists, some degree of inferiority complex is necessary to stimulate our improvement. In our case, the fact that we were looked down upon by the people of other prefectural backgrounds was the propelling power. We were always filled with great ambition not to be behind those of the other prefectures and to become persons of consequence in the future. Sometimes, we gathered on the hill of Punchbowl or on the top of Tantalus and engaged in discourse and debate, or practiced public speaking and, thus, greatly enhanced our spirit.[60]

The Okinawans had an effective social organization based on their locality clubs, which represented their native localities such as village, town, city, or Aza, to facilitate mutual aid and intimate fellowship as well as close spiritual ties with their birthplaces in Okinawa. The locality clubs were independent of each other. They took care of visitors from Okinawa and also had a special interest in their children's welfare. They sponsored the Nisei interlocality club baseball tournament and the annual interisland tournament. Some of the clubs rented a building for educational and recreational activities for their children. Before World War II, the locality clubs were very active and meaningful for the Okinawans. In contrast, however, attempts to organize an overall Okinawan prefectural association did not last long.

When the news of the fall of Okinawa reached Hawaii in June 1945, and subsequently the extent of the devastation was reported by Taro Higa, a veteran just returned from Okinawa, the Okinawans on all the islands launched an all-out relief effort collecting clothing, food, medicine, school material, and so on. The Okinawa Relief Committee, composed of Caucasian church leaders as well as Okinawan community leaders, secured the help of the U.S. Navy for transportation of these relief goods to Okinawa. The most dramatic and practical relief project was the sending of 550 pigs purchased with $50,000 collected in Hawaii. Eight representatives of the Okinawan community including a veterinarian went to Oregon and purchased the pigs and accompanied them from Portland to Okinawa in 1948. Later, a Nisei group sent 500 goats as well as vegetable seeds, school material, and other goods to Okinawa. After having actively participated in relief work for Okinawa, Nisei leaders organized the Hui Makaala in 1946 for social, educational, and service activities among the Nisei men and women.

The United Okinawan Association was formed among the Issei in 1951 in order to continue to help the reconstruction of their homeland and for the education and training of its future leaders. Dr. Shimpuku Gima, the first president of the Association, described the process of its formation:

> Since the Okinawan community was made up of those from many localities of Okinawa, the proposed organization must have representatives from their locality clubs. At first there was strong opposition to formation of such an exclusively Okinawan organization as reversing our past effort to eliminate anything which made the Okinawans a separate group from the other prefectural people. For this reason, only fourteen locality clubs joined when the United Okinawan Association was formed. Because of the significant role it was assuming, however, by 1955 the number of member clubs increased to twenty-seven and within a year a total of thirty-six clubs including thirty-four locality clubs and two clubs representing those in Kailua and Kaneohe joined. The remaining fifteen locality clubs have never joined it. This fact shows the freedom and independence of each locality club.[61]

Although deeply hurt by the discrimination and humiliation accorded them by their fellow Japanese immigrants who arrived earlier, the Okinawans never lost their collective self-respect and determination to excel. Within a decade after World War II, they became a thriving group. Their collective achievement was conspicuous, particularly in the field of business. Many Nisei became prominent in the political area as well as in various professions. Their demonstrated ability not only impressed the people of the other prefectural backgrounds, but also increased their confidence in themselves and pride in their Okinawan background.

Part II
Work

5

Plantation Laborers

AFTER Hawaii's annexation to the United States, plantation laborers became more positive in expressing their grievances and demands. There were more work stoppages in 1900 than ever before. Of twenty-two work stoppages in that year, twenty involved Japanese laborers, according to the U.S. Labor Commissioner.[1] Their demands for the immediate discharge of lunas who inflicted injuries to laborers and reinstatement of discharged laborers became more insistent. In addition, their frustration at being Hawaii's lowest-paid plantation workers became increasingly overt.

According to the report of the president of the Board of Immigration for the period from 1888 to 1890, the monthly wages paid to contract laborers by ethnic group were $19.53 for Portuguese, $18.59 for Hawaiians, $17.61 for Chinese, $15.81 for South Seas Islanders, and $15.58 for Japanese. The differential wage scale for different ethnic groups for the same type and amount of work continued after Hawaii became a United States territory. The discrepancy in daily wages applied to skilled workers in 1905 was cited by William L. Abbott, educational director of the United Rubber Workers, AFL-CIO, as follows: $4.38 for Caucasians, $1.68 for Hawaiians, $1.61 for Portuguese, $1.06 for Chinese, and 97 cents for Japanese.[2] As late as 1909, Japanese plantation laborers were paid $18 a month while Portuguese and Puerto Rican workers received $22.50 and were given better housing as well. Also, the Portuguese, Spanish, and Russians who were brought to the Islands under the *Induced Clauses* of 1907, whose objective was to curb the numerical predominance of the Japanese plantation laborers, were paid a wage one-third higher than that paid to the Japanese.[3] Considering such discrimination unfair and unjust, the Japanese laborers became rebellious.

Their frustration was articulated by the Japanese-language press. In May 1908, Motoyuki Negoro, who studied law at the University of California, wrote a series of articles criticizing the disproportionately low wages of Japanese laborers in comparison with the large profits of the sugar industry and its policy of racial discrimination in setting wages. He asked the *Hawaii Shinpō* of Honolulu to publish it, but its editor, Sometarō Shiba, declined on the grounds that an effort should be made to induce the planters to take the initiative to eliminate racial discrimination, and any difference between the laborers and the planters could be settled peacefully through conciliation. Negoro then took his article to the *Nippu Jiji*, whose editor, Yasutarō Sōga, published it. Thus, the wage issue became the subject of bitter editorial battles between the *Nippu Jiji* and the *Hawaii Shinpō*, the former calling the latter a traitor while the latter criticized the former as an agitator and disturber of the peace. The *Pacific Commercial Advertiser* and the *Evening Bulletin* made accusations against the *Nippu Jiji*. Eventually, the vernacular papers on the other islands became involved, siding either with the *Nippu Jiji* or *Hawaii Shinpō*, attacking each other vehemently, and dividing opinions within the Japanese community.[4]

Advocates for racial equality in plantation work met together under the sponsorship of the *Nippu Jiji* at the Asahi Theater in Honolulu in November 1908. At a second meeting, held at the Japanese YMCA, the Higher Wage Association (Zokyu Kisei-kai) was organized and its officers were chosen: Fred Makino was named president, Motoyuki Negoro secretary, and Matsutarō Yamashiro treasurer.[5] The group discussed ways to help the Japanese plantation laborers take an active role in improving their status as workers. The *Nippu Jiji* was to be responsible for arousing public concern in its editorials and articles while Makino and Negoro were to visit the plantations after work hours and in the evenings to meet with the laborers. They also decided that strikes must be limited to Oahu; the plantation workers on the other islands would continue to work and make monetary contributions to support the Oahu strike. In view of such preparations on the part of the Higher Wage Association leaders, plantation authorities mobilized plantation policemen and lunas to prevent the "agitators" from entering their premises, some of whom even carried pistols to shoot them for trespassing. Evidently, however, the meetings with the plantation laborers were without incident. Makino and Negoro were popular speakers among the laborers, Makino for his witty sarcasm and Negoro for his earnest legal deliberation. The plantation laborers were instructed firmly that they must never resort to violence in the event of a strike.[6]

The Plantation Strike of 1909

In January 1909, the Higher Wage Association of Honolulu submitted its demand for equal wages for Japanese laborers to the Hawaiian Sugar Planters' Association (HSPA). With no favorable response after repeated negotiations, the plantation workers took action themselves in the form of a labor strike, beginning on May 9, 1909, by 1,500 Japanese workers at Aiea Plantation, joined by those of Waipahu, Kahuku, and Waianae plantations. Ewa and Waialua plantation laborers, who had struck but returned to work on the advice of Japanese priests and merchants, walked out a second time. The Waimanalo Plantation laborers decided not to strike but helped the strikers by donating $600. Monetary and material assistance came from plantation workers on Kauai, Maui, and Hawaii. The strikers were ejected from plantation housing, and most of them made their way to Honolulu. By the end of June, about 5,000 workers and their families were in Honolulu, being fed and sheltered by the Higher Wage Association. When there were no more housing facilities for refugees, the Ewa and Waialua plantation laborers returned to work.[7]

While the vernacular papers on all the islands acknowledged racial discrimination in wages, during the actual strike the *Nippu Jiji* was the only one that advocated raising the wages of the Japanese laborers. In Honolulu, the *Hawaii Shinpō* and the *Hawaii Nichi Nichi* as well as the vernaculars on Maui, Kauai, and Hawaii all opposed the *Nippu Jiji*. Dr. Saburo Hayashi's *Kona Hankyo,* which openly supported the *Nippu Jiji*'s stand, was the only exception.[8] Consul General Senichi Uyeno issued an official statement on May 25 expressing his regret that the Japanese laborers resorted to strike and urged them to seek conciliatory means to settle their grievances against their employers. His message was published in all the vernacular papers in Hawaii except the *Nippu Jiji.*[9]

At its director's meeting on May 27 the HSPA reiterated its determination to make no concession to the laborers until they returned to work. In the meantime, the HSPA employed Chinese, Hawaiians, Koreans, and Portuguese as strike-breakers, paying $1.50 a day, and the Japanese laborers' strike took on the appearance of the Japanese versus other ethnic groups.[10] Moreover, the strike funds were dwindling, and some of the strikers were beginning to return to work. It appeared that the strike might break up from within. Realizing this, the Higher Wage Association held an emergency meeting on July 31 at which the decision was reached to call off the strike. Within a few weeks, almost all the strikers had returned to their old plantations. Thus ended the first large-scale plantation labor strike on Oahu. It lasted nearly three months and cost the planters about $2 million and the supporters of the strike about $40,000.[11]

The Commissioner of Labor in his report on Hawaii pointed out that the weakness and eventual failure of the strike lay in the absence of full support from the Japanese community in addition to the fact that the demands for higher wages were initiated by the educated Japanese elite and not by the laborers themselves.[12] Yasutarō Sōga acknowledged the fact that the strike could not get wider support because it was taken to be a Japanese nationalistic movement, since its purpose was to secure higher wages for the Japanese laborers to make their pay equal to that of the other nationalities and the Japanese were the only strikers. The strike was opposed from the beginning by the Japanese consul general, whose job since the start of Japanese contract labor was to see to it that the Japanese plantation laborers worked without stoppages; by most of the Japanese merchants, whose businesses were bound to be curtailed by the prolonged large-scale work stoppage; and by a considerable portion of the Japanese community, including intellectuals.

Although the strike was unsuccessful, by the end of the year the minimum wage for plantation laborers had been raised from $18 a month to $20, more feasible contract conditions were set up, and the bonus system was introduced to provide extra pay for workers who worked a certain number of days per month for twelve months, along with improved housing and sanitation and increased contract payments to independent cane growers.[13]

Punishment of Strike Conspirators

After the strike, a series of arrests were made; leaders of the Higher Wage Association were arrested on various charges and detained many times. The "most ridiculous" charge, according to Yasutarō Sōga, resulted from an incident that occurred during a hearing for conspiracy to strike. On the morning of August 3, Sōga and the other defendants were in court and Motoyuki Negoro was on the witness stand. The plaintiff's representative, William A. Kinney, suddenly announced that Sometarō Shiba, editor of the *Hawaii Shinpō,* had been attacked by an assassin and seriously wounded. Sōga described the scene:

> The court was adjourned immediately. When we went outside, the street was noisy with the newsboys shouting "Extra, Extra!" We felt that everybody was staring at us. The culprit was Tomekichi Mori, aged twenty-two, one of the seven delegates from Maui who came to attend a special meeting of the Higher Wage Committee. Evidently, Mori happened to come across Shiba on King Street and got into an argument. Then he suddenly attacked Shiba with his pocket knife. While they were grappling in blood, a Caucasian carpenter who happened to pass by separated them, and Mori was taken to the police station while Shiba was taken to the hospital. Fortunately, Shiba's neck artery escaped the knife thrust. After ten days at the hospital, he returned home to recuperate. Mori served two years in prison and was released on the condition that he return to Japan. He died in Yokohama soon after his arrival there.[14]

Fred Makino, Motoyuki Negoro, Sōga, Matsutarō Yamashiro, and reporters Keitaro Kawamura and Yokoichi Tasaka were arrested on charges of co-conspiracy in the attempted murder of Shiba. They were released on bail, paying $400 each. The attack on Shiba was the only incidence of violence associated with the strike.

Those who were arrested after the termination of the strike were released on bail through the efforts of attorney Joseph Lightfoot, and several were subsequently acquitted. However, editor Sōga of the *Nippu Jiji,* reporter Tasaka, Negoro, whose articles were published in the *Nippu Jiji,* and Fred Makino, president of the Higher Wage Association, were found guilty of conspiracy by the circuit court and sentenced on August 22 to ten months of imprisonment and fined $300 each. They appealed to the Supreme Court of Hawaii, which rejected their appeal on March 20, 1910. Thus they began to serve their terms in Oahu Prison.[15]

As soon as imprisonment became inevitable, the residents of Honolulu who had supported the higher wage movement for Japanese plantation workers held a meeting and decided to provide the prisoners with decent food during their stay in prison. Sōga recalled that "people of all prefectures formed the Prisoner-Assistance Society and obtained permission from the warden to send in three meals for us every day. So, from the first day we had a feast of food which we shared with the other prisoners, including those of other nationalities. Until the day we were released, we did not eat prison food."[16]

Sōga, Tasaka, Negoro, and Makino set about trying to adjust to life in confinement, which Sōga described vividly:

> I felt an indescribable sensation of hopeless desolation when I put on the prison uniform for the first time. Oahu Prison was an old building and generally unsanitary. An old bed was the only equipment each of our solitary cells had. At night we were given a pail each to use as a toilet. There was a tiny window on the door through which a dim light from the electric light in the corridor came in. Although reading was permitted, it was difficult because one had to stand close to the door. Every time the guard changed he peeped in through that tiny window.
>
> Except for three meals, we were not permitted to go out of our solitary cells, which wasn't good for our health. There was, however, a provision that those who observed the prison rules faithfully and were willing to do any kind of work were to be permitted to be out in the courtyard from 5:00 A.M. to 5:00 P.M. So, we volunteered to work right away. Makino was assigned to work in the prison store. Negoro was to polish all the brass objects. Tasaka was assigned to do yard work, and I was to clean the office of the chief warden. Our work was not heavy, taking only a couple of hours, and we were permitted to do reading or anything we liked for the rest of the day. I decided to do as much reading as I could. Warden Ash and the guards treated us very kindly.
>
> Among the variety of prisoners was a Chinese who was a heroin addict. He seemed lifeless, but when the doctor gave him a tiny bit of heroin, he immediately became lively. I seriously wondered if the prison was a right place for him to receive the treatment.
>
> There was an elderly Japanese. Evidently, he was a repeater of petty

theft and was a familiar figure to the guards. This time, he was arrested as he was leaving the market with a bunch of vegetables. He seemed to be a good-natured old man. He has money, but he seems to steal for sheer enjoyment.

Another unusual case was a group of Russians. They were imported by the Planters to restrain the Japanese laborers. However, they had complaints as soon as they landed and they wouldn't go to the fields. As a result, those who were the leaders were imprisoned. Then, they began a hunger strike, rejecting all food. After several days, however, they conceded to the prison doctor's order to eat. Soon after that they were all released, and almost all of them left Hawaii for the mainland.[17]

Outside the prison, friends of the prisoners, Caucasians and Japanese, including those who had firmly opposed the strike, launched a campaign for their release. The Reverend Takie Okumura, who had been against the strike, was especially active in securing signatures from the leading citizens of the dominant white community, including James Cooke, then president of the Hawaiian Sugar Planters' Association, on a petition to the governor for a special pardon for the prisoners. Undoubtedly, James Cooke's signature added special significance to this petition and influenced Acting Governor Ernest A. Mott-Smith in making his decision. As a result, the prisoners were released on July 4, 1910, after serving three months of the original sentence of ten months. The fine was revoked also. Another young man also serving time in connection with the strike, Heigo Fuchino, evidently was not included in this special pardon.[18]

There was a large crowd of people waiting in front of the prison gate to greet the ex-prisoners. "We were almost buried with beautiful leis," Sōga recalled.

After the pictures were taken, we walked to King Street and crossed Aala Park to the Yamashiro Hotel in front of which was a still larger crowd waiting, and Mr. Torakichi Kimura gave an impressive speech to welcome us back, which was followed by three cheers of "Banzai," making us feel overwhelmed. Then we were taken to Palama Tetsurei Tea House for a welcome luncheon. For the first time we felt relaxed. We discovered that all four of us gained weight during our imprisonment. I gained seven pounds. A week later, a dinner party was given at Isshinro Tea House by more than 150 people to celebrate our special pardon. In thanking them, I told them that the strike may have caused some ill-feeling between the Japanese and Americans and disturbed the peace of the community, but it called the attention of the general public to the fact that the Japanese were not an ignorant people contented with a discriminatory slave-like existence, but they were a people with human dignity and aspiration.[19]

The Plantation Strike of 1920

After World War I the cost of living continued to rise while the basic wage for Oriental laborers remained what it had been since the 1909 strike: $20 for twenty-six work days a month or 77 cents a day for a ten-hour work day. Housing for Oriental laborers was exceedingly inferior compared with that provided for the Portuguese and other non-Orientals. A retired teacher who was familiar with Kahuku Plantation at the time of the 1920 strike remembered that "all the Japanese plantation workers and their families had to use the community toilet and bathhouse. There was a long line of people standing outside the toilet, waiting for their turns. The whole sight was beneath human dignity. The toilet was partitioned by a thin board, one side for men and the other side for women. The bathhouse was in the same order."[20]

Yasutarō Sōga had observed the plantation housing situation since 1896, and he said the conditions "not only shocked me but made me angry."

> The living area of the laborers . . . was like a hog pen unfit for human housing. Several hundred men and women lived in shacks built of rough boards white-washed with cement. Each shack was over-crowded, without privacy and with no sanitation facilities. The multi-tiered bunks were used by single men while a small room was used by a married couple, but they were often compelled to share it with single men. While there was a facility for drinking water, there was no sewage system, and the whole camp stank with an unbearable stench. All the plantations had the same conditions.[21]

In 1919, plantation laborers on all the islands began to organize in an effort to have their wages raised. The Youth's Association was formed on Hawaii on October 19; the Waialua Young Buddhists' Association (Oahu) had a rally on October 25; and a Committee to Support the Campaign for Higher Wages was organized in Honolulu on October 27. On Kauai, the workers organized the Kauai Labor Federation on November 23. The workers of both east and west Maui organized the Maui Labor Unions Federation on November 23. On Oahu, the Japanese workers of Ewa, Waipahu, Waimanalo, Aiea, and Waialua plantations formed a labor federation in mid-November, and Kahuku Plantation workers joined the following year. The first meeting of the Japanese Federation of Labor in Hawaii was held in Honolulu early in December 1919, at which it was decided that all requests for wage increases would be channelled through the Federation and that the negotiations would be aimed at raising the basic daily pay to $1.25 for men and to 95 cents for women for an eight-hour workday instead of a ten-hour day, and that prices paid to contract cane growers would be increased correspondingly. A request to this effect was submitted to the secretary of the HSPA on December 6, 1919. Thus began the negotiation, which went on for two months. The request was denied and the two months of negotiation failed.[22]

When the HSPA rejected the demands of the Federation, on February 1, 1920, the Japanese workers went on strike. Ten days earlier, on January 19, Filipino plantation workers on Oahu had gone out on strike in response to a call from their union, the Filipino Federation of Labor, headed by Pablo Manlapit, in support of similar demands, which the HSPA had also rejected. Thus began the 1920 Oahu-wide labor strike involving two thousand Filipino and four thousand Japanese workers from Kahuku, Waialua, Waimanalo, Ewa, Waipahu, and Aiea plantations.[23]

Manlapit issued an order for the Filipinos to stop their strike on February 9, accusing Japanese strikers of conspiring to cripple Hawaii's sugar industry and declaring that the Filipino laborers would save the industry from strangulation by the Japanese. Not all the Filipino strikers returned to work, and Manlapit resumed the strike again on February 14. His fickle leadership resulted in the breakdown of the Filipino union organization, however.[24]

In the meantime, the HSPA, on February 14, issued an eviction notice. Those who failed to report for work on February 18 were ordered to leave the premises of their respective plantations. Ten thousand Japanese men, women, and children left their homes on the plantations, and only about thirty families remained. Evicted strikers were taken care of by friends and acquaintances who were in independent enterprises, but three-fourths of the Kahuku and Aiea strikers sought refuge in Honolulu.[25]

The strike coincided with a worldwide influenza epidemic. Accommodating six thousand strikers and their families who came to Honolulu was the most difficult task for the Japanese Federation of Labor, because the epidemic was at its peak. The Japanese Physicians' Association issued two thousand free medical tickets for them. Over 20 percent of the strikers contracted influenza, and a large number of them never recovered, including one of the leaders of the Federation. The epidemic spread rapidly in rural Oahu also, and school buildings were converted to hospitals. In spite of such adverse circumstances, however, the strikers were firm in their determination to carry on.[26]

Japanese Consul General C. Yada maintained a hands-off policy, regarding labor disputes as the domain of employer-employee relationships and not a diplomatic concern. With the large number of strikers in town, the general atmosphere in Honolulu was disquieting, and for the Japanese residents it was disturbing. Both the planters and the English-language press accused the strikers of aiming to take control of Hawaii's sugar industry. The Japanese-language vernaculars were more objective about this strike, however, in contrast to their attitude in 1909, because it was started by the laborers themselves without persuasion from nonlabor outsiders, including newspapers.

In the middle of the anti-strike mood, leaders of the Hawaiian Board of Mission of the Congregational Church openly criticized the planters and the English-language newspapers for treating the strike as a Japanese nationalistic movement, stating that there was not a shred of evidence of connection between the Japanese government and Hawaii's plantation strike. The editors of *The Friend,* the organ of the Hawaiian Board of Missions, urged the planters to get the viewpoints of the workers and the causes of disagreement and to create an agency that would have the confidence of both, the planters and the laborers, to undertake arbitration. Such forthright statements at that time required tremendous courage in view of the fact that many of the large contributors to the Hawaiian Board of Missions were top officials of the HSPA. According to historian Albertine Loomis, the editors of *The Friend,* Dr. Frank Scudder, Dr. Doremus Scudder, Orramel Gulick, Norman Schenck, J. P. Erdman, Lloyd R. Kilam, and

Theodore Richards represented the best minds and stoutest hearts in the Christian community.[27]

The Palmer Plan

In view of the danger of the strike turning into a racial conflict, Dr. Albert W. Palmer, pastor of the Central Union Church, called a meeting with Dr. Arthur L. Dean, president of the University of Hawaii, Dr. Iga Mori, Dr. W. C. Hoddy, Masao Kawahara, a businessman, and Goro Nakayama, the manager of Sumitomo Bank, to discuss the strike situation. He proposed the so-called Palmer Plan to dissolve the Japanese Federation of Labor, call off the strike, and form a bargaining group representing all ethnic groups to negotiate with the management of the plantations to settle the present dispute as well as all grievances in the future. Dr. Palmer presented the proposal his group had worked out from the pulpit at a Sunday morning service. Then he presented it to the Japanese Federation of Labor and the HSPA. The directors and secretary of the Japanese Federation of Labor met with the Palmer group and, after discussion, agreed to accept the plan as the basis for peaceful settlement. Federation leaders also agreed to disband the Federation and reorganize under the new name Laborers' Association, with members from any ethnic group. The HSPA, however, rejected the whole idea. While the strike dragged on, the influenza epidemic took a heavy toll on the strikers and their families, making it impossible to continue the strike. Accordingly, the delegates of the Laborers' Association met with John Waterhouse, the president of the HSPA, and other HSPA officials in a meeting at the Young Hotel arranged by Bishop Hosen Isobe of the Soto Sect Buddhist Temple and explained the situation.[28] As a result, the strike was called off on June 30. It had lasted six months, involved 13,000 men and their families, and cost the Japanese community at least $200,000 and the planters $12 million.[29]

Without any promises from the planters, most Japanese and Filipino strikers had returned to their respective plantations. Shortly thereafter, however, the wage and bonus differential based on ethnicity was eliminated; the minimum wage was increased from $20 a month to $23, the bonus was increased, and extensive improvements were made in housing, sanitation, and the water system,[30] although the concept of collective bargaining failed and paternalism continued.

Gradual improvements in the working and living conditions of the plantations also began after the 1920 strike. The difficult physical work of loading cut sugar cane onto railcars, called "hapaiko," was mechanized in 1925, according to HSPA personnel. A tremendous change in housing had been achieved by 1930. Yasutarō Sōga described the improvements he observed during an all-day inspection tour of plantations at the invitation of the HSPA:

> When I saw Frank C. Atherton [president of HSPA] at some meeting, he said that he noticed frequently in what I wrote [in the *Nippu Jiji*] inaccurate accounts about the present conditions of the plantation and that he would like to take me and my son [a *Nippu Jiji* reporter] to a couple of plantations to see the conditions myself and that I could ask him any question. It was one day in September 1931. From early in the morning my son and I made an observation tour of a couple of plantations with Mr. Atherton driving his car as our guide. I was not familiar with the technical aspects of sugar production, but I noticed that much of the labor was mechanized, although there was some work done by manpower. Those who were receiving the minimum wage of one dollar a day were only five percent of the total labor force.
>
> The living area was tremendously improved. It looked more like a village (with houses) than a camp. It was certainly a different world since the contract labor era. The greatest change was not in the outside appearance but in the psychology of the people living there. In the past the reason that the majority of young people [immigrants] disliked the plantation life was not necessarily the work itself but the oppressive atmosphere and racial discrimination in the plantation system, with the manager like a feudal lord. There was no longer that kind of barrier between the manager and laborers, and equality was prevailing in everything. The very fact that Mr. Atherton, the most important official of Hawaii's sugar industry, spent the whole day driving his car as our guide was the proof of the change.[31]

The 1920 strike caused a deep resentment toward the Japanese. After the strike, many left the sugar plantations. In 1920 there were 19,474 Japanese male plantation workers in Hawaii; in 1922, their number decreased to 16,992. By 1930 their number had decreased to 8,955.[32] Also, the change in labor-management relations along with other social changes resulted in a higher status for plantation jobs, making them attractive enough for native-born men and women. According to the survey of HSPA in June 1931, there were 56,411 laborers in Hawaii, of whom 12,050 were U.S. citizens. The total number of Japanese was 10,268, of whom 8,062 (7,063 males and 999 females) were aliens and 2,207 (1,999 males and 208 females) were Nisei working as production technicians, surveyors, accountants, carpenters, painters, and so on. The Filipinos eventually became the largest field labor force, replacing the Japanese. In turn, the Japanese seemed to be following the Portuguese and taking over minor positions of responsibility such as field overseer.[33]

The harmful effects of the policy of treating Oriental laborers as inferior to non-Oriental laborers had long been criticized by Caucasians in responsible positions. The U.S. Commissioner-General of Immigration, in a report in 1911, denounced the HSPA policy of lower wages and poor living conditions for Oriental laborers as detrimental to the Americanization of Hawaii, keeping them below the American standard of living.[34] Hugh V. White, pastor of Kahului Union Church on Maui, asserted in January 1921 that the sugar industry was organized on the condition of industrial feudalism, which was fundamentally undemocratic, although it was often benevolent and generous; that it was hard to teach the ideals of political liberty and democracy and to instill the American idea of independence and self-respect in the children at school when they lived under the conditions that were contrary to those ideals. Another minister, Royal G. Hall, on Kauai stated in March 1923 that the American standard of life and the present economic system of Hawaii were in large measure incompatible; that in a democracy no man was simply an economic tool but a person with rights.[35]

The long-term impact of the strike on the Japanese was their gradual withdrawal from plantation labor and seeking independence as vegetable growers or in other nonagricultural occupations. By 1922, the Filipinos had become the largest labor force on the sugar plantations.[36]

6

Japanese in Other Major Industries and Commerce

The Pineapple Industry

PINEAPPLES were introduced to Hawaii by a Spaniard, Don Francisco de Paula Marin, in 1813. Captain John Kidwell started to raise pineapples on five acres of land in Manoa, Oahu, in 1885, and in the following year he imported a superior pineapple, Smooth Cayenne, from Jamaica. In 1898, when Hawaii became a territory of the United States, farmers from California settled in Wahiawa, Oahu, to start pineapple plantations. One of these farmers, Alfred W. Eames, founded Hawaiian Island Packing Company in 1906 and built a cannery in Wahiawa. In 1917 it became part of the California Corporation of San Francisco, which became known later as the Del Monte Corporation. In 1899, James D. Dole, a young New Englander, a Harvard graduate, arrived in Hawaii and in 1901 he founded the Dole Hawaiian Pineapple Company with plantations and cannery in Wahiawa.[1] Pineapple growing, the novel agricultural enterprise, attracted many Japanese in Hawaii, who became involved in pineapple production as independent growers very early.

Yasuke Teshima of Fukuoka-ken was the first; he started raising pineapples in Wahiawa in 1901. The Japanese cultivated pineapple mostly in central Oahu in the Kipapa, Waipio, and Wahiawa areas and in north Oahu. Some individuals leased from 250 to 400 acres and subleased their lands to smaller pineapple growers. There were also cooperative enterprises of small groups working on leased lands in the vicinity of Pearl City. When the Oahu Pineapple Growers Association was formed in 1913, more than 200 Japanese pineapple growers joined. By 1915 the Japanese had invested approximately $700,000 to raise pineapples on about 8,000 acres on Oahu alone.[2]

102

On Maui a group of Japanese started the Pauwela Cannery in 1910 with capital of $20,000 to process pineapples grown by independent farmers. This cannery was sold to the Baldwin Company in 1917, which later sold it to the Dole Company. On Kauai, defying the depression of the early 1930s when Caucasian-owned canneries were curtailing their operations, a group of pineapple growers from Okinawa-ken organized a cooperative in 1932 and built a canning factory on Kauai Homestead near Kapaa to can their own produce. This cannery proved to be successful, and by 1936 it produced annually 40,000 cases of canned pineapples. The company was sold to Caucasian-controlled interests in 1937 and continued under the new name Hawaiian Fruit Packers. The number of Japanese pineapple growers had increased to 3,000 by 1930, but during the Depression years many of them returned to the sugar plantations, which, with improved working conditions, provided more stable employment.[3]

Not all of the Japanese pineapple growers were successful. The most ambitious pineapple enterprise, the Waipio Pineapple Company, known among the Japanese as Hyakunin Compa ("One Hundred Men's Company"), was organized with capital of $50,000 by Gensho Hasegawa of Haleiwa, one of ten physicians who came from Japan in 1902 or 1903.[4] Dr. Hasegawa had been considering founding an all-Japanese pineapple plantation when he met Nihei Okazaki, a young sugar plantation worker from Fukushima-ken who made a strong impression on him. Finding him to be a "man of character," Dr. Hasegawa spoke to Okazaki about his plans to start a pineapple plantation to help Japanese immigrants. Okazaki was interested, and the venture got under way in 1908. In 1952, Dr. Hasegawa reminisced about the ambitious enterprise and its sad fate:

> Mr. E. Tokimasa, who used to be an interpreter for a plantation manager, was one of the few Japanese who could speak English in those days. Since his service would be indispensable in negotiation with Caucasians, we invited him to join us in our venture as our vice-president. Mr. Nihei Okazaki was the executive vice-president in charge of all the business matters, especially soliciting investors as well as recruiting laborers. We asked Mr. Soichi Nakashima, originally from Kumamoto-ken, who had experience in raising pineapples on his own farm, to be our field luna.
>
> We leased in my name 808 acres of land in Kipapa from a Caucasian

for a period of twenty years. We organized our company as a joint-stock company. Our shareholders were mostly those of Tohoku, principally Fukushima-ken. . . . We paid our workers 80 cents a day. We opened our company store, and we also employed a cook to feed us all. Thus, our company was organized as a pineapple plantation in form, calling attention from both the Caucasian and Japanese communities. Then, we worked very hard, piling up effort upon effort. When we saw our crop, however, whether it was due to our lack of technology or fertilizer, our fruits were inferior to those grown in the fields of the neighboring Caucasians. Ours were to be rated the third or fourth grade, and were no match for theirs. With the sale price so low because of the inferior pineapples, our accounts were minus. Every year our company's minus account increased. We could not keep our laborers without paying them wages. Mr. Okazaki and I went around on horseback to borrow money from the likely Japanese who might lend us money.

Finally, in desperation, we borrowed a large sum of money from Libby, McNeil & Libby Co., which had 3,000 acres under cultivation at that time. . . . As we were unable to pay back the money as we agreed (in one year), Libby Company took over all our leased land along with all the rights connected with our business. In utter dismay, our laborers did not know what to do. Those who wanted to stay and work for Libby were accepted, but all the others had to leave our familiar farm right away. Already, a Caucasian luna on horseback was inspecting our premises while new field lunas were posted in various places and new laborers carrying their *kori* [wicker suitcases] were arriving rapidly to replace us. In a short time we who had worked together with a united purpose were separated and scattered. . . . As Mr. Okazaki and I stood in . . . Wahiawa [looking on our farm] . . . tears of chagrin rolled down on our cheeks.[5]

The officers and directors of the bankrupt company were idealists rather than practical farmers. They were greatly influenced by the Puritan spirit; they had built a church at the beginning and held their business meetings there, which usually ended as prayer meetings. Dr. Hasegawa gave up the pineapple business completely after this bankruptcy, but Nihei Okazaki continued to dedicate his time and energy to pineapple cultivation.

In 1922 James D. Dole purchased the whole island of Lanai from the Baldwin family of Maui for a pineapple plantation. Of the total of 90,200 acres, 15,000 acres were cultivated as pineapple fields. Practically all of the population of about 3,000 people of various ethnic backgrounds were the company's employees and their families. The small town of Lanai City grew up with stores, churches, banks, movie theaters and other recreational facilities, schools from kindergarten to high school, a hospital, post office, and community organizations such as the PTA, Kiwanis Club, Boy Scouts, and Girl Scouts.[6]

Dole Pineapple Company's plantation on Lanai was a large-scale operation similar to a sugar plantation, but no brutal treatment of the laborers was ever recorded. Russ and Peg Apple described the plantation life as follows:

> The plantation manager in 1936 was a virtual king on all Lanai. The majority of 237 married workmen were Japanese. There were 1,045 single laborers including the Japanese, Filipinos, Koreans, Chinese, and Hawaiians, and they boarded for $12 a month in mess halls, each of which served ethnic foods. Everybody including the manager got up long before dawn. Then men and women, and children during the vacation, were loaded on trucks at dawn six days of the week for field labor and brought back by 4 P.M. The field bosses or lunas were young Caucasians and under them were straw bosses most of whom were Japanese. The chief problem was the damage by the bugs that killed the pineapple plants, and another was a minor problem that some lazy laborers slept during their work hours.[7]

During World War II practically all the sons of military age of the Japanese workers served in the U.S. Armed Forces. Most of those who returned took advantage of the G.I. Bill for further education on the mainland and pursued professional careers or entered the business world. As a result, the majority of the retired Issei moved to where their sons and daughters lived and worked—Honolulu. By 1960 there were only a small number of Japanese, all in nonlabor occupations such as storekeepers, on Lanai. Practically all the field laborers were Filipinos.

Pineapples not being essential food, pineapple growing waned during the war, and independent pineapple growers, including the Japanese, were phased out. After the war, the pineapple companies made efforts to "rehabilitate" plantations and canneries, which had suffered from the wartime shortage of labor and general neglect.[8] However, the postwar period was a different era with new challenges for the prewar paternalistic plantation system. Large pineapple companies succeeded in reviving the pineapple industry, but conditions were changed. As in the case of the sugar plantations, the pineapple plantation workers were unionized as early as 1945–1946 by the ILWU.[9]

Japanese Coffee Growers

In 1892 or thereabout, Japanese began to settle in Kona on the island of Hawaii to work for the Hawaii Coffee and Tea Company. Climatically and topographically, Kona is well suited for the production of superior coffee. When the Japanese became interested in coffee growing, they needed money for the initial expenses. They had to lease from five to fifteen acres of land for ten years from the Bishop Estate or other landowners, paying rent of $300 to $1,000. Then they had to buy coffee seedlings to plant. It took approximately four years for seedlings to mature and bear coffee beans. During these years there was no income, but expenses for tending the young trees were ongoing. To assist these farmers at this initial stage, Sanshichi Ozaki, a businessman in Honolulu, and Kenji Imanishi, then manager of the Honolulu Branch of the Yokohama Specie Bank, with the aid of Consul General Miki Saitō, negotiated with the Japanese government to release $10,000 of the unclaimed savings of contract laborers that was still in the custody of the bank in Honolulu to subsidize the Kona coffee growers.

Since the price of coffee depended on the world market, which was affected principally by the production of coffee in Brazil, coffee growing in Hawaii was not a stable or lucrative industry. In 1901, when the price of coffee dropped from about $10 to $12 per 100 pounds in the world market to $7, most coffee growers left this unprofitable industry. An American named Brunner, however, made a contract with the Japanese to have them cultivate several hundred acres of coffee by providing them with housing and water tanks, and collecting one-third of their yields as rental. When the price rose to $11.50 per 100 pounds in 1912, Brunner sold his interests to the Captain Cook Mill. After that, the coffee growers paid the rental for land and sold all their produce to the company. There were 273 Japanese coffee growers in 1909. In 1914 more than 80 percent of the Hawaii coffee crop was produced by the Japanese, grown on more than 3,780 acres in the Kona district. By

1931 there were 1,300 Japanese families engaged in growing coffee. That year a total of 2,448,000 trees, grown on 5,500 acres, bore 8,846,500 pounds of coffee. Each family owned an average of 188 trees, collecting about 3.95 pounds from each tree.[10] Anthropologist John F. Embree, who made a study of the Japanese in Kona in 1937, observed that each family harvested about 125 bags worth about $625, which hardly covered the year's living expenses for the family. Often the entire crop was mortgaged to grocery stores in exchange for food.[11]

Unlike sugar plantation work, the coffee industry among the Japanese was in the nature of a family venture. While there were financial risks, crop failure, perpetual poverty, and so on, coffee workers did not encounter the indignity experienced by the immigrants who worked on the sugar plantations of earlier years. Moreover, since all members of the family worked together as a team, there was an intimate understanding of the nature of the work involved, mutual role-taking, and, as a result, closeness of the family members.

Helen Oyakawa, who grew up in a coffee-growing family, described her experiences during the 1937 harvesting season from August to mid-November in the *Honolulu Star-Bulletin*.[12] In Kona, the school vacation was scheduled during the coffee harvesting months so that the children could help their parents. Father and mother and three elementary school children, including Helen, worked together as a team for ten or more hours a day. Each carried a basket and a large hook to pull down tall branches. When the basket was filled with coffee beans, they emptied it into 100-pound burlap sacks. Then the farmer who was the employer sewed up the mouths of the sacks. They were paid from $1 to $1.50 for each 100 pounds of coffee beans. When the children were small, the Oyakawa family picked only four bags a day, but when the children grew older, together with their parents they were able to pick fifteen bags a day. Since they were paid by the amount they picked, there was no time for relaxation. For lunch, however, the family sat together to eat. Their meal generally consisted of a pot of hot rice and some meat or a can or two of salmon or corned beef, vegetables, cocoa or fruit juice, and a large jug of water to drink and wash hands.

At the end of the day Helen and her brothers would watch the coffee beans emptied into and rinsed in a large tank at the mill, and then another machine hulled the bright outside skin, which was later recycled into fertilizer, while the inside beans were carried through the moving chute to topside ceiling to be dried in the sun. The roof that covered the ceiling was movable, and in good weather the coffee on the ceiling was uncovered for airing and drying. Several times a day one of the farmer's family would rake the coffee beans with long-handed wooden rakes. At sundown the roof was rolled back to cover the coffee beans.

After the family returned home between 4:30 and 5:30 P.M., one of Helen's brothers would heat the *furo* bath, and she and her mother would cook dinner or attend to heavy laundry. She or her brother would also babysit their younger sisteer, and her father would work in the vegetable garden. After taking a bath and eating supper under the kerosene lamp, the family read the newspaper, books from the library, or listened to the radio. Exhausted from the day's work, they went to bed by 9:00 P.M.

Although Kona coffee was known for its superior quality, the amount produced was not enough for local consumption. The consumers in Hawaii were more used to various brands of coffee from the mainland. Also, when the world market price was very low, it was disastrous for coffee farmers in Kona. Their predicament prompted Governor William F. Quinn to make a special appeal to the State legislature on April 3, 1961, to act on an emergency measure to save Kona coffee farmers. He explained that coffee growing in Kona, which was the basis of livelihood for eight hundred to a thousand families, was in serious trouble because the world market prices were the lowest since early 1950s. Coffee fields were neglected and even abandoned. Coffee farmers had exhausted their credit resources and were heavily in debt. He urged the legislature to make emergency loans with very low interest available to coffee farmers along with other measures to improve the production and quality of Kona coffee and promotional programs to attract a larger market in Hawaii and on the mainland.[13]

The official assistance resulted in the revival of coffee growing in Kona and in the opening of Honolulu branches of a number of mainland coffee companies. Through their agents in Kona, these companies buy green coffee beans from the farmers' cooperatives and roast and grind the beans in their factories in Honolulu to make Kona coffee ready for consumers in Hawaii and on the mainland. According to the Department of Agriculture of the State of Hawaii, Kona coffee farmers, who are the second and third generation of the original Issei coffee growers, are doing very well in the 1980s.

The Hog Industry

Hog-raising in Hawaii was a monopoly of the Chinese in the early years. Since hogs multiply fast and mature quickly, and cheap feed in the form of garbage and waste could be obtained from slaughterhouses and restaurants, hog-raising was a feasible enterprise for those who had scanty capital. For this reason, ambitious young immigrants who saw no future in plantation labor turned to hog-raising as an independent business. Hog-raising flourished on Oahu, especially on the outskirts of Honolulu. In the early years Japanese hog farmers were largely from Yamaguchi, Hiroshima, Kumamoto, and Fukuoka prefectures. By 1930, however, the number of Japanese hog farmers on Oahu had increased to 243, of which 119, or 49 percent, were from Okinawa-ken.

By 1940 Okinawans constituted 62 percent of the total of 264 Japanese hog farmers and 44 percent of the total of 349 commercial hog farmers on Oahu. Hog farmers as well as truck farmers were frozen to their jobs during World War II, being considered essential for the production of food for civilians and the armed forces. After the war, Okinawans continued to dominate the hog industry in Hawaii until the City and County of Honolulu and land develoment companies forced the removal or closing of most of the large-scale hog farms near Honolulu during the mid-1960s.[14]

The Fishery Industry

After their contracts with the sugar plantations expired, many immigrants from the coastal areas of Wakayama-ken and Yamaguchi-ken turned to fishing for a livelihood, and it became a thriving industry among the Japanese. Having heard of the good prospects in fishery in Hawaii, Gorokichi Nakaji of Wakayama-ken built a boat 32 feet long and 5.8 feet wide especially constructed and equipped to catch tuna in deep-sea waters. His arrival with this boat in 1899 resulted in a phenomenal change in the fishing industry in Hawaii. Before the Japanese entered the market, fishing in Hawaii had been dominated by Hawaiians. Their catch had been enough to meet the local need. With the arrival of the fish-eating Japanese immigrants, the need increased. When the Japanese began deep-sea fishing, the quantity and variety of the catch increased, resulting in a sharp drop in the price of fish—a welcome change for consumers but a threat to Hawaiian fisherman that caused bitter feelings.

In 1913 there were 300 Japanese fishermen in Hawaii, using gasoline-powered wooden fishing boats or sampans. In the 1920s Kiyoshi Kashiwabara helped to reduce the cost of fishing by one-fourth by installing diesel engines and using No. 2 oil. Both types of boats were used by Japanese fishermen. According to Sanno-suke Ōnishi, a retired fisherman and skipper of a fishing boat 40 feet long and 8.5 feet wide with three crew members, his boat carried 600 gallons of gasoline for ten to thirteen days of fishing, taking 60 pounds of ice for refrigeration of the catch. A larger sized boat 60 feet in length and 10 feet in width had one or two additional crew members. The market price of the catch fluctuated daily, depending on kind, quality, and quantity of fish as well as the high bids of the buyers representing fish markets. By 1930 fishing was yielding more than $2 million annually, with approximately 1,000 Japanese engaged in this business. By 1935 the Japanese operated more than 140 fishing vessels. To curb Japanese fishing activities, Italian fishermen were brought from the mainland by the government, but they did not stay long in Hawaii. Fishery became almost a monopoly of the Japanese until World War II when it was suspended for the duration of the war.[15]

The Tuna Packing Industry

The abundance of fish brought in by fishermen stimulated the development of the canning industry in Hawaii. A young enterprising man named F. Walter Macfarlane founded the Macfarlane Tuna Co. in 1916 at Ala Moana and Cooke streets, employing thirty-nine Japanese fishermen and constructing two gasoline-powered boats, *Tenjin Maru I* and *Tenjin Maru II,* in addition to sailing sampans. The people in Hawaii who had easy access to fresh fish had no inclination to make use of canned tuna, and it was exported to New York and other mainland cities. In 1922 a group of local stockholders incorporated the company as Hawaiian Tuna Packers, Ltd., with increased capital and ten more privately owned sampans. In time, local consumption increased also. In 1929 this cannery moved to Kewalo Basin, where sampans could bring their catch right to the cannery door. With technological improvements in addition to approximately five hundred workers, the company produced nearly ten million cans a year by 1937. In 1941 about 300 fishermen were bringing in tuna in a fleet of twenty-six sampans. With the outbreak of war with Japan, the sampans were confiscated by U.S. authorities and the cannery was converted to war work for the duration of the war.[16]

The Emergence of Non-Chinese Fish Markets

A fish market is an extension of fishery, although it is a commercial organization. During the early years fish markets in Hawaii were operated by the Chinese, and the Japanese fishermen took their catch to the markets for auction to fish dealers. In 1908, however, the Chinese refused to buy fish from Japanese fishermen as a result of the boycott of Japanese goods and anti-Japanese feelings in China aroused by the *Tatsu Maru* Incident. On February 5, 1908, the *Tatsu Maru,* a cargo ship owned by a shipping company in Kobe, Japan, carrying 94 cases of firearms and 40 cases of ammunition ordered from a firearms company in Macao, had anchored at Macao Port. Regarding the ship as a tool of smugglers, the Chinese authorities confiscated it along with the firearms and ammunition and detained the crew. The Japanese government protested, and the Chinese government released the crew and the ship on March 5 and paid for all the firearms and ammunition.[17] In Honolulu, in order to help more than 300 fishermen dispose of their catch during this crisis, twenty Japanese and Caucasian businessmen and professionals founded the Hawaii Fishing Company with capital of $50,000 and opened the King Fish Market on Kekaulike Street. The company kept 10 percent of the selling price as its share. While the company president and other officials were drawn from its interracial shareholders, the personnel in charge of actual business, such as the manager of the fish market, its auctioneer, and divisional heads, were Japanese—three Wakayamans, one Yamaguchin, and one Okinawan—all of whom were experts on fish.

In Hilo, the Hawaii Island Fishing Company, owned by Japanese, was founded in 1910. In the same year, in Honolulu, the Pacific Fishing Company was founded by Chinese and Japanese businessmen with capital of $10,000. In 1914, the Honolulu Fishery Company, a Caucasian–Japanese-owned joint-stock company, was founded. The competition between these companies was beneficial to the fishermen in the sense that they were not at the mercy of a single company.[18]

Matsujiro Ōtani and the Otani Seafood Company

While the fish markets were founded by those who had sufficient capital, the Otani Seafood Company evolved step by step under the leadership of a young immigrant from a fishing island in Yamaguchi-ken who had no money but who was charged with determination to succeed, had persistence, vision, courage, and ingenuity for new ventures and a strong sense of independence—the characteristics possessed by American business and industrial pioneers. That young immigrant was Matsujiro Ōtani, who arrived in Hawaii in 1908, three months before his eighteenth birthday.

Matsujiro Ōtani was born in 1890, the second son of a proprietor of a store on Okikamuro, a small island of about one square mile in the Inland Sea off the coast of Ōshima county of Yamaguchi-ken, where the Japanese government had sought contract labor emigrants to Hawaii since 1885 to relieve its overpopulation and impoverished condition. The population of Okikamuro Island was about one thousand, or about three hundred families, mostly fishermen, while some operated small stores like Ōtani's father.[19] Matsujiro was a frail child. When he was small, his father had taken him to the shrine in Taga to pray for his health. After elementary school in Okikamuro, he was sent to the Kōtō-ka (higher grade school) in Nishikata on the mainland and he lived at the home of the principal in Shimoda along with other students from faraway districts. He left school at age thirteen, despite the pleas of Principal Fujimoto that he remain in school to graduate, and returned home to work with his father. His job was to receive and weigh the fish off the twenty or so fishing boats in Niihama Bay that went out to sea daily. He also did some fishing himself and worked as a delivery boy and carpenter.[20]

Many years later, he wrote in his memoirs, "I became aware that there was no hope for the future for me on this isolated island." He decided to emigrate to Korea to make money, but just at that time Isojiro Kitagawa, recently returned from Hilo, visited the Ōtani home. "Without hesitation I asked him what he was doing in Hawaii," Ōtani recalled. "He said he was a fish peddler and that he could earn a net income of $2 a day easily. That made me decide to go to Hawaii."[21]

Once he made up his mind to go to Hawaii, Ōtani was determined to succeed, and he set out to realize his goal.

> I went to Bōchō Emigration Company in Yanai to apply for emigration to Hawaii. A young clerk came out. I told him that I wanted to go to Hawaii and requested his help. He asked me if I had a wife. When I answered "No," he said that I was not qualified, since his company did not handle single men. Feeling dejected, I returned to my island by the next boat. . . . While feeling disgusted, I still felt that there should be some way for a single man to go to Hawaii. So, I wrote to Mr. Hyōtayu Shimanuki, editor in charge of emigration problems, of Hakubundō, the publishing company of the magazine *Shōnen Sekai* [World of Youth] in Tokyo. I received his answer right away. He explained that the rejection of single men by the emigration company was because of the profit. A couple paid 20 yen for application fee while a single man paid only 10 yen.[22]

Ōtani did not give up. Instead he went back to the emigration company to negotiate with its manager. He was again informed that the company handled only married couples. Considering himself too young to need a wife, Ōtani volunteered to pay the 20 yen fee for a married couple. Told that he would be charged that anyway, Ōtani said he would pay 30 yen, and the manager could write down 10 yen on the receipt. The manager agreed, and Ōtani's name was entered on the list of those leaving in December. Ōtani was jubilant, and the whole family shared his happiness and congratulated him on his success.[23]

The date set for Ōtani's departure was January 10, aboard the S.S. *Hong Kong Maru*. The family gathered at the Ōtani house to wish him well. It was New Year's Day and as the family ate together the special breakfast his mother had cooked to celebrate her son's departure as well as New Year's Day, he felt sad. It was the last time the whole family would have a meal together. Carrying a wicker suitcase filled with the personal effects his mother had prepared for him, Ōtani left the island for Yanai Port, where he took the train to Kobe.[24] In Kobe, the young emigrant reported to "Police Headquarters for instruction, to the doctor's clinic for health examination, to the eye doctor's for trachoma, to the American consulate for visa," and took care of other last-minute preparations.[25]

At last, it was time to leave Japan.

On January 10 the S.S. *Hong Kong Maru* arrived. . . . Since I passed the health and eye examinations and completed all the required business for sailing, I was allowed to go on board. I bought ten cases of Kishu oranges from a salesman and had them brought to the cabin. . . . That night when we were sailing on the Sea of Enshū, it was rough, but I was too excited to be sick. We arrived at Yokohama next morning. Many passengers went to Tokyo for sightseeing, but I spent the whole day watching the streets of Yokohama and the harbor from the deck of the boat. At the end of the day the *Hong Kong Maru* sailed for Honolulu. From the boat I looked up high in the sky at the snow-covered, sacred Mount Fuji, thinking that I was really leaving Japan and feeling sort of sad. We had a calm voyage and I enjoyed eating the oranges I bought at Kobe with the friends I made on the boat."[26]

Matsujiro Ōtani arrived in Hawaii on January 24, five months before free immigration from Japan was terminated by the so-called Gentlemen's Agreement between the governments of Japan and the United States.

On the morning of January 24, 1908, the *Hong Kong Maru* arrived outside Honolulu Harbor. A boat which seemed like one of the Harbor Police came, bringing a physician and immigration officials. We waited for them on B deck, standing in rows. The doctor ordered us to show our hands. We stretched our hands forward to show him. Then he looked at our faces, and he left. That was our health inspection. It was very simple. Just when we were ready to land, we were told that a Chinese passenger on our ship was suffering from smallpox, and that we were all (steerage passengers) to be quarantined for two weeks. At about 9:00 A.M. each of us carried on our backs the heavy wicker suitcase and walked on the long wooden bridge and the road to the so-called Sennin Goya [Barrack for One Thousand People]. About 150 passengers had to spend two weeks there. Mr. Tōichi, whom I met at the Yanai Railway Station, and I spent every day watching the countless automobiles passing on the bridge. . . . Thus, we did sightseeing of Honolulu from Sand Island, thinking that it was a big town.²⁷

After two weeks in quarantine, the new arrivals were transported "little by little on a small boat to the Immigration Service in Kakaako." There they had a brief interview with a Japanese customs inspector to determine whether or not they had friends or relatives in Hawaii, and money. Ōtani was prepared. "When I said that I had 100 yen [$50] . . . he said aloud, 'You won't become a public charge' and laughed. Evidently I had passed the inspection. Later I heard that he was that famous Dr. Tomizō Katsunuma." Ōtani went to the Kawasaki Hotel and later to the Suzuki Employment Agency to look for a job. "A yard boy for $3 a week, a first-class cook for $7 a week, and several other jobs were listed on the bulletin board, and many men were waiting there." He soon met other young men from Okikamuro and was invited to live with them in Kakaako, where many others from Okikamuro lived. He moved out of the Kawasaki Hotel. "I felt relaxed in the atmosphere of my old island, as if I were back home." After paying his bills, he decided to send $20 home to his parents. That left him with 35 cents for himself. "I did the right thing," he said to himself. "From now on I am on my own. I will work hard to earn money." He felt new courage within himself.²⁸

Ōtani had made up his mind to be successful in the new world, and he began preparing himself for that goal, first learning English while supporting himself. His experiences were a succession of uncertainties.

I thought that the first thing I must do was to learn English. . . . So, I started to attend the Pacific Mills Institute on the corner of Nuuanu and Beretania streets. I commuted by street car for 5 cents for both ways, going and returning. In the meantime, I got a part-time job as a school boy at a Caucasian home, receiving $1 a week. Every day before going to the afternoon class I went to Wo Fat to eat a bowlful of noodles as my lunch for 5 cents. To make myself full, I put a lot of soy sauce and water on it. After a month, I decided to work full time in the daytime and attend the evening school for English. So, I quit this school. I got a job as a janitor at Wall, Nichols Co. for $7 a week.

There was a night English school at Jōdo Mission (a Buddhist temple) on South Street. I borrowed $15 . . . and bought a bicycle to attend this night school. . . .

I got another job in the wholesale department of Y. clothing store as a truck driver. After working for a month or so, there was no sign of paying me a wage. When I asked for pay, the proprietor said, 'You don't need money. What are you going to do with it?' So, I decided to quit this store, but since it seemed ridiculous to have worked for nothing, I asked through my friend who introduced me there to have six dozen undershirts delivered to me at my lodging. At $3 a dozen, I got $18 for my monthly wage.

Mr. K from my home island told me that Mr. Y, also from my island, was doing a successful business in Lahaina, Maui. Introduced by him, I went to Lahaina with my scanty belongings. Maui was a completely backward country. At the beginning I was assigned to cut the leaves of the sugarcane, with permission from the sugar company, and to bring them home on the mule for feed for the horses. After a while I was assigned to take orders from the customers of various plantation camps. The senior clerk of the store, Mr. M, took me to a couple of nearby camps and introduced me to chief cooks and others and taught me how to get orders. The orders were chiefly rice and other foodstuff. . . . Since the roads were narrow, everything had to be carried on horseback. . . . I got up at dawn and washed seven horses and fed them with cane leaves. Then, I cleaned up the store. After I had breakfast, I started on horseback to get orders from the customers. It took four hours to reach some of the camps. . . . Next day I tied four sacks of ordered goods to the horse and, with a small piece of hard biscuit for my lunch, I went to deliver them to our customers. On their paydays I went to collect money, returning home after midnight sometimes. Since I was still an inexperienced apprentice, I was not paid a regular wage except some spending money. . . . Since there was no future for me on Maui, I decided to return to Honolulu. . . . A letter came from my friend, informing me of a new fish market which was looking for someone to take charge of buying fresh fish from fishermen, suggesting that I come back to Honolulu. . . .[29]

The Opening of a Fish Store: the Road to Otani Seafood Company

After more than two years of working in various jobs as a janitor, yard boy, sales clerk, and so on while studying English, Ōtani opened a small fish store in the King Fish Market of the Hawaii Fishing Company in Honolulu in 1911. That same year he married Kane, the nineteen-year-old Hawaii-born daughter of Roku-suke Yanagihara, who was from Okikamuro.[30] In 1913 he got a license for fish peddling, and in 1918 he moved the store to the Aala Fish Market, owned by Mr. Ahoi, a Chinese, for a monthly rental of $100. He described his entry into the fish business in his memoirs.

I opened a small fish store as a tenant at King Fish Market on Kekaulike Street in 1911. It was a small store but my future looked bright and every day was a happy one for me. I got up at five every morning and returned home at six in the evening. In May that year Mr. Tamura who used to live in Kakaako asked me if I were interested in buying houses on a lot owned by Bishop Trust Co. Without money I was hesitant at first, but Mr. Hamada, a boat carpenter, and I decided to buy them together. I paid $190 for a house while Mr. Hamada bought two houses and a boat-carpenter shop. I was naive like a small child. I borrowed money by joining a Tanomoshi-kō with $15 monthly payment. . . .

In 1913 I got a license for fish peddling. I bought a horse-drawn peddling car from Mr. Yamasaki. I tended my store at the fish market from 5:00 A.M., and from about 11:00 A.M. I went around the city selling fish to my customers, and when I went to Wahiawa, I returned home after 7:00 P.M. and even as late as 9:00 P.M. As soon as I returned home, my wife fed the horse and cleaned the car. When I bought an automobile for peddling, she was glad that all she had to do was clean the car. We already had two children, but my wife employed Miss Aki F. as a baby-sitter, and she herself worked at the American Fish Cannery. Even now I wonder how she managed to work so hard.[31]

With the assistance of his younger brother Usanosuke whom he had invited from home, Ōtani founded the Otani Seafood Company in October 1920 with capital of $500 in order to expand his business by importing seafood from Japan and the United States mainland. He contracted with the Crab Canning Company of Japan to be its sole agent in Hawaii, and he also started manufacturing *kamaboko,* Japanese fish cakes. Participating in the bidding on canned crabs at Armstrong Army Barracks, the Otani Company won the bid to become the purveyor for the U.S. Armed Forces, and in February 1925, when a fleet of 125 naval vessels arrived at Pearl Harbor for a large-scale maneuver in Hawaiian waters, the Otani Company was assigned to supply them with fresh fish as well as other seafoods. Encouraged by his success Matsujiro Ōtani expanded further by founding the Taiyo Company jointly with Yoshio Tagami with $5,000 in capital to import dried abalone from Mexico. Subsequently, Ōtani and Tagami traveled to San Francisco, Seattle, and Los Angeles and made contracts with various companies to import a variety of seafoods, including fresh salmon, salted salmon, smoked salmon, cod, and Alaskan herring roe. By then the Otani Company employed a Caucasian salesman named Steiner to be in charge of the orders from the Armed Forces.[32]

In 1929, Ōtani decided to expand the manufacture of fish cake. He built a concrete structure in a corner of the Aala Market Place and employed a specialist in kamaboko as the chief cook and ten cooks to work under him. Kamaboko with the Otani Company label became popular and was in tremendous demand all over Hawaii. Then in March 1933, a sudden windspout took away the roof and the newly built chimney of the kamaboko factory along with the bicycles on the streets and carried them high in the air toward Nuuanu Pali and Alewa Heights, leaving behind in 15 minutes great damage and loss to his business. To add to his troubles, Ōtani learned that the monthly rental at the Aala Market was going to be raised from $390 to $1,300. He consulted his company's legal advisor, attorney William Heen, and with his assistance the outrageous rent hike was averted. Realizing the precariousness to future expansion of renting his place of business, in 1938 he bought the whole Aala Market Place, including the remaining one year of Mr. Ahoi's lease, for $150,000. At the same time he leased the land the market place occupied for twenty-five years from the Dillingham Corporation and its subsidiary, the Oahu Railway Company.[33]

In 1940 the Otani Company was reorgnized as a joint-stock company with Aala Market Place as its subsidiary, and Attorney Heen was elected president of both companies.[34] The Aala Market had a monthly income of $2,400 from rent from its fifty-six tenants who had stores there, but since repairs and additional refrigeration facilities to the old building were too costly, the construction of a new building was launched to replace the old one. On November 14, just two weeks before the completion of the new building, the Aala Market had a fire, started from the leakage of a gas pipe in the refrigeration room, which burned three-fourths of the market place. As chemical material was used to extinguish the fire, the stores there were ordered closed by the Board of Health. At that time Ōtani was recuperating from a heart attack at his Kaneohe home. A few days later the inspector of the Board of Health visited him at Kaneohe, expressed his sympathy for the fire, and promised to permit opening of the stores as soon as the inspection was completed.[35]

Realizing the fire hazard, Ōtani decided to build a concrete building to replace the wooden structure. After the ground-breaking ceremony in February 1941, the construction work was speeded up so that the market place could open within the year. On December 4, a three-day open house got started, and all the Otani Company business connections from the West Coast as well as in Hawaii were invited. On the fourth day of the celebration, December 7, an elaborate luncheon party was planned for several hundred guests and employees. Despite his recent heart attack, Ōtani went to the market place early in the morning, and President Heen of the Otani Company was there also, helping and advising the staff preparing for the big luncheon. The celebration never took place. Ōtani described the unexpected incidents of that day.

> There was a confused atmosphere on the streets, and many people said that they saw black smoke rising up in the vicinity of Pearl Harbor with occasional big fires shooting up, something like the explosion of gas tanks. At about 7:00 A.M. some people saw five planes with the Rising Sun insignia flying toward Pearl Harbor. Some asked, "Could it be war?" Others said, "That's ridiculous. It must be a maneuver." When we heard the repeated radio announcement that the ships at Pearl Harbor were attacked and sunk, everybody was shocked. At about 10:00 A.M. Governor Poindexter announced that the Japanese Air Force bombed Pearl Harbor suddenly and that the war with Japan had started. Attorney Heen who heard this announcement gave this news to all of us in the market. . . . Our hearts were filled with pain and agony. When those of us who had trucks were asked over the radio to come to Pearl Harbor immediately and help take the wounded sailors and officers to hospitals, I sent two trucks, each manned with two employees, to Pearl Harbor. But they were refused entry to the gate despite their permits because they were Japanese. So, they headed to Schofield Barracks to help, but there too the Japanese were refused. So, they brought back the trucks at about 4:00 P.M. I left the market

with my wife at about 4:00 P.M., headed for our home in Manoa. On our way we were stopped by soldiers five times and questioned. Reaching home at about 4:30 P.M., so tired and feeling sick, I was ready to rest. Just at that moment, an FBI agent and two soldiers came into our house. With a pistol thrusting at me, they asked me, "Are you Matsujiro Ōtani? Don't you know America is at war with Japan?" and they started dragging me out of the house. My wife and my son-in-law were right there. My wife pleaded with them, saying, "Please wait a moment. I must dress him in proper clothes and have him wear shoes." But they shouted, "Don't you know there is war?" and they pushed me into their car. My wife threw my shoes into the car.[36]

Ōtani was interned for the duration of World War II and separated from his family for four years. The Otani Company continued under his eldest son, Jiroichi, and its president, Attorney Heen. In the meantime his four other sons served in the U.S. Army.

In 1952 Ōtani founded the United Fishing Agency, Ltd., to revive the fishing industry in Hawaii. During World War II there was no fishing in Hawaii. After the war, Issei fishermen were too old to undertake deep-sea fishing. Concerned people, including Ōtani, tried to urge Nisei and Sansei to enter into fishing, but they showed no interest. Finally, Ōtani, accompanied by Judge William Heen, advisor to his company, went to Japan three times to urge the Foreign Office of the Japanese government to permit Japanese fishermen to come to Hawaii. But his efforts failed. In 1957, together with Shinsuke Nakamine, a prominent Nisei businessman who was a leader of the Okinawan community as well as the Japanese community, and Katsuichi Shinsato, the Issei Okinawan expert in fishery, Ōtani secured the cooperation of the Territorial government of Hawaii and the U.S. Immigration Service and succeeded in getting the consent of the Ryukyu government, which was still under the Commissioner of the United States Army,[37] to permit young Okinawan fishermen to come to Hawaii. As a result, forty young fishermen came to Hawaii in February 1962 on a three-year contract. Since then several hundred fishermen have come from Okinawa. In the course of the three-year contract, each fisherman earned from $5,000 to $6,000 to take home.[38] According to Nakamine, many of them gained permanent residence and are contributing to Hawaii's fishery in 1980s. Ōtani was naturalized in 1954 and became an American citizen.

In summary, the Japanese immigrants worked in Hawaii's major industries—pineapple, coffee, the hog industry, fishery, as well as sugar. World War II interrupted their careers. Pineapple and coffee growing waned. Fishing was completely stopped, because all the fishermen became enemy aliens in addition to the fact that the Pacific Ocean was a war zone. Hog-raising was the only industry urged by the military because it provided an essential source of food for the army as well as the civilians. After the war, however, because of land development, this industry too waned.

7

Issei in Professions

DURING the early years Japanese in professions in Hawaii were mainly connected with the plantation laborers, most employed by the Bureau of Immigration. In 1894, a year after the overthrow of the Hawaiian monarchy, the Immigration Convention signed in 1886 by Japan and the Hawaiian Kingdom was annulled. Joji Nakayama, chief inspector of the Japanese section of the Bureau, and all the Japanese inspectors and physicians on his staff resigned in 1895, and the separate Japanese section was closed.[1] They remained in Hawaii, however.

An Issei Lawyer

The only lawyer from Japan in Hawaii was Keigoro Katsura, born in Ishikawa Prefecture in 1860, who died in Honolulu in March 1891 at the age of thirty-one and was buried in the Makiki Japanese Cemetery. He studied law at the University of Tokyo and practiced in Yokohama. He came to Hawaii from the West Coast of the United States, where he had heard about the slavelike treatment of the contract laborers, sometime around 1885.[2] His efforts to help the laborers branded him as a troublemaker, and he was once beaten and locked up for three days in the warehouse of the Hamakua Plantation. Because of his incessant protests against the treatment of the immigrants, the planters complained to the Bureau of Immigration. Considering it wiser to make use of Katsura's ability instead of making him an enemy, Chief Inspector Joji Nakayama appointed him to be his legal advisor. It was during his tenure that the lynching of Hiroshi Goto took place in Honokaa

on the island of Hawaii. Goto had come to Hawaii from Kanagawa-ken in 1885 as a member of the first group of government
contract immigrants. He spoke English and always helped as an
interpreter in court or in negotiations when Japanese laborers
were involved. He was a source of irritation to planters and others
on the island of Hawaii. On October 29, 1889, his body was
found hanging from a telephone pole in Honokaa by a passerby.
Katsura dispatched Eijiro Tatsumi to the Big Island, who determined that the knots of the cord used to tie the body of the victim
were tied neither the Hawaiian nor the Japanese way, leading to
the arrest of five Caucasian offenders. Katsura passed the bar
examination brilliantly and was licensed to practice law in the
Kingdom of Hawaii.[3]

Japanese Physicians in the Pioneer Era

The first Japanese doctor to come to Hawaii, Kosai Yoshida,
arrived in 1885 as an employee of the Hawaiian Bureau of Immigration, accompanying the first group of government contract
labor immigrants. Following him about twenty Japanese physicians were invited by the Hawaiian government to serve as physi-
cian-interpreters. They were assigned to various plantations with
a monthly salary of $125. After resigning from the Bureau in
1895, many of them went on to build distinguished medical
careers in the islands. Dr. Sansaburō Kobayashi came to Hawaii in
1889. After passing the examination to practice in Tokyo, he went
to Cooper Medical College in California to major in surgery and
practiced in San Francisco for a while before relocating to Hawaii.
He was regarded as a brilliant surgeon, known particularly for
brain surgery for epilepsy. Another was Dr. Iga Mōri of Ishikawa
Prefecture who graduated from the Naval Medical Academy in
Japan, went to Cooper Medical College, and specialized in internal medicine. He came to Hawaii in 1890. Besides his medical
career, he participated in various activities of the community. In
the Japanese community, he was the president of the Japanese
Benevolent Hospital as well as the Japanese Benevolent Society
and also the chairman of the Board of the Directors of the United
Japanese Society. In the larger community, he was a director of the
Institute of Pacific Relations and a member of its Division of Sci-

ence. He was also a member of the Board of Directors of the Mid-Pacific Institute. He was an honorary member of the Honolulu County Medical Society.

Dr. Shobun Gotō, president of the Goto Hospital for Leprosy in Tokyo, was invited to the Islands by the government of the Kingdom of Hawaii in 1886 and served as a government leprosy specialist until 1895. His appointment was a by-product of King Kalakaua's visit to Japan in 1881. After a short stay at the Kakaako leper clinic, he went to Kalaupapa Settlement on Molokai. Dr. Gotō used two types of treatment for his patients: pills made from a compound of which Chaulmoogra oil was the principal component, and a bathing treatment two to three times a day in warm water of 70° to 100°F in which four to five ounces of Chaulmoogra oil was dissolved. Chaulmoogra trees grew in east India and oil taken from the seeds was used to treat skin diseases. Dr. Arthur L. Dean, former University of Hawaii president and chemistry professor, succeeded in 1918 or thereabouts in emulsifying Chaulmoogra oil to be used for injections. The use of this new medicine was discontinued after a couple of years when more effective sulfa-drugs became available.[4]

Not all the Japanese doctors in Hawaii at this time had come at the invitation of the government or as employees of the Immigration Bureau, however. Dr. Katsugoro Haida first came to Hawaii as a contract laborer, and after completing his medical training at Cooper Medical College in California in 1898, he returned to Hawaii to practice in 1902. In the meantime, more doctors came from Japan.[5] Dr. Ichitarō Katsuki, son of an industrialist in Osaka, graduated from San Francisco High School in 1888, returned to Japan to teach English in colleges in Kobe and Osaka, and later studied medicine at the University of California School of Medicine, graduating in 1896. In 1900 he was sent to Hawaii by the San Francisco Department of Health to investigate the outbreak of bubonic plague in Chinatown, which was regarded as a potential threat to the West Coast. He worked closely with Drs. R. W. Wood and F. Trotter while in Honolulu and went to China to make an on-the-spot study of the localities where the plague was rampant. He decided to make his home in Hawaii. His earliest patients were plantation laborers who came to his clinic from Ewa, Waipahu, Waimanalo, and even as far as Kahuku. They complained that the plantation doctors were too busy to give each patient much attention and that they were sent to work when they were still sick. Dr. Katsuki retired after sixteen years of practice, but he continued to read and travel extensively, pursuing his scientific interests, particularly in genetics. He was made a life member of the American Red Cross in 1919. In 1963 the Hawaii Medical Association presented him a special award as dean of Hawaii's medical profession. Many old-timers remember him in his business suit, wearing a hunting cap and carrying a cane, taking his daily walk of three miles to Waikiki from his Keeaumoku Street Victorian residence. He died on January 13, 1967, at the age of 101. His three sons became physicians.[6]

The Japanese Physicians' Association was formed in 1896 with about a hundred physicians. As Nisei physicians began to emerge the number of doctors of Japanese ancestry increased. In 1934 there were fifty-nine, including twenty-nine in Honolulu, three in rural Oahu, nine on Maui, four on Kauai, and fourteen on Hawaii. In 1940 their total number increased to seventy-nine: forty-four in Honolulu, four in rural Oahu, nine on Maui, four on Kauai, and fifteen on Hawaii.[7]

Japanese Dentists

Dr. Umekichi Asahina, the first Japanese dentist in Hawaii, was one of eleven from Shizuoka Prefecture among the first contract labor immigrants who arrived in Hawaii in 1885. He worked as a cattle ranch hand on Niihau for several years before he moved to Honolulu to practice dentistry. He was officially licensed by the Hawaiian government in the early 1890s. His first dental clinic was in Chinatown, but later it was moved to Nuuanu and Beretania streets during the reign of King Kalakaua and remained in the same vicinity throughout his career. He died in 1943 at the age of eighty-eight. In 1978 the Asahina family was in its third generation in the dental profession.[8] The Japanese Dentists' Association was formed in Honolulu with eighteen members in 1919. The total number of Japanese dentists in 1934 was fifty-eight, including thirty-eight in Honolulu and rural Oahu, eight on Maui, six on Kauai, and eight on Hawaii. In 1940 there were seventy-nine dentists: fifty-four in Honolulu and rural Oahu, seven on Maui, six on Kauai, and twelve on Hawaii.[9]

Midwives

Among the wives and picture brides who emigrated to Hawaii from Japan were women who were trained in midwifery. They played an important role. In Japan they had attended schools of midwifery attached to hospitals, and after graduating they took the prefectural examination; if they passed it, they were given a license to practice by their respective prefectural government. When they came to Hawaii they had to pass an examination given by the Territorial Board of Health to receive a license to practice midwifery. They operated under the Board of Health and were required to observe strictly American standards in sanitation as well as in their professional practice. Most of the pregnancies and childbirths of the Issei women were taken care of by them.

Where there was no midwife or doctor, however, the more capable of the women helped the other women. The following statement made in 1959 by Grandma Inaba of the Kona Hotel reveals the way the immigrant women helped other women at childbirth.

I am eighty years old now. I have been in Kona for sixty years. I think I know almost everybody in Kona. If I don't remember them, they know me and greet me. In the early years when there was only one doctor and no midwife in Kona the people asked me to help them whenever there was a childbirth. I think I delivered 117 babies. Among them were twenty Portuguese, three Chinese, four Hawaiians, and many Japanese. Once I came across a twin birth. I told the woman that she was going to have twins, but she insisted that she had only one baby inside her. So, I told her husband that his wife was going to have twins and that she had better get the help of the doctor. The nurse came from the hospital and told her that the babies must be born by operation. I told Mr. X that one baby was already coming out, but the nurse insisted on taking her to the hospital. Sure enough, both babies were born on the way before they even went half-way to the hospital. Since then, this Portuguese man trusted me completely, saying, "You know better than the nurse. You are like the doctor." I told him that I had no education and not even a midwife's license. Later, a licensed midwife came from Japan. So, I didn't have to help in any more childbirth.

In the early years the Japanese did not register the births of their children. So, when the Nisei needed birth certificates to prove their

Hawaiian birth before and during World War II, they had none. They had to have someone who knew them at the time of their births as a witness. Oh, I was a witness for so many, many of them. They were very thankful.[10]

Practically all the Hawaii-born women resorted to physicians and hospitals for care during pregnancy and childbirth. "Nisei all go to doctors" was the major complaint among the midwives in the 1930s. Thus, their clientele shrank as Issei women passed the child-bearing age. There were twenty-two midwives in Hawaii in 1940, sixteen in Honolulu, three in rural Oahu, and three on the island of Hawaii. Except that two on Maui and one on Hawaii moved to Honolulu in 1928, there was no change in the total number of midwives.[11] Some had non-Japanese clients, such as Hawaiians in rural Oahu. Honolulu midwives were members of the Japanese Midwives' Association, which held a monthly meeting at the International Institute of the YWCA to hear a doctor or Board of Health personnel and to discuss their professional problems. As their Japanese clientele declined, some began to take other kinds of jobs such as taking care of elderly members of well-to-do Caucasian families. With the outbreak of World War II, the Midwives' Association was closed like all the other organizations of enemy aliens, and their professional practice was suspended.

Other Professions among the Issei

The Issei were involved prominently in other major professions and, in fact, played important roles in the lives of the immigrants. They worked as Japanese language school principals and teachers, Buddhist and Shinto priests and Christian ministers, as well as editors and reporters of the Japanese vernacular papers. They will be discussed in later chapters.

Part III
Family and Social Life

8

The Growing Independence
of the Immigrants

Relations with Resident Japanese Officials

IN 1883, when negotiations for the resumption of Japanese immigration to Hawaii were under way, Consul General Robert W. Irwin and Kalakaua's special envoy to Japan, Curtis P. Iaukea, interviewed two of the Gannen Mono who had come to the Islands in 1868. On the basis of the interviews, Irwin recommended to the planters that lunas to supervise the Japanese laborers were unnecessary, since the immigrants had been experienced farmers for generations.[1] Irwin's advice was completely ignored, however, as evidenced by the fact that problems arose on various plantations soon after the arrival in 1885 of the first group of contract Japanese immigrants. In fact, the actual conditions under which the Japanese immigrants were to work and live were never discussed in the negotiations. There was not a single word about the kind of treatment they would receive. If the Japanese government had known about the situation awaiting them, it would have refused to send labor immigrants to Hawaii. Japanese officials visualized plantation work only in terms of Japanese rural villages. In recruiting emigrants, they described Hawaii in terms of its geographical location, climate, peoples, language, food, and customs, assuring the emigrants that they could live comfortably. Concerning their jobs, there was only superficial information such as wages, hours, and days of work, although they did note that there was work even on rainy days and no time for rest or smoking except during a half-hour of lunch. The send-off messages by the governors of Hiroshima-ken and Yamaguchi-ken, the largest emigration prefectures, made no mention or warning of humiliating and brutal labor practices in Hawaii. Their advice consisted solely of expressions of kind, fatherly sentiments such as "Observe the laws of the host country; never disgrace your homeland by your bad conduct; serve your employers faithfully; don't drink; don't gamble; don't fight among yourselves but help each other as brothers; don't join the crooks and lose money; consult always immigration officials about money; be economical and save money, and after the three-year contract is over, come home with wealth so that you will live comfortably. . . ." The immigrants were unprepared for the humiliation of being yelled at and the physically frightening prospects of being whipped, beaten, and kicked. Such violent practices were unknown in the rural communities in Japan.

Rural life in Japan was known to be peaceful, with warm and cordial human relationships. Farmers worked hard, but with free will. Disputes were settled by the village council. Only for punishment of criminals were such methods used by prison guards in the olden days. Being treated like criminals in their daily work in the cane fields caused anger and rebellion among the immigrants, which were expressed in heavy drinking, gambling, and licentious living. Their anger was twofold, against their slavelike existence and against the Japanese government, which had "deceived" them by not having told them about labor conditions in Hawaii. The Japanese government, through its consul in Hawaii, Jiro Nakamura, prevailed upon the immigrants to stop their wild behavior, but they had no intention of doing so just because the consul told them to. Nakamura was replaced by the brilliant Tarō Andō, who was displeased with his new assignment, which was mainly to take care of labor immigrants. The immigrants, in turn, found him to be high-handed and arrogant.

When these immigrants were recruited for emigration to Hawaii, their direct contact was with the local officials of their villages who knew them and spoke their colloquial languages. These officials never used insulting words in addressing the farmers. In Hawaii, for the first time in their lives the immigrants came directly under the authority of high-ranking government officials like Consul General Andō and Chief Inspector Nakayama of the Japanese section of the Immigration Service. Moreover, both Andō and Nakayama had been active samurai during the Tokugawa Era when class distinction was rigid. If their language and manners were haughty and arrogant from the standpoint of the plantation laborers, they were merely following their old customs and habits of acting and talking to farmers in Japan.

The role of the Japanese consul in Hawaii during the early years of Japanese immigration was to help the plantation laborers to work and complete their contracts. The consul was involved in disputes between the laborers and the planters, his job being like that of an arbitrator. At the same time, as a representative of a foreign nation, the consul had to be a diplomat. Hawaii was not a high diplomatic post in those days and, regardless of the efforts of the Japanese government to raise his rank, Andō regarded his assignment to Hawaii as a demotion.

As a youth, Tarō Andō studied at the prestigious Sokuzen Yasui school in Yedo (Tokyo) and was considered to be a genius. He later became the principal of an English school in Waseda. During the civil war that followed the collapse of the Tokugawa Shogunate and the Meiji Restoration of 1868, Andō served under Buyo Enomoto and four other officers, fighting for the Tokugawa regime against the Imperial Army. They escaped to Hokaidō by boat and defended their position in Goryokaku Castle in Hakodate, the last stronghold. Andō was wounded in the right arm. Enomoto and his small remnants of the Tokugawa royalists surrendered in the second year of Meiji, 1869. While the Tokugawas and their leading officers as well as those feudal lords who sided with the Tokugawas were purged in the process of Japan's political and social reorganization, the leaders of the Meiji government who had foresight began to make use of able individuals of the Tokugawa Era. One such wise leader was Kiyotaka Kuroda, prime minister from 1888 to 1889 and also acting prime minister four times, who recommended Enomoto to serve in the new government. Enomoto became minister of communication. Tarō Andō, Enomoto's former junior officer, eventually joined the new government. He accompanied Ambassador Plenipotentiary Tomomi Iwakura as an interpreter on his official 1872–1873 visits to the United States and Europe. Andō had a brilliant career in the foreign service.[2] He was considered by the Japanese government to be the only man in the diplomatic service who could bring order to the Japanese plantation laborers in Hawaii. He served as consul general from 1886 to 1889.

Joji Nakayama was a captain of cavalry during the Tokugawa Era. He was appointed the chief of the customs office of Yokohama in 1872 by the Meiji government. After six months, in the same year, he was appointed to serve as consul general in Venice, Italy. In 1876 he was appointed minister of the Department of the Imperial Household. Later, he left that department to concentrate on foreign commerce and colonization. He came to Hawaii in December 1885 at King Kalakaua's invitation, recommended by Consul General Irwin, to become the chief of Japanese immigration. He was considered the most powerful Japanese in Hawaii during the period of government contract labor immigration. He remained in his post until after the overthrow of the Hawaiian monarchy, resigning in 1894.[3]

In spite of the fact that Nakayama's job was to help the immigrants, especially in their disputes on the plantations, he was disliked because of his unsympathetic attitude and arrogance. For example, there was the incident involving the more than 160 Japanese laborers at Heeia Plantation in 1890. Since the immigrants were on three-year contracts, their employer tried to get out of them as much work as possible within that time, beating them up, knocking them down, reducing their pay to a half or even no pay at times. When they appealed to the manager to improve their working conditions, the situation became worse. The manager explained that they were disobedient. They felt that they had endured the limit and decided to strike; at the same time they selected three delegates to approach Consul General Taizō Masaki, appointed to the position after Tarō Andō returned to Japan, and Chief Nakayama with two copies of a petition stating that they would refund to the Hawaiian government the travel fare it paid from Japan to Hawaii and that they wanted to be discharged from Heeia Plantation. The consulate secretary informed them that news of the situation at Heeia had already been received and the consul general would visit the plantation soon and advised them to see Nakayama also. When they appeared at Nakayama's office, he was angry, and without listening to their pleading, he grabbed the copy of their petition and threw it to the floor, shouting rudely, "You who are contract labor immigrants have no right to appeal about your problems. No matter what reasons you have, during the period of contract, you must perform your labor without incident and you have a duty and responsibility to serve the plantation company." In dismay, the three delegates said to Nakayama, "Now, there is no other way but to appeal to the consul general and to the Japanese government to solve our problem." Incensed with their declaration, Nakayama said, "Don't quibble. Let's go to the consulate," and he left in his carriage. At the consulate, Nakayama's attitude changed and he listened to their complaints with Consul General Masaki.[4] Masaki was known to be a scholarly type who did not like showy displays, and Nakayama respected his opinion.

In the meantime, the Heeia Plantation officials in Honolulu became seriously concerned about the labor strike on their plantation and proposed to settle it peacefully. The Japanese laborers insisted, however, that they would rather be discharged than return to work there. Since the Heeia Plantation had a constant problem of shortage of labor, the officials reasoned that if all the Japanese laborers should leave, their plantation would have to be closed. Accordingly, they proposed to accept all proposals from the laborers, including the discharge of bad lunas. With the mediation of Consul General Masaki and Chief Nakayama, everything the laborers wanted was accepted, three undesirable lunas were fired, and the strikers returned to work. The labor conditions on Heeia Plantation changed completely.[5]

Independence of the Issei from Consular Advice

The plantation laborers learned by experience to be persistent in their demands and to be assertive and independent of Japanese officials in order to achieve their desired goals. Not only laborers but also nonlabor immigrants and intellectuals showed independence from consular advice by taking action on their own, with fruitful results. One such case of independent actions occurred when the S.S. *America Maru* arrived from Yokohama on July 25, 1901. Because of a suspicious case of the bubonic plague, all the Oriental passengers, including women travelling first- and second-class as well as the steerage passengers, were ordered to strip for physical inspection while the Caucasian passengers merely walked in front of the physicians. Taking this as outright racial discrimination and humiliation to the Oriental women, the leaders of the Japanese community, including doctors, newspaper editors, and others, requested that Consul General Miki Saitō make an official protest to the U.S. authorities. When he expressed his desire not to

make an issue out of this incident, they were outraged and called a
mass meeting attended by more than two thousand people. A petition generated at the meeting was sent to the Japanese ambassador
in Washington, to the president of the United States, and to both
houses of Congress demanding that female immigrants be examined by female physicians. The United States government expressed regret over the incident and promised to provide female
physicians.[6]

Saitō, who was acting consul general from September 1898 to
July 1902 and consul general from March 1903 to July 1908,
encountered bitter opposition from the immigrants again in 1903
when he objected to their leaving the Islands for the West Coast. In
May of that year, he organized the Central Japanese Association in
order to get the cooperation of the entire Japanese community on
all Islands to achieve two objectives: (1) to stop the mass migration of the Japanese to the West Coast and (2) to curb the frequent
plantation strikes. Discovering that many of the directors of the
Central Japanese Association were officials of the Keihin Bank of
the Emigration Companies, which refused to pay back the deposits of the immigrants until after their return to Japan, the indig-
nant immigrants held a mass meeting sponsored by the vernacular
papers and organized the Reform Association, which sent a
detailed report of the activities of the Keihin Bank and the Emigration Companies to the Japanese government along with a petition
requesting an investigation of their operation and the recall of
Consul General Saitō.[7]

Saitō was called to Tokyo temporarily to explain the state of
affairs in Hawaii. In August of that year the Foreign Office of
Japan invalidated all the outstanding deposit contracts between
the immigrants and the Keihin Bank. In the spring of 1905, the
officials of the bank and the Emigration Companies left Hawaii
permanently. Before leaving, they donated $10,000 to the Japa-
nese community in addition to land and a building for the Japanese Benevolent Society. Having achieved its purpose, the Reform
Association was disbanded in September 1905.[8]

Whenever the Japanese consul general was asked by the planters to intercede with the workers when a strike was pending, he
always urged them not to strike, and if they had already struck, he
urged them to return to work. On the other hand, the Japanese
strikers always rejected such advice. When the secretary of the

Japanese consulate went to Wailuku, Maui, to help solve a labor dispute, the Japanese laborers told him that he had no authority to interfere with their disputes with their employer. In 1905, the Commissioner of Labor reported on Hawaii that "the Japanese laborers are not quite so subservient to authority, even of their own government."[9]

During the 1909 plantation strike the Japanese consular officials stayed away from the disputes until the English newspapers misreported that Consul General Senichi Uyeno was supporting the strike. He then tried to act as a mediator, sending out his official message advising the strikers to return to the plantations and to seek a peaceful means of settling their grievances. The strikers paid no attention to his advice, however.[10]

Despite the bitter accusation of the English-language press and the white community as well as the planters that the 1920 plantation strike was a Japanese nationalistic movement to control Hawaii and its industry, Japanese consular policy was not to get involved in the strike issue, regarding it as an employer-employee dispute and not a diplomatic concern. When the English dailies reported that the consul was supporting the strike, however, Acting Consul General Eiichi Furuya issued a public statement that the Japanese government had absolutely nothing to do with the strike and its leaders.

In 1922, when 87 of 144 Japanese language schools decided to litigate to test the legality of the restrictive laws against them, which allowed the Department of Education to supervise them, determine the contents of texts, the ages of students, and otherwise strip them of autonomy, Consul General Keiichi Yamasaki urged them to respect the policy of the Hawaiian government and cooperate with the authorities. The litigating language school leaders defied his advice and went ahead with their lawsuit.[11]

The Japanese in Hawaii respected the consul general as the official representative of the Japanese government as long as he was functioning in accordance with their interests, but if they considered him failing to be so, they did not hesitate to denounce him severely and even to demand that the Japanese government recall him. Sogā explains:

> During the very early years the Japanese immigrants relied upon the consul general and consular officials for protection and guidance. As

the Japanese community became more organized and self-sufficient, they became independent of the Japanese consuls for such purposes. Japanese consuls were transferred too often, staying in Hawaii only for a couple of years. The local Japanese felt that they knew about their problems much better than the consular officials did. They were confident about their ability to take care of their own problems. They were sure that they could go directly to their Caucasian employers, if necessary, to discuss their problems. They could even employ able Caucasian attorneys to defend their cases.[12]

Vice-Consul Keizo Naito, who was in Hawaii in 1922–1923, was an exception among the consular officialdom. He undertook an active campaign to help young immigrants to improve their public appearance. He urged them to stop wearing in public the loose yukata (a lightweight kimono) with only a narrow cordlike belt and with the bottom tucked up, showing their underwear, because they looked sloppy and ill-mannered. He spoke at meetings at all the Young Men's Associations and language schools in Japanese neighborhoods in Palama, Kalihi, Makiki, Moiliili, and Kakaako as well as at the YMCA and YMBA on the theme, "Sloppily-Clad Persons Are Embarrassing to Everybody and to All the Japanese," showing slides of such persons in the Japanese neighborhoods. As a result of his untiring crusade, more men began to wear American-style clothes when going out of their houses. Vice-Consul Naito had a close, informal relationship with the common people in the Japanese community rather than just with its leaders and intellectuals.[13]

The Japanese Press and Consular Officials

The Japanese vernacular papers had a history of independence from the consular authorities and never hesitated to criticize the official positions taken by the latter on crucial issues. Yasutarō Sōga of the *Nippu Jiji* recalled that when Consul General Uyeno asked the Japanese vernaculars to publish his admonition "Not to Strike" in 1909, he refused to do so. Immediately, the vice-consul called him up and severely reprimanded him for not carrying out the consul general's order. Sōga retorted that to publish it or not in his paper was his prerogative, and that it made no difference whether or not the order came from the consul general or the ambassador.[14]

A major incident involving the press and consular officials occurred in 1940, when Rev. Yasuzo Shimizu, a Christian educator and founder of Sutei Gakuen, a school for Chinese orphans and delinquent children in Peking, came to Hawaii to raise money for his school. At the time, Japan was engaged in a serious and costly war in China. Shimizu arrived on January 5 and stayed for about a month as Sōga's house guest. He arranged a series of lecture-meetings in Honolulu, Ewa, Waipahu, and Wahiawa and on Kauai, Maui, and the Big Island as well. An admission fee of $1 per person was charged for the Honolulu meetings and 25 cents per person for those given in rural Oahu and on the neighbor islands. The meetings were announced daily in the *Nippu Jiji,* where Reverend Shimizu explained that the money raised in Hawaii would be used only for support of the school. He also announced that his lectures would reveal not only his own observations about the Chinese after having lived and worked in China for more than twenty years but the feelings and thoughts of the Chinese people as personally conveyed to him. Sōga wrote an editorial note before the first meeting with the title "Dissecting the Saint of Peking, Yasuzo Shimizu."

Shimizu was an experienced speaker who was eager to address the issues of the Sino-Japanese conflict for an audience used to having news of the war only from Japan. In addition to his lectures, he wrote sixteen articles on Sino-Japanese relations that were published in the *Nippu Jiji* throughout January. In the first article, he indicated that the Japanese people believed that China had rejected Japan's proposal of friendly cooperation, which had forced Japan to wage war with China. Thus they believed Japan was fighting for a just cause. He noted that it was Japanese military aggression that caused the Chinese to take action. The Japanese invasion resulted in the evacuation of many Chinese cities and the movement of the government further inland. Intellectuals, including professors from Peking University, he reported, were moving to sparsely populated provinces to help with development in remote areas.

In ensuing articles, he cited China's contributions to Japan from the time of Shōtoku Taishi (Prince Shōtoku, A.D. 574–622) in terms of Buddhism, government, and the moral and ethical teachings of Confucius, all of which had a fundamental influence on the culture and thinking of the Japanese. Since the Japanese were known for remembering *on* (great indebtedness) and endeavoring to repay it, he suggested that it was time for the Japanese to express their appreciation to China for what they had received.

It was Shimizu's articles on the Nanking atrocity, however, appearing in the *Nippu Jiji* on January 22 and 23, that raised the ire of the consular officials and caused a disturbance among some Issei. Immediately after Japanese military forces captured Nanking, the capital of Chiang Kai-shek's Nationalist government, on December 27, 1937, the troops went on a rampage of violence and pillage, raping and murdering without constraint. Reports by foreign correspondents spread the news around the world. Shimizu stated that this outrageous behavior was reported not only in Nanking but in Peking and other cities that the Japanese army invaded, making the peoples of the world very angry. He added that since the greatest crime a man could commit was murder, war, whose purpose was to kill, changed the human being into a brute without the moral or ethical sensitivity of man.

Acting Consul General Binjiro Kudo made a strong protest to Reverend Shimizu and accused Sōga of publishing damaging news about Japan. Sōga criticized Kudo for acting "as if he were the incarnation of the Japanese military, meddling with our affairs, resulting in my clash with him."[15]

Shimizu's lecture-meetings in Hawaii were very successful and raised more money than had been expected. He went on to Los Angeles, raising more money and delivering the same speech. He returned to Japan directly from the mainland. Upon landing in Yokohama, he was taken into custody by military authorities. Even after he was allowed to return to his school in Peking, he was subjected to constant interrogation, which resulted in a near nervous breakdown on his part. Only when he turned over to the military the $5,000 he had raised in Hawaii and Los Angeles was he left alone.[16]

In Hawaii, Acting Consul General Kudo retaliated by withholding information about the arrival of dignitaries from the Japanese press and the United Japanese Society, which normally welcomed such visitors at the pier or at a reception given at the consulate. There was no hope of reconciliation between him and the Japanese community, particularly the press. He was finally transferred.[17]

A consul general who completed his tour of duty in Hawaii without experiencing major friction with the local Japanese indicated in an interview in 1939 that Hawaii was regarded as one of the toughest assignments because of the critical attitude of the resident Japanese toward consular officials and their independence from consular advice. For the majority of the Japanese immigrants, their contacts with the Japanese consulate were mainly for official business such as getting family records from their village offices, consulting about expired passports, and so on. When Japan suffered major catastrophes such as earthquakes or tidal waves, relief money and materials collected by the local Japanese were sent by way of the Japanese consulate. The local Japanese were invited along with non-Japanese residents to the consulate for annual celebrations such as New Year's and the emperor's birthday, and many Japanese, particularly community leaders, attended such functions. Most of the Japanese, however, celebrated such occasions in familiar places such as language schools in their areas, where they were usually followed by picnics, sports, and games. Thus, as time went by, the Japanese immigrants developed a collective sense of self-confidence, which in turn made them independent of the consular officials.

9

The Emerging Issei Community

The Period of Summoning Kin and Picture Brides

THE rush of more than 35,000 Japanese plantation laborers to the West Coast after Hawaii's annexation to the United States intensified the anti-Japanese mood and agitation already present there. In 1907, President Theodore Roosevelt stopped the immigration of the Japanese to the U.S. mainland by way of Hawaii, Canada, and Mexico. The following year, 1908, the so-called Gentlemen's Agreement was made between the United States and Japan. The Gentlemen's Agreement severely restricted Japanese immigration. Except for certain categories of nonquota immigrants, only the close kin of immigrants already residing in the United States and its territories were allowed to emigrate. This condition of immigration continued until June 30, 1924, when immigration from Japan was completely stopped by an act of Congress.[1] The period of summoning kin from 1908 to 1924 is called the *Yobiyose Jidai,* and the immigrants who came during this period were known as *Yobiyose,* the Summoned.

Picture Brides

During the Yobiyose period, 62,277 Japanese immigrants came to Hawaii to join their kin, including 26,506 men, 30,633 women, and 5,138 children. Among the women were the so-called "picture brides." The immigration of picture brides had been going on before Hawaii became a territory of the United States, but it accelerated during the Yobiyose period. According to the U.S. Immigration Service, 14,276 picture brides came to Hawaii between

142

1907 and 1923.² The immigration of picture brides to Hawaii continued until the Japanese Exclusion Act became effective on July 1, 1924, although the Japanese government stopped issuing passports in 1920 to picture brides of the laboring class on the U.S. mainland because of rising anti-Japanese agitation, intensified by the high birthrate of the Japanese.³

The practice of sending for picture brides got started when many immigrants, realizing that they would be unable to accumulate money within a short time to return home, began to send for brides from their villages and towns. The picture bride was chosen by the immigrant's parents or close relatives. Photographs were exchanged between him and his prospective bride, and if the proposition was agreeable to both sides, it culminated in a wedding ceremony, with the groom in absentia, either at the village shrine or before the miniature altar at the groom's home. Close relatives of both families were present, and a Shinto priest officiated. The ceremony was followed by registration of the marriage in the village office. Thus, the picture brides came to Hawaii legally married to their picture husbands.

The U.S. government accepted such marriages as legal until April 1904. From May of that year, however, the wedding ceremony with the bridegroom in absentia was no longer recognized by the government. Consequently, it became necessary to hold a group wedding on the wharf upon the arrival of the picture brides, sometimes involving sixty to a hundred or more couples at a time, at which a Christian minister officiated. Mrs. Raku Morimoto recalled that Rev. Gennosuke Motokawa, the pastor of the First Japanese Methodist Church in Honolulu, officiated at so many marriage ceremonies on the wharf that he acquired the nickname "Kekkon Bozu" (priest specializing in weddings).⁴ The Japanese couples objected to these unceremonious "wharf weddings," and from 1912 on picture brides were permitted to go with their husbands to have wedding ceremonies at a place of their choice, usually shrines or churches or homes of ministers or priests.

Issei women who had been picture brides often recalled the scene of their arrival in Hawaii, as each woman, in apprehension and excitement, tried to find her husband by his photo in her hand, asking one another, "Have you found your man?" While most of the picture brides went with the men who claimed them, some refused, asserting that the men were not the right ones. Most men, without money or time to take new pictures, sent the old photographs of their younger years, such as those used for their passports. Some of them even borrowed the photographs of their friends to send home. Disappointed picture brides who could afford the return trip went back to Japan immediately, while others ran away. The Japanese vernacular newspapers of those years constantly published requests for help in locating missing wives.[5]

The Susannah Wesley Home in Honolulu, founded by the Women's Society of Harris Methodist Church, the first Japanese Methodist church in Honolulu, as a dormitory for orphans and children from rural Oahu and the other islands, became a temporary home for many runaway picture brides. A Nisei who was fourteen years old and living there in 1910 or thereabout recalled an eighteen-year-old picture bride who came to the Susannah Wesley Home at four o'clock in the morning, explaining that she had run away from her husband after discovering that everything she had been told about him was false.

Sōga remembered such cases of falsehood, especially regarding occupational status, for instance, a yardman describing himself as a gardener or landscape architect. Such misrepresentations caused marital trouble, which sometimes resulted in injuries and even suicide. Most cases, however, ended in peaceful adjustment. Many picture brides remembered their feelings of disbelief and disappointment at the first sight of the dingy-looking shacks that were to be their lodging on the plantation and on learning of the hard labor they would have to perform in the fields. They spoke of crying behind the tall sugarcane while they worked.[6]

The Sex Ratio and Stabilization of the Japanese Community

In the early years of Japanese immigration, the unbalanced sex ratio was a major cause of instability and crime in the Japanese community. The first time the death penalty was invoked against Japanese in Hawaii was in an 1896 case involving two men and the murder of a woman and child.[7] Because of the unbalanced sex ratio, the giving and selling of wives, as well as elopement, were common phenomena, and there were "brokers" who took advantage of the situation for monetary gain. Gradually the female population increased with the arrival of picture brides and the birth of female children, and the sex ratio became more balanced. Table 1 shows the growth in the number of women to men in the Japanese population in the period from 1890 to 1930.

The arrival of women, particularly a large number of picture brides, resulted in the establishment of family life, which stabilized the Japanese community. Accordingly, there was a marked increase in the number of births among the Japanese. Wakukawa noted that in 1912 more than 39 percent of the total births in Hawaii were Japanese, and it rose to more than 46 percent in 1915, more than 48 percent in 1918, and 51 percent in 1923. The largest number of Japanese births was recorded in 1925, although the ratio to total number of births in Hawaii that year was 4 percent less than that of 1923. From 1925 the number of Japanese births decreased continually, indicating that the large proportionate births of the Japanese was a temporary phenomenon. According to Romanzo Adams, the birthrate of the Japanese in 1921–1922 was 48.1 per thousand, but it decreased to 30.3 in 1931–1932. The death rate of the Japanese was 12.0 per thousand in 1921–1922, while it was 7.2 in 1931–1932. The fact that many elderly Japanese returned to Japan caused the death rate to be lower than it might be. At any rate, the population increase of the Japanese was 36.1 per thousand in 1921–1922, while in 1931–1932 it decreased to 23.1 per thousand. Adams explained that the high birthrate of the Japanese during the years following the arrival of women in large numbers was due to the very favorable age distribution of the women: an unusually large number of married women of childbearing age, from twenty to forty-four years of age, with a small number of women of forty-five and older and girls of nineteen and younger. However, their fertility rate was not as high as that of the Chinese or Portuguese, and as

Table 1. Number and Percentage of Male and Female Japanese Immigrants per year from 1890 to 1930 with ten-year intervals

Year	Male	Percent	Female	Percent	Total	Percent
1890	10,219	81.0	2,391	19.0	12,610	100.00
1900	47,508	77.7	13,603	22.2	61,111	99.9
1910	54,784	68.7	24,891	31.2	79,675	99.9
1920	62,644	57.3	46,630	42.7	109,274	100.0
1930	75,008	53.7	64,683	46.3	139,631	100.0

Source: Adapted from Adams, *Peoples of Hawaii,* Table 1, pp. 8–9.

their Hawaii-born daughters became mature, they tended to follow the American middle-class pattern of family size, resulting in a lower birthrate and lower rate of population increase among the Japanese.[8]

Crime among the Issei

The Japanese in Hawaii were generally regarded as law-abiding, but there was criminal activity among them in the early years of immigration. Organized gangs, made up mostly of deserters from the plantations and antisocial individuals who came as free immigrants, emerged as early as 1895. They operated vice quarters in downtown Honolulu in the Pauahi-Maunakea and River Street areas. These gangs had approximately 350 members and some 200 prostitutes working for them. Many of the prostitutes were kidnapped wives or women sold by their husbands, runaway picture brides, or women who had been engaged in a similar "occupation" before coming to Hawaii. Racketeering, intimidation, extortion, and fraud were common practices.

Leaders of the Japanese community sought to eliminate this vice district, and gang leaders retaliated by threatening the vernacular newspaper editors who exposed their activities as well as prominent leaders of the reform movement like Rev. Takie Okumura, who spearheaded the clean-up project with the aid of Christian leaders of the white community such as Dr. Theodore Richard. Yasutarō Sōga, then still manager of the Shiozawa Store, was shocked by the presence of this vice district, which he considered a national shame for Japan. He wrote articles in the vernacular newspapers for which his life was threatened repeatedly. There was a plan to deport about thirty of the ringleaders to Japan, but because victims and witnesses were afraid to come forth for fear of retaliation, nothing came of it. The great fire of Honolulu in 1900 wiped out the Japanese vice quarters completely.[9]

In 1900 another red light district, organized by Japanese and Caucasian promoters, was started in Iwilei. It was registered at the Police Department and its prostitutes were regularly examined by the Board of Health. A large majority of the more than 200 prostitutes in this enclosed quarter were Japanese. Because of incessant attacks by Christian leaders, this quarter was forced to close, and its operator, a Japanese, moved to the U.S. mainland and eventually died in New York.[10]

In 1898, a violent crime involving Chinese and Japanese took place. After a scuffle between a small number of Chinese and Japanese on Kahuku Plantation, a large group of Japanese laborers, armed with cane knives, raided the Chinese camp and killed three and injured more than twenty. Six who were leaders were charged with murder, and the rest were charged with violence. One was sentenced to death, later reduced to life, and all served terms in prison.[11]

Violence and homicide resulting from labor-luna conflict on the plantations continued after Hawaii became a territory of the United States. In connection with the first general strike of 1909, four Issei men, all intellectuals and non-plantation workers, were convicted of conspiracy and imprisoned but pardoned after serving three of ten months. No violence was involved in this conviction. During the 1920 general plantation strike, the house of Jusaburo Sakamaki, the interpreter for Olaa Plantation on Hawaii, who was a strong opponent of the strike, was dynamited. Fifteen men were arrested and tried in the court in Honolulu. One died in a car accident but the rest were sentenced to serve from four to ten years. Two were released in 1925 on condition that they return to Japan, and the remaining twelve were released in 1926.[12]

During Prohibition, from 1920 to 1933, the Japanese broke the law as much as any other ethnic group. Some Hiroshimans recalled that some from their prefecture became rich by peddling sake that was produced by moonshining. The guilty who were caught and convicted served their terms in Oahu Prison. An elderly Okinawan remembered that the meals in the prison were better than those he had at home. The Japanese vernaculars published the names of those convicted along with their prefectural backgrounds. That bothered the nondrinkers from the same prefectures, but in general, the Japanese were not as guilt-conscious when it came to drinking as they were in other kinds of offenses.[13]

When Immigration Inspector Katsunuma visited Oahu Prison in March 1922, he found 150 Filipinos, 60 Hawaiians, 29 Japanese, 20 Portuguese, 18 other Caucasians, and 17 Chinese. He noted that the Japanese offenses were largely homicide or aggravated assault inflicting serious injury but very few cases of robbery or theft. One from Hiroshima-ken was serving a life sentence.[14]

Although the following crime was not committed by an Issei, it horrified all of Hawaii and stunned the Japanese community and thus behooves a mention. The Fukunaga incident of 1928 involved kidnapping, ransom, and murder by the nineteen-year-old son of a poverty-stricken Japanese family. Myles Fukunaga was among the brightest students in his class up through intermediate school, but because of poverty he had to work instead of going to high school. After watching a trust company agent take away the only money his mother had to feed the family, ignoring her pleas to allow her to pay half of the rent on their house later when her daughter brought home her earnings, Fukunaga decided on revenge. He spent most of his time in the library reading the records of crimes in Chicago and Los Angeles to plan his revenge. Fukunaga was arrested five days after he kidnapped and murdered the ten-year-old son of the trust company official.

As soon as the news of his arrest spread over the city, a great crowd gathered in front of the Honolulu Police Station, many shouting for Fukunaga to be lynched. Sirens were screeching from Aloha Tower, and the National Guard was called in for an emergency blockade of the area from King Street to the Police Station. The *Nippu Jiji* offices were in this blockaded area. Editor Sōga was in communication with the Police Station and received a copy of the more than twenty pages of confession made by Fukunaga during the questioning that night, which enabled him to know for the first time the scope of the crime.[15]

Fukunaga was indicted for first-degree murder. The court was crowded to capacity during the trial. Sōga, sitting in the newspaper reporters' section, recalled that when asked about his religious beliefs, Fukunaga answered that he had no specific religion but he found religion in all phenomena in nature. Fukunaga had two government-appointed defense attorneys. The jury found him guilty of murder and the judge sentenced him to death. Governor Farrington signed the execution order. In the meantime, two specialists, both Caucasians, a navy doctor at Pearl Harbor and a professor of philosophy at the University of Hawaii, declared that Fukunaga was legally insane. This led to a movement among a segment of the Japanese community, spearheaded by Kinzaburo

Makino of the *Hawaii Hochi Daily,* for a retrial on the grounds that Fukunaga was a minor and was suffering from mental derangement. This appeal was rejected by the Ninth Circuit Court of Appeals in San Francisco and the United States Supreme Court in Washington, D.C. The group then appealed to Governor Lawrence Judd to commute the death sentence to life imprisonment. This appeal for clemency was rejected. During his one year and two months of imprisonment, Fukunaga became an ardent Christian under the guidance of Rev. Tokujiro Komuro of Harris Methodist Church. Fukunaga was executed on November 19, 1929.[16]

According to Romanzo Adams' Tables of Convictions, in each of seven major categories of crime per 1,000 civilian males of eighteen years and above in all the Territorial Courts for two six-years periods, the first ending December 31, 1924, and the second ending December 31, 1930, the Japanese showed the lowest number of convictions and the least increase. The next lowest in convictions was the Chinese. The Chinese had no convictions for murder in the first period and none for manslaughter in the second period.[17] In robbery, burglary, fraud, embezzlement, forgery, and sex crimes, the Japanese showed the least number of convictions, followed by the Chinese. Adams explained that the low rates for the Japanese and the Chinese were due to the persistence of the standards of conduct of their home countries. The crime committed by a person affected adversely the members of the whole family as well as marriage prospects, for the go-between was committed to scrutinize the family records. Adams also pointed out that both the Japanese and the Chinese were sufficiently numerous to maintain effective social organization through which individual deviation from behavior norms was effectively controlled.[18]

Inter-Ethnic Relations

There were certain collective feelings of animosity on the part of the Chinese and Koreans toward the Japanese, principally because of Japan's aggression toward their homelands. However, such feeling was submerged in Hawaii's general atmosphere of tolerance and good will among the multiethnic population. Being the earliest Asian arrivals (1852), the Chinese were well-established economically and otherwise when the Japanese were just arriving.[19] The Chinese were collectively secure and self-confident and knew their seniority to the Japanese, and the Japanese recognized this fact and consciously and unconsciously they followed in the footsteps of the Chinese. The Japanese immigrants had been looked down upon by the Chinese, but the news of Japan's victory in the Sino-Japanese War of 1894–1895 relieved them of their so-called "inferiority complex." In Honolulu and Hilo, merchants celebrated the victory, parading downtown with lanterns at night, and with men masquerading as Japanese army officers.

The closest Chinese-Japanese cooperation in the history of Hawaii was demonstrated in the fire claims following the devastating fire of Honolulu in 1900. On January 20, 1900, the Board of Health decided to burn the portion of Chinatown that had been affected with bubonic plague since mid-December, claiming seventy-nine lives. Unfortunately, the fire spread out of control because of strong winds and burned fiercely all day. More than six thousand people became homeless. American community leaders set up evacuation centers for the victims in the old armory, Kawaihao Church, as well as in the Kakaako and Kalihi districts near town. The Japanese Benevolent Society and the Japanese Physicians' Association, along with Japanese living outside the fire area, helped with evacuees. The number of fire claimants by ethnic group were 3,720 Chinese; 2,574 Japanese; 728 Hawaiians; 19 Portuguese; 128 others; and 21 insurance companies, with a total claim amounting to more than $3.1 million. As a result of Governor Dole's request for federal assistance, President McKinley approved payments for losses suffered by the fire victims.[20]

A special Court of Claims assigned by the government to process the fire claims announced that a $20 filing fee must accompany each claim and that the court's decisions would be final, with no rights of appeal on the part of the claimants. The penniless fire victims were indignant. The Honolulu Chamber of Commerce was also critical of the court. To protest this requirement as unreasonable and unfair, the Chinese and Japanese held a joint mass meeting on April 6, 1901, at the Central Institute, a Japanese language school, on Nuuanu Street. Several thousand people attended the meeting. Three speakers from each national group spoke alternately, addressing their compatriots in their respective native tongues. Two speakers, one Chinese and one Japanese, followed, who spoke in English for the benefit of the Caucasians, Hawaiians, and others present. Resolutions were made to the effect that the rules and regulations issued by the court should be changed. The resolutions were signed by the Japanese and Chinese joint committee of thirteen members and were presented to Governor Dole by Yasutarō Sōga and Quon Yim on April 9. This effort resulted in closer and more friendly relations between the Japanese and Chinese communities. Not long afterward, Chinese community leaders invited about sixty prominent Japanese, including the consul general, to a sumptuous banquet in the elegant hall of the Chinese Association on King Street. Sōga recalled the cordial atmosphere, delicious food, and the delightful music by Chinese musicians and the Royal Hawaiian Band. After prolonged proceedings, Congress finally passed a bill on January 26, 1903, to release $1 million from the federal treasury and authorized the territorial government of Hawaii to issue fire-claim bonds for the repayment of the remaining claims.[21]

The Japanese immigrants had little chance to develop a close relationship with immigrants from Korea. Japan annexed Korea in 1910, and the Koreans were political refugees determined to help their homeland regain its independence from Japan. They were patriots who resented the treatment they received from Japan as subjugated nationals. Among the Koreans, the worst insult was to be called "Japanese." In general, the Koreans ignored the local Japanese, while the Japanese were insensitive to the feelings of the Koreans.[22] The situation of the Korean homeland continued until the end of World War II, when Japan was defeated.

Regardless of the undercurrent of animosity toward the Japanese, it was not directed toward individual immigrants nor did it disrupt Hawaii's multiethnic community. Moreover, since all the immigrants had scaled the same occupational ladder, the various ethnic groups were sympathetically disposed to each other's problems. Also, occupational status on the plantations was determined by the plantation management and not as a result of ethnic competition. The Japanese never replaced any other ethnic group by accepting lower wages. On the contrary, they demanded higher wages equal to those of the Portuguese and Puerto Ricans, the non-Asian plantation laborers. In labor disputes, the organized efforts of the Japanese were directed toward the plantation authorities and never against the Portuguese or the Puerto Ricans.

Moreover, rather than being bothered with the numerically large and aggressive Japanese, the Portuguese were preoccupied with the differential treatment accorded by "Other Causacians" and their exclusion from the category of "haole."[23] Their collective effort was to prove that they were "Caucasians." In 1940, the separate classification of the Portuguese was eliminated from the Census, and in 1947 the Board of Public Instruction eliminated the ethnic identification of students by their parental origin, nullifying automatically the Portuguese identification of their children.[24]

Since all the nonwhite immigrants who constituted a large portion of Hawaii's population were ineligible for naturalization, the Japanese never suffered a feeling of complete isolation or rejection in relation to the white people who had citizenship. Moreover, except for political rights, the Japanese immigrants as well as the other nonwhite immigrants were entitled to all the privileges of citizenship, including the ownership of land. In fact, the ownership of real property was encouraged as an indication of permanent residence.

10
Religion

Traditional Japanese Religions

THE majority of the immigrants from Japan were Buddhists, and although there was no need for missionary work involving their conversion, without Buddhist priests and temples, they felt that they lacked a spiritual link with their ancestors. Moreover, in time of death there was no one to officiate at the funeral according to their customary rituals. The earliest deaths were merely burials by friends. In 1889, when Soan Kogai of Honpa Hongwanji came to Hawaii, he was received enthusiastically by the immigrants, but he did not stay long. In 1897 Kenjun Miyamoto of Honpa Hongwanji came to prepare for a ministry in Hawaii. Honi Satomi arrived in the following year as the first priest. He was succeeded by Yemyo Imamura in 1900 when he left for Japan.

The Rev. Imamura was one of the most influential and respected leaders of the Japanese community in Hawaii until his death in 1932 at the age of sixty-five. Despite the fact that most of the Japanese immigrants were Buddhists, however, he experienced almost insurmountable difficulties during the early years of his ministry.

Due to lack of women, plantation laborers were extremely wild. Since there were no recreational facilities, the only outlet after returning from long hours of hard field labor was drinking and gambling. Drinking was taken for granted and gambling was openly done and those who did not join them were not treated as human beings. I went to see these drinkers and gamblers in the evening with the Gospel of Buddha's teaching. But some of them would say right into my face, "It is a bad omen to have a Bozu [Buddhist monk]," "Throw salt at him," or at times such a violent expression as "Tatande shimae" [Down with him].[1] I felt as if I were in the cave of tigers and wolves or in water full of sharks and crocodiles. Even when I managed to talk to some of them, I was afraid of violent attack by roughnecks to prevent my religious talk. I did not know how to handle them. Finally, I was able to talk to four or five men gathered in a room about the good tidings of Buddha. But drinking parties with loud singing and gambling were going on in the adjoining rooms.

After my talk I needed to stay overnight. The bed in the camp was a hanging tier, hard to sleep on, but being tired I fell asleep. With the bell at four o'clock in the morning everybody got up. I too got up in a hurry, picking up my briefcase, and went to a nearby Chinese restaurant to have breakfast. Then I walked to the station to wait for the train to return to Honolulu. While waiting at the station, I pondered over my work, which was hopeless, like a drop in the ocean. But every time I pondered, I thought of hardships experienced by Saint Shinran, the founder of Hongwanji Sect, and his teaching that all such hardships were for one's own sake. Inspired by Buddha's grace, I continued my missionary work, hoping that some day those drunkards and gamblers will come under the grace of Buddha and change to gentle, humble, faithful individuals.[2]

Even in Honolulu Bishop Imamura had difficulty getting Buddhists to attend religious services. "It was not the lack of believers of Hongwanji Sect," he later wrote, "because most Japanese immigrants came from such prefectures as Hiroshima, Yamaguchi, Kumamoto, and Fukuoka where the Hongwanji Sect was predominant. It was due to self-humiliation because the immigrants were sensitive to the fact that they came to a Christian country. And earlier even Consul General Andō and his consulate staff became Christian. Christians seemed to enjoy priority in everything. It appeared that only stupid people came to Hongwanji."[3] Bishop Imamura perceived that even those who were faithful believers tried to be inconspicuous when attending services at the temple. He decided that in order to overcome this religious self-deprecation there was no other way but to secure the help of people from outside of the Japanese Community.

After all considerations concerning ways and means, I heard that the queen [Liliuokalani] of Hawaii had favorable feelings toward Japan and some interest in Buddhism. So, through someone we invited her to our service commemorating the [730th] birthday of Saint Shinran, the founder of Hongwanji Sect, on May 19, 1902. She accepted our invitation and attended our service with Miss Foster. This was the first time for the Hawaiian queen to attend a gathering of a Japanese institution and the news was published in the *Jiji Shinpo Daily* of Tokyo and in the *Osaka Mainichi Daily* with big headlines. This helped to increase self-respect in our Buddhist believers.

Also, when a Caucasian Buddhist scholar, Dr. O., who spoke on Buddhism in various countries in the Orient including Japan stopped here, we asked him to speak. In February 1902, with *Hawaii Shinpō's* publisher Mr. Shiozawa as the interpreter, he spoke on the theme "Buddhism is Superior to Christianity" for more than one hour. Even those who had never attended Buddhist service came to hear him. His lecture was published in the *Advertiser* next day, giving the Japanese encouragement to attend Buddhist temple and reducing prejudice on the part of the American public toward Buddhism.[4]

The turning point in the role of the Buddhist Mission in Hawaii came, according to Bishop Imamura, with the strike of the Waipahu Plantation laborers in 1904.

The reasons for their strike were usual ones, such as the brutality of lunas, demand for higher wages, improvement of the living quarters, and so on. Since it was during the Russo-Japanese War, the strikers were irritable and the strike was unusually violent. Although Consul General Saitō went there several times to calm them down and to stop their strike, they did not accept his advice. Because of my missionary work among the plantation laborers, I was asked by the plantation authorities to help them. So I went there and spoke before the excited audience. I spoke entirely from the religious standpoint to calm them. The result of my advice was helpful and the strikers returned to work (after eleven days of strike). I felt the great power of Buddha. The English papers reported this news.

After this incident, the planters and the Caucasians in general recognized the fact that Buddhism had important meaning to the Japanese and was necessary to stabilize the labor population on the plantations. Since that time the plantations provided land for a preaching center [temple] and when the temple was newly built or rebuilt, they made monetary donations and also they helped us in various ways, thus enhancing our spirit as Buddhist missionaries.[5]

The Honpa Hongwanji Sect became in time the most active and influential of all the Buddhist sects in Hawaii because of the ingenious leadership of Bishop Imamura, who made many innovations in the worship service and other activities of his temple to meet the needs of Issei believers and their Hawaii-born children. In order to become a meaningful institution, the Honpa Hongwanji temple began to include in its regular program Boy Scouts, social activities for the youth, and wedding ceremonies. It established a dormitory for students, a Young Men's Buddhist Association (YMBA), and a Japanese Language School. In 1935 the Honpa Hongwanji Mission in Hawaii had thirty-six branch temples and preaching centers and twenty-eight language schools.

As the Nisei generation matured, they began to assume lay leadership in the affairs of the temple. Beginning in 1926, five Nisei high school graduates were sent to Japan for seven years of study and training at Ryukoku University in Kyoto to prepare for the priesthood. Upon their return, they were assigned to various islands. The last one to return to Hawaii, in 1941, was Keigan Yoshikami. He was assigned to the main temple in Honolulu. During World War II he worked for U.S. Military Intelligence and at the same time took care of funerals because practically all the Buddhist priests were interned.

Another able and active Buddhist priest was the Rev. Entei Itoh of Jodo Sect, who came to Hawaii in 1900. The other sects that began ministries in Hawaii were Higashi Hongwanji branch of Jodo Shin, Nichiren, Soto (Zen), Shingon, Kannon-kyo, and Hokekyo (a Nichiren sect).[6] Jodo came in 1894; Higashi Hongwanji in 1899; Nichiren in 1900; Soto (Zen) in 1904; Shingon in 1914; and Tendai in 1918. The number of temples or preaching centers of these sects increased as they gained constituents all over Hawaii. Most of them operated language schools.

Unlike Buddhism, Shintoism is exclusively Japanese in origin and beliefs, ranging from the worship of natural phenomena as the revelation of supernatural deities—most having protective power, some with healing power, and a few with destructive power—the worship of deified heroes, scholars, persons of high moral principles, and so on. The state Shintoism of Japan differs from this popular Shintoism in the sense that it enshrines Amaterasu Ōmikami (Supreme Sun Goddess), the ancestor of the imperial family of Japan. The shrine is called Daijingu. The first Daijingu shrines in Hawaii were built in Hilo in 1898 and in Honolulu in 1905. The other major Shinto shrines, built in subsequent years, were

Izumo Taisha, Ishizuchi Jinja, and Kotohira Jinja. All enshrined mythological figures of Kamiyo (the Age of Gods), believed to be related to the imperial ancestry.[7]

The Japanese immigrants were both Buddhists and Shintoists at the same time, Shinto shrines taking care of celebrations concerning birth, marriage, prosperity, happiness, health, harvest, groundbreaking, and dedication of new buildings—all aspects of life in this world—while Buddhist temples took care of funerals, burials, and memorial services for the deceased—activities largely related to death and life after death.

Tenrikyo and other faiths of more recent origin were also introduced to Hawaii before World War II. Tenrikyo, a non-Buddhist, non-Shinto popular faith among the Issei, was officially recognized in 1933. Konko-kyo was introduced to Hawaii in 1929. After World War II, a number of new religions from Japan were introduced in Hwaii. Among the best known were *Seicho no Ie, Sekai Kyusei-kyo* (religion to save the world), and *Tensho Kotai Jingu-kyo,* commonly known as *Odori no Kamisama* (dancing goddess).

The Role of Christianity in the Japanese Community

In contrast to the traditional Japanese religions, Christianity (Protestantism) was a completely new religion to the Japanese immigrants. There was freshness and vitality in its message. Moreover, the ministers who brought this new message were dedicated individuals endowed with the ability to inspire and lead as well as a deep understanding of human nature and sensitivity and insight into the situations at hand. Many changes in individuals and in the social order in Hawaii were the outcome of their positive leadership.

Bible classes were started for the Japanese immigrants by the Congregational Board of Missions in 1885. Kenjiro Aoki, a theological student from Doshisha University in Kyoto, assisted Dr. C. M. Hyde in preaching and teaching the classes. In need of a Japanese-speaking minister after Aoki's departure for the United States in 1887, the Congregational Board sought help from the Methodist Conference in California, where Japanese ministers were active. Rev. Kanichi Miyama and five younger ministers arrived in Hawaii in September 1887. Miyama remained in Honolulu while the young Methodists went to the other islands.[8]

News of the hardships of the Japanese plantation laborers and their disorganized way of life had already spread on the West Coast. Just before Miyama's departure a group of students gathered for a prayer meeting and offered $25 to be used for his work in Hawaii. Thus, from the beginning Miyama was committed to saving the plantation workers from degeneration. He visited all the islands. Knowing that practically all of the Japanese immigrants were Buddhists, he did not try to convert them to Christianity. Instead, aiming at restoring in them human dignity and self-respect, he pleaded with them to remember that they were Japanese subjects and that they must not disgrace their homeland by their behavior, and he urged them to stop drinking, gambling, and their wild way of life. His earnest, heartrending pleading soon won their respect and trust, and hundreds of them gave up drinking and gambling. Miyama would return to Honolulu with his pockets full of discarded dice and sake mugs. Deeply inspired by Miyama's successful mission as well as his sermons, Consul General Tarō Andō supported his work wholeheartedly.[9] After three months of dedicated service, Miyama left for San Francisco in December 1887.

At the invitation of Consul General Andō, Miyama came to Hawaii again in March 1888, accompanied by his wife Toyoko and two young ministers, both from Tokyo, to assist him in ministry. The first Japanese Christian church was started in July 1888 at the Miyama residence on Nuuanu Street near Beretania under the name of the Japanese Mission Society. Among the first group of Japanese who were baptized on July 15 at the old Central Union Church were Consul General Andō, his wife Fumiko, and the consular staff. Soon the Miyama residence became too small for its congregation. Having heard of it, John Waterhouse, a wealthy businessman, offered the lyceum he owned to be used free of rent. The Japanese Mission Society moved there and from September of 1888 it operated as a regular church. Mr. Waterhouse also helped the church with a monthly gift of $25.[10]

Reverend Miyama carried on in his work to improve the situation of the plantation workers. In April 1888, as an outcome of prayer meetings at his home, the Temperance Society of Hawaii was organized, with Andō as its president. In his decision to become active in temperance work, Andō was strongly influenced by his wife. The Andōs had received the previous December two barrels of Nada, a choice sake, from Japan. Mrs. Andō consulted Miyama, who advised her to throw it away. The consul general was hesitant, since it was a gift from his former superior officer, Buyo Enomoto, then a government minister. While Andō was out, Mrs. Andō had a servant empty the barrels in the rubbish pit in the backyard and burn the sake. When the consul general heard about it on his return, he was deeply impressed by her determination and from then on he never again touched alcoholic beverages. When a Japanese navy ship called at Honolulu, he gave its crew and officers a tea party.[11] Concerning the effects of the Temperance Society, he wrote in his memoir:

> Since the membership included plantation laborers on all the islands, it increased within less than a half year to more than 1,000, which further increased to more than 2,000 with tremendous influence, completely changing their customary way of life. The lazy ones became hard workers; the sickly became healthy; the gambling areas were cleared; fights disappeared. Consequently, the reputation of the Japanese immigrants among their Caucasian employers suddenly rose, with increased demand for their labor. . . . After temperance was practiced among the Japanese, their savings increased greatly. As proof, the remittances sent home by more than 6,000 immigrants through the Japanese Consulate [later through the Yokohama Specie Bank] came to over 340,000 yen.[12]

The consul general and Reverend Miyama visited the quarantine barracks of the Immigration Bureau every time an immigration ship arrived to give the new arrivals help and advice. The Miyamas left for San Francisco in August 1889 and returned to Japan in February 1890. Consul General Andō and his family returned to Japan in 1889.[13]

In 1891, the Methodist Board of Missions of the California Conference requested the Board of Missions of the Congregational Church in Hawaii to take over all their work among the Japanese. In Honolulu, however, thirty-four persons who had been converted by Reverend Miyama refused to join the Congregational Church. They gathered nightly at the Kawasaki Hotel for a prayer meeting and circulated among themselves mimeographed devotional materials to keep their faith. Finally, in 1894, the California Conference recognized the Japanese Methodist group and sent Rev. Soshichi Kihara to be their pastor. The church was named Harris Methodist Church, honoring the bishop of the California Conference at that time. The Methodists organized the Japanese YMCA, visited the prison and hospital, and engaged in evangelistic campaigns. The Harris' Women's Society founded the Susannah Wesley Home in 1900 to take care of needy families, orphans, children and young people from rural Oahu and other islands who came to attend school or work in Honolulu, and women in need of temporary protection. In about 1905 the Methodist Mission took over the operation of the Susannah Wesley Home.[14]

The Congregationalists began their missionary work among the Japanese immigrants in 1889, when Rev. Jiro Okabe came from San Francisco to work on the island of Hawaii. Five graduates of the Doshisha Theological Seminary arrived from Japan the same year. Okabe, a dedicated, enterprising minister, began his ministry at his parsonage in Hilo with a congregation of sixty-nine from the nearby plantations. As a travelling minister on horseback and by boat, he visited the plantations along the coast. In January 1891, he founded the Church of the Holy Cross in Hilo, with seventy-two charter members. Okabe organized the Mutual Aid Society, with seventy-three members paying 25 cents a month and twenty-three special members, mostly Caucasians, who paid 50 cents a month but claimed no benefits. Sixty-six persons received help in the first six months. Later, Okabe was transferred to Honolulu and sent to Japan to recruit more ministers. As a result, two Doshisha graduates already experienced in ministry arrived in Hawaii in 1894: Takie Okumura, who settled in Honolulu, and Shiro Sokabe, who went to Honomu on the island of Hawaii. In the same year Orramel Gulick, a missionary in Japan for eighteen years, became the head of the Japanese Department of the Hawaiian Board of Missions of the Congregational Church.[15]

The Ministries of Takie Okumura and Shiro Sokabe

As the pastor of the Nuuanu Congregational Church, Okumura helped it to grow from a mission church to a self-supporting church. He later founded the Makiki Christian Church. From the beginning he was deeply concerned about the Japanese vice quarters of lower Nuuanu and spearheaded the campaign to eliminate them despite threats of violence from the ruffians.[16] He organized the the first Japanese language school, the Central Japanese Institute, in Honolulu, as a result of his baffling experience with the unintelligible pidgin Japanese of Hawaii-born children. With one teacher who had a Japanese license to teach and thirty pupils the school started in a room in Queen Emma Hall which was made available by Mrs. H. C. Coleman. In order that children could attend regardless of their religious backgrounds, Okumura made it an independent nonchurch-affiliated school to be supported by their parents. A spacious site was purchased after three years when the number of students increased to eight hundred.[17]

Okumura was active in relief work in the devastating fire of Honolulu in 1900. He and his wife opened a Christian dormitory called the Okumura Home for students from rural Oahu and the neighbor islands who attended schools in Honolulu. He was actively concerned with practically all of the important issues involving the Japanese. He was, however, an ardent opponent of labor strikes, believing that strikes would result in nothing but hurt feelings. Regardless of this firm stand, Okumura was the key figure in getting signatures from Caucasian businessmen, including the president of the HSPA, on the petition to the governor seeking a pardon for four men serving time as conspirators of the 1909 plantation strike.[18] Through quiet persuasion he almost always succeeded in getting support from the Caucasian community for his propositions.

Reverend Okumura was also the founder of the New Americans' Conference of the Nisei, which was held every year in Hawaii from 1927 until the summer of 1941. Being deeply concerned about the increasing anti-Japanese feeling among the non-Japanese, mainly due to labor strikes, Okumura began making a biannual tour of the islands in January 1921, visiting any area where fifty or more Japanese resided to hold informal meetings with them to discuss the need for the Americanization of the Issei. Realizing, however, the greater importance of Americanization for their Hawaii-born children, he began in 1926 to focus on the Nisei. He observed that because the Caucasians on the plantations were mainly managers and other high-salaried personnel and schoolteachers, the Japanese, both Issei and Nisei, could not associate with them on an equal basis. As a result, the Japanese had developed an inferiority complex in relation to the whites. He felt that such self-humiliation would generate dissatisfaction and frustration, which might lead to various problems and incidents.[19] He also noticed that the large majority of the Nisei had little interest in political issues and were lukewarm about voting. He felt keenly the importance of developing in the Nisei self-confidence, self-respect, and a sense of civic responsibility as American citizens.

To achieve these goals, Reverend Okumura decided to have representatives from among the Nisei of various rural districts of all the islands come to Honolulu to meet the governor and other officials and leading citizens of Hawaii; talk freely with specialists on Hawaii's industry, government, and social problems; and visit in Caucasian homes. To qualify, a delegate had to be an American citizen who had finished the ninth-grade compulsory education and who had a job, regardless of sex or religious background. Where there was no Nisei organization to select the delegates, the plantation managers or previous delegates were requested to assist in selecting them. All the expenses for the conference and part of the delegates' travel and living expenses in Honolulu during the conference were paid for by generous donations from individuals and business firms in the Caucasian community. The executive committee responsible for the conference consisted of six men: John F. Erdman, secretary of the Hawaiian Board of Missions; Yasutarō Sōga, editor of the *Nippu Jiji;* Dr. Iga Mōri, a physician; Dr. Tasuku Harada of the University of Hawaii; attorney Wade Warren Thayer; and Reverend Okumura. They were assisted by an associate committee made up of Nisei such as Earl Nishimura, Masuo Ogoshi, Umetaro Okumura, Jiso Sanjume, Clarence Shimamura, Natsuichi Yamamoto, and Shigeo Soga.[20]

At the beginning, many feared that the conference would not last. Some mature Nisei businessmen objected to its name, asserting that the term "New Americans" should apply to newly naturalized foreign-born persons, not to Nisei who were native-born Americans.[21] The first conference was held August 1 to 6, 1927, at the Honolulu YWCA with fourteen delegates. The morning hours were spent on discussions of various social issues. At the luncheon, the governor, the commanders of the army and navy, professors from the University of Hawaii, businessmen, social workers, and newspaper editors were among the guests invited to speak and to meet the delegates. Afternoons and evenings were spent on visits to private homes, Schofield Barracks, and Pearl Harbor Naval Base, and in recreational activities, including movies and sports.[22]

The *Honolulu Star-Bulletin* and the *Nippu Jiji* supported the conference from the beginning, and it was customary that at the end of it the two papers gave a banquet honoring the delegates. Later the Yokohama Specie Bank, Sumitomo Bank, and Pacific Bank joined in sponsoring the banquet. Each year an English-language report of the conference was printed and circulated for the interested public. Beginning with fourteen delegates in 1927, the conference was held every summer until 1941, when the number of delegates reached eighty-eight, including sixty-one men and twenty-seven women. Their political party affiliations were thirty-nine Republicans, one Democrat, thirty-two independents, and eighteen who had never voted. Forty-eight had American-only citizenship, while twenty still had dual citizenship, and twenty-five had already applied for expatriation of Japanese citizenship. Fifty-one were employees of sugar plantations in various capacities; five were employees of pineapple companies; and thirty-two were in miscellaneous jobs. Their religious backgrounds represented Christianity, Buddhism, and Shintoism, but the large majority were Buddhists.[23]

Shiro Sokabe's assignment to the island of Hawaii took him first to the Hamakua Coast and later in the same year (1894) to Honomu where a small, crude board house of 30 by 20 feet, built by the sugar company, became his chapel, school, library, and recreation hall as well as his parsonage. During his early ministry on the plantations he found the homes of the laborers unfit for the upbringing of their children. Because of the long hours of hard labor, when men and women came home to the crude barracks, they were often too tired to give their children full parental care. Drinking and quarreling were a daily scene in the barracks, and even when married couples were given separate cottages, their work schedules left no time and energy for adequate care of their children. Sokabe resolved to make his parsonage into a Christian home and school. He walked all over the island seeking donations. Then Superintendent Gulick gave him a leave of absence to go to Japan to observe kindergartens and to obtain books and materials.

While there he married a devoted Christian woman. Sokabe also brought back with him an experienced teacher, Mrs. Tamie Susumago, whom the Board of Missions employed as his assistant in the new venture. The Sokabe Boarding School opened with an enrollment of twenty boys, while twenty more children came as day pupils. Their parents were mostly Buddhists. The children attended school daily, and they studied Japanese language, history, and culture two afternoons a week. The Bible was read in the morning and evening, and before each meal a blessing was said, following the Christian pattern of home life. The school was so successful that young delinquents were sometimes sent there as an alternative to reform school. When the place became too crowded with sixty pupils, the plantation donated an acre and a half of land, and with donations from individuals, additional buildings were built. Later young adults, thirty-seven men and even a few married couples, came to stay.[24]

Reverend Sokabe was referred to as the "Saint of Honomu" or "Christ-like Christian" among non-Christians as well as Christians because of his selfless service to all people, regardless of their religious affiliation. Sokabe used his salary to support his boarding school and was so often in debt that it became customary for the concerned people of various faiths to collect donations every few years to defray his debt. Sokabe was extremely patient in dealing with troubled persons. Once a woman of about fifty years of age, mentally disturbed, came to the Sokabe Home with a truck loaded with twenty sacks of rice (one sack contained 100 lbs.), shouting, "Where is *Bozu* Sokabe?" *Bozu* is a derogatory term for Buddhist monks. "*Bozu* is poor. So, I give you all this rice. Feed all your children with it." Surprised, Sokabe called the woman's husband who came and explained that since she was emotionally disturbed, he let her do whatever she wanted to do and that it would be a blessing if her donation of rice to the Sokabe Home helped to improve her condition. "Please accept it," he pleaded. This woman had accumulated some $10,000 by peddling fish. When her husband tried to take her home, she insisted on staying at the Sokabe Home. For several days and sometimes even at night, she "preached" to Sokabe, calling him *"Bozu, Bozu."* Sokabe always said, "Yes, Yes," and never disturbed her. Fortunately, she eventually recovered from her mental disorder. In 1915 when Zen Buddhist priest Mokusen Hioki visited the island of Hawaii on his way back to Japan from the United States, there was a tremendous reception honoring him in Hilo. Reverend Sokabe gave the greeting of welcome to him on behalf of all present.[25]

In 1942, due to a drastic curtailment of funds and wartime complications, the Sokabe Boarding School was closed, but Sokabe continued his ministry as pastor emeritus and lived among the people he loved in Honomu.[26]

Rural Ministers

In reality, all the Japanese ministers in Hawaii except those serving in Honolulu were rural ministers, whether in rural Oahu or on the other islands, living in the plantation communities and observing daily the experiences of the laborers, often helping the people in solving secular but crucial problems. Rev. Shigehide Kanda of Kohala on Hawaii, for instance, worked as a luna while the plantation manager looked for a replacement for the brutal luna who beat up a laborer and who Reverend Kanda demanded be dismissed in twenty-four hours. There are many examples of the social service activities undertaken by rural ministers and their wives.

The Rev. Eisaku Tokimasa and his family lived on Kahuku Plantation from 1903, receiving $40 a month from the Methodist Mission. For his services as an interpreter for the manager, his family was given a rent-free house with a bathroom, toilet, and telephone. It was not rare in those days that women strapped their infants on their backs while performing the hard labor of the cane fields. Day care centers were crucially needed for the married plantation laborers. Reverend Tokimasa's daughters described how he filled this need in his rural ministry.

In those days both men and women worked in the fields. Women took their babies and small children with them and left them on mats or in boxes near the fields while they were working. It was hard for them as well as for the babies, so my father and mother started a nursery to take care of their children. The plantation was interested in this project and built a sizable building in the large open lot next to our house and put the fence around it so that the children could not wander out. We named the building Adams' Children's Home in honor of the manager of the plantation. The women brought their babies and small children as early as five o'clock in the morning on their way to the fields. They handed them to my mother over the fence. The children were all crying when their mothers left them. There were usually about twenty-three to thirty children. So our mother was very, very busy. The children were picked up by their mothers when they returned home. Later, the plantation employed a few women to take care of the children and my mother supervised the work without pay.

We had the weekly prayer meeting at our house, but all the other Christian services, including those of the Portuguese and Filipinos as well as the Japanese, were held in the Nursery Building. At Christmas we had a big Christmas party there and all the children of the plantation, regardless of their parents' religions, were invited and everybody received a package of Christmas present.

In 1920 or thereabout [at the time of the second plantation strike on Oahu] we moved to Kaneohe. Our father continued his Christian ministry, and we had the Sunday service and weekly prayer meeting at our house. By that time our eldest sister and I (Aiko) were teaching at the same public school in Kaneohe. Our principal allowed us to use the school building on Sunday for our Sunday school. Thus, our father and our family continued the Christian work in our house and in that general area. That became later the Parker Memorial Methodist Church where Chimpei Goto, a young lay leader of Harris Church, became the minister in charge.[27]

Rev. Chimpei Goto, the Village Master of Kaneohe

Chimpei Goto came to Hawaii in 1898 at the age of eleven with his parents, who were labor immigrants from Iwate Prefecture in northern Japan. They had never done farm work before, and plantation labor was too hard for them. "After two years they moved to Honolulu," recalled Mrs. Goto, speaking about her husband's early years in Hawaii.

They happened to live as tenants of the Kawasaki Camp. Chimpei was a brilliant boy and he always remembered *kodan* [stories of actual or legendary heroes or events] and also the history of Japan, which his parents used to tell him. The people of the camp used to come to their house to listen to Chimpei tell them the stories. Since his parents were frail, unable to work hard, Chimpei helped them by earning money as a paperboy or as a store clerk while attending the public school.

Mr. Kiyozo Kawasaki, the landlord and the owner of the Kawasaki Hotel, was a remarkable Christian and had the greatest influence on young Chimpei. He introduced the Goto family to the Rev. Chuzo Nakamura of the Japanese Methodist Church, which was on River Street then. Very soon Chimpei became a Sunday school teacher and was also active in *"Yagai Dendo"* [sidewalk ministry] every Sunday, regardless of the weather.[28]

When he was twenty-nine years old, Goto visited his birthplace in Iwate-ken, where he met the young woman, a distant relative by marriage, who was to become his wife. "He proposed to me," Mrs. Goto remembered, "but my parents opposed it, because I was too young, and their only child." Against their wishes, however, the couple became engaged. She went to Tokyo to attend the Aoyama Jogakuin, a prestigious Methodist Mission girls' high school. "After graduation, I came to Hawaii in 1921 at the age of nineteen years to marry him. I was a very naive young girl," she said.[29]

In the meantime, Chimpei Goto had been persuaded by the ministers and elders of his church to become a minister. Soon after the wedding, he was assigned to Lahaina, Maui, where he, assisted by his dedicated young wife, developed Sunday schools and built a church with strong adult membership during the seven years of his ministry there. In 1927 he was assigned to Parker Memorial Church in Kaneohe and to serve in the general area of windward Oahu. He acquired the nickname "Soncho of Kaneohe" (Village Master of Kaneohe) because he had to take care of a variety of problems pertaining to the Japanese immigrants, mostly plantation workers, ranging from personal or family problems and disputes between individuals and groups to remittances to Japan, expatriation of the children from Japanese citizenship, and obtaining copies of family records from village registration offices in Japan. Once a week he would go to Honolulu with loads of papers and documents on behalf of the residents in Kaneohe and other areas of windward Oahu to deliver filled-out forms to the Japanese consulate, to discuss cases with consulate officials, or to consult with the U.S. Immigration Service officials.[30]

Reverend Goto established churches in Kahuku, Kahaluu, and Waimanalo also. While he welcomed the Issei to church membership, his major effort was for the Nisei generation. In the plantation communities there was nothing in terms of recreation for teenagers or young adults. Goto organized baseball teams for rural youths as a healthy outlet. On special occasions such as Christmas the rural churches overflowed with 400 to 700 or more young people. Mrs. Goto said that she and her husband were very busy with their regular work in the four churches and with visitations to families and the sick. But Sunday schools were the most important part of their church work.[31] Mrs. Goto herself was an ingenious Sunday school teacher in that she created hymnal dances to be performed at Christmas, Easter, and Thanksgiving by young people. "For children and young girls, dancing is more expressive and meaningful than just singing hymns," she said. "I had no training in dancing, but because I was eager to make the hymns meaningful, I created dances suitable to the words of the hymns. Evidently, they enjoyed dancing to the hymns and even now after they passed the age of sixty, they remember the dances very well and can dance."[32] Mrs. Goto also taught the Japanese language to the young members. Parents were eager to have their children learn proper Japanese.

When Rev. Goto died in 1954 after thirty-three years of rural ministry, of which twenty-seven years were spent in windward Oahu, Mrs. Goto spent two years on the mainland, visiting her two sons, then she visited Japan for the first time since she came to Hawaii thirty-five years earlier to observe the completion of the new church building in Sashi in Iwate-ken, the home town of the Gotos.[33] It was when she returned to Hawaii that Mrs. Goto received her own call to the ministry, which she later described in an interview:

> When I returned to Hawaii in 1959, the Lahaina Church of Maui did not have a Japanese-speaking minister. The old members wanted me to go there to be their minister. My husband and I were there from 1921 to 1927 and they remembered us very well. So, the Methodist Board assigned me to serve there. I had no academic background to become a minister. I only wanted to do my utmost in whatever capacity God chose for me. I served in Lahaina for six years. Those were the happiest years of my life. The old members were so generous in assisting me both in church work and in visitation to homes and patients in the hospital. Mr. X, one of the elders of the church, drove his car to take me for my pastoral calls, but I realized that it took too much of his time, and often when I had to visit the patients in the middle of the night, I felt that it was too much of imposition on him. So I took a

driving lesson from Mrs. Jōshō Nakamura, another pillar of the church and the leader of the women's group. [Mrs. Nakamura was the first woman to get a taxi driver's license on Maui.] Having become able to drive a car myself, I felt free to work harder.[34]

High blood pressure eventually obliged Mrs. Goto to retire from Lahaina and return to Honolulu, although she continued to go to the Lahaina Church once a month, at the members' request. A heart condition finally forced Mrs. Goto to retire in earnest. She remained active, however, with Harris Methodist Church in Honolulu, attending the Rōyūkai gathering (senior citizens' group) and holding informal meetings of church members in her apartment.[35]

Eventually, various denominations began missionary work among the Japanese in Hawaii. In 1940, just before World War II, there were forty-two Japanese Christian churches of seven different denominations in addition to the Quaker church, which was interracial. All the Caucasian churches had a limited number of Japanese, mostly professional Issei and Nisei, attending their services.

11

Major Organizations and Institutions

The Japanese Benevolent Society and Benevolent Hospital

THE oldest Japanese organization in Hawaii, the Japanese Mutual Aid Association, was founded in Honolulu in October 1887 through the joint efforts of Consul General Tarō Andō and the Rev. Kanichi Miyama. It was organized to assist those without savings to meet such emergencies as sickness, injury, loss of jobs, and death and funeral expenses. Mrs. Fumiko Andō, wife of the consul general, was elected president, and Mrs. Joji Nakayama, wife of the chief of the Japanese section of the Immigration Bureau, became vice-president. The membership was solicited from among the immigrants, at a monthly fee of 20 cents. Japanese contract laborers on all the islands were eligible to join. If the member did not receive assistance, $3.80 was returned to him at the end of his contract with the plantation. Combining the dollar that each immigrant paid on landing for emergencies with the donations of $50 from Consul General Andō, $25 from Mrs. Andō, and $3 from Reverend Miyama, the Mutual Aid Association had $323.55 in its treasury from the beginning.[1]

In 1892 the Association was reorganized as the Japanese Benevolent Society, with a new slate of male officers, to expand its services to include the entire Japanese community and to form a close association with the Japanese Physicians' Association. When Dr. Iga Mōri became its president in 1899, the service of this Society was expanded further to give 30 cents a day to each of its members in distress, and a person without money who wanted to return to Japan was given half of his travel fare. In the meantime, one acre of land was obtained in Palama to build a Japanese Benevolent Hospital. In 1900 its two-storied building was completed with

170

two large rooms as 38-bed wards, three rooms for surgical patients, an operating room, a room for nurses, a room for a pharmacy, a business office, a caretaker's room, and a laundry room.[2] The hospital was moved to Liliha Street in 1902. In need of further expansion, it was moved to Kuakini Street in 1917 and renamed the Japanese Hospital, which was renamed again during World War II. As Kuakini Hospital, its services were available to all races and nationalities.

By the middle of the nationwide depression years of the early 1930s some thirty elderly Japanese were being aided by the Territorial Department of Welfare and about twenty were in the Japanese Hospital, assisted by the Japanese Benevolent Society. Realizing the growing need for the care of elderly indigents, the Benevolent Society launched a fund-raising campaign in 1931 to build a Home for the Aged. The large donations included $5,000 from the Hawaiian Sugar Planters' Association, $1,000 from the Pineapple Companies' Association, $5,000 (10,000 yen) from the Department of the Imperial Household of Japan, $15,000 (30,000 yen) from the Japanese Red Cross, and $2,267.67, which was the balance of the funds used for the celebration of Emperor Hirohito's coronation in 1928. The construction of the Home began in February 1932 and was completed in May that year to accommodate ninety elderly people. Forty-five men and three women were cared for that year.[3]

Similar organizations were founded elsewhere in the islands. On the island of Hawaii, in Kona, the Japanese Association was formed in 1899 by members of the former Japanese Labor Union. In Hilo and Honomu, the Kyodo Club was formed in 1894 for mutual help among its members, with a monthly fee of 25 cents each. Poor members were assisted, but if their poverty was the result of misconduct, no help was awarded.[4] Prefectural associations also assumed responsibility for the welfare of their respective members.

The International YMCA (Nuuanu YMCA)

The Japanese YMCA was founded by the Rev. Takie Okumura in 1902.[5] In February 1912, Mitsushige Matsuzawa of the National YMCA of Japan was invited to Honolulu to be in charge of it. It became a branch of the Honolulu YMCA in 1917 and a truly international YMCA, when Lloyd R. Killam became its executive secretary and Ko Fong Lum, a Chinese, Tai Sung Lee, a Korean, and B. T. Makapagal, a Filipino, added to its staff. In 1918, with Frank Atherton as chairman, the YMCA raised money from leading businessmen in Japan and Honolulu to construct a building on the corner of Fort and Beretania streets. It cost about $70,000, of which $35,000 was raised in Honolulu, while $35,000 was raised in Japan. The building was completed in the same year and thus provided a place where Chinese, Japanese, Koreans, and others could participate in activities regardless of their national backgrounds. In 1921, another campaign was carried out in Honolulu to build additional facilities, which resulted in $25,000 from leading Caucasian businessmen, $6,000 from Japanese residents, and $4,000 from Chinese and Korean residents.[6] Because of its location near Nuuanu Avenue, it became known as the Nuuanu YMCA.

The Thursday Luncheon Club *(Mokuyō Gosankai)*

The Thursday Luncheon Club, proposed by Consul General Rokuro Moroi, had its first meeting on September 19, 1918, at the Nuuanu YMCA. It was a very informal gathering with no set membership. Anyone could attend it, bringing his own lunch from the YMCA cafeteria, to hear a speaker, often an interesting person who happened to be in Honolulu on his or her way to Japan or to the mainland United States. Katsutaro Yasumori of the YMCA was in charge of the program. He was succeeded by Seinosuke Tsukiyama, who was followed by Choki Kanetake. The Thursday Luncheon Club celebrated its sixty-fifth year in 1983 with the publication of a book compiled by Kanetake honoring the late Consul General Rokuro Moroi, its founder.[7]

Tanomoshi, a Mini-Savings and Loan Club

Tanomoshi, which is also called *mujin* in eastern and northern Japan and *moai* in Okinawa, is a folkway long practiced in villages and small towns in Japan. In Hawaii it began when there were no financial facilities on the plantations for immigrants to borrow money to meet emergencies such as sickness, injury, death of their family members, or birth of a baby. Their meager earnings were barely enough for their subsistence. Later, after their contracts with the plantations expired, when they wanted some capital to start small stores or independent farms or to send money to bring their close kin such as wives, children, or picture brides to Hawaii, tanomoshi was commonly utilized for borrowing money. The following illustrates the way tanomoshi works.[8]

X needs $200 to start a small store. He asks his trusted friends to help him by forming a tanomoshi with $10 monthly dues for each member. Thus he needs twenty members to get the desired $200 at the first meeting of his tanomoshi. He will pay back the $200 he borrows in twenty months by paying $10 every month. It also means that it takes twenty months for each of the twenty members to have his turn to receive a share of money. The one who proposes organizing the tanomoshi is called the Oya, the parent. He is responsible for the continuation of his tanomoshi group until the last member gets his share. He decides a time and place to meet convenient for the members. When the Oya receives his needed $200 at the first meeting, he has a co-signer on his receipt. In fact, every member who receives his share of money is required to have a co-signer on his receipt as a witness and at the same time to insure implicitly that the receiver will continue paying his monthly dues until the end. If he fails to pay after he gets his share of the money, the co-signer will have to take the responsibility of paying his unpaid dues.

After the first meeting the receiver of the money is determined by bidding on the amount of *modori-kin* or interest he is willing to give each of the members, except the Oya and himself. The Oya, who has already received his share of money is not eligible to make a bid on the *modori-kin* or to receive it. At the second meeting each of the eligible members, numbering nineteen in this case, writes the amount of his or her bid on a slip of paper and puts it in a box. The amount of each one's bid is secret. When everybody has put in his or her bid, the box is opened and the highest bidder gives the amount of money he bid every member except the Oya and himself. This means that if a member's bid on the *modori-kin* is $1 and all the other bids are smaller than that, he pays $1 to each of the eighteen members and gets his share of $182 ($200 minus $18). It seems unfair that he receives only $182 instead of the $200 that all the other members receive, but it is accepted as a part of the game. Sometimes, one who needs a sum of money in a hurry will purposely make a high bid even if he does not get the full $200. At any rate, after he has received his sum of money, he is not eligible to bid on or receive *modori-kin*. The number of members who can bid on or receive *modori-kin* decreases as this process is repeated. The last member does not make a bid or receive *modori-kin* because there is no one to pay. He gets his $200. In the meantime he has received *modori-kin* for eighteen months. Thus, the longer one waits the more *modori-kin* one gets. Because tanomoshi provided a social occasion with the fun and excitement of a game while helping a friend in need of money, it was popular among the old-timers.

Japanese Banks

During the years of government contract labor immigration 15 percent of the laborers' earnings was automatically deducted from their wages every month by the planters and handed over to the Japanese consulate for safe-keeping. The remittances the immigrants were urged to send to their homes were also handled by the Japanese consulate. When the Japanese population reached more than 60,000, Consul General Taizō Masaki (1889–1891) requested the Japanese government to establish a bank to handle the immigrants' financial matters. As a result, a small office of the Yokohama Specie Bank was opened in Honolulu in 1892, which was upgraded to a branch bank later to expand its services to increasing numbers of Japanese merchants.

With mostly government contract plantation laborers as its customers, the remittances it took care of in the first year amounted to $1,384.39, and their savings were only $236.40 altogether. When private emigration companies took over the emigration of the Japanese to Hawaii in 1894, nonlabor immigrants, including merchants, increased, which meant an increase in business. In 1901 the savings of the Japanese increased to $230,598.02. In 1917 they reached $1,428,650.57. In 1931 the savings account showed $2,496,659.47.[9] All the major officers of the bank came from Japan but also a small number of Nisei University of Hawaii graduates were employed.

Sumitomo Bank of Osaka opened its branch in Honolulu in 1916. Its major officials were from Osaka but it also employed a few Nisei University of Hawaii graduates. The savings account in 1917, a year after it was open, was $315.72. In 1931 it had increased to $4,724,914.00. The Pacific Bank opened in 1913 with capital assets of $200,000 raised by nine local businessmen to promote the businesses of Hawaii. They also solicited investments from among the leading businessmen in Japan, but they ended up in 1921 being controlled by their Japanese investors, with Soichiro Asano, a business tycoon, as the head of their bank under the new name Asano Chuya Bank. In 1925, however, through the efforts of Kazusuke Motoshige and Tajiro Sumida, the bank was returned to the control of Hawaii's Issei businessmen and resumed its original name, the Pacific Bank. The savings accounts during the Asano Bank years ranged from $600,000 to $700,000, but after it again became the Pacific Bank, savings increased to more than one million dollars and continued to increase.[10]

The Keihin Bank was set up in 1897 by three emigration companies, Hiroshima, Morioka, and Kumamoto. The immigrants who came through these companies were the victims of extortion. Before leaving Japan, each immigrant was required to deposit $90 to $100 in the Keihin Bank for return passage, just in case he should fail the physical examination and be ordered to return to Japan. When the immigrants who were permitted to land—the majority of them—asked for their money, they were told that it was on fixed deposit and they were to withdraw it when they returned to Japan three years later. Moreover, each immigrant was required to deposit 15 percent of his wages every month as savings and $2.50 monthly for his return trip to Japan after he finished his three-year contract with the plantation. Each immigrant was also required to pay the bank $4.50 for life insurance. In spite of all these forced deposits, the immigrants were not allowed to withdraw funds from their accounts, even in cases of emergency.

When Consul General Miki Saitō organized the Central Japanese Association as a means to reduce plantation strikes and to stop the mass exodus to the West Coast, the Issei noticed among its leaders the directors of the Keihin Bank and the emigration companies. Infuriated, the Issei organized in May 1905 the Reform Association and reported to the Japanese government about the practices of the Keihin Bank and the emigration companies. Consul General Saitō was recalled temporarily. Subsequently the Japanese government invalidated all the deposit contracts between the Keihin Bank and immigrants in 1905 and the bank was closed and the emigration companies left Hawaii forever.[11]

These banks played an important role in the Japanese community in Honolulu. In Hilo small-scale local banks and loan associations started, but they were all short lived. In 1941, just before World War II, the savings deposited in the Japanese banks amounted to approximately $3 million in the Yokohama Specie Bank, $2.8 million in the Pacific Bank, and more than $2 million in the Sumitomo Bank. It was estimated that the Japanese had about the same amount in savings accounts in American and Chinese banks.[12] All the Japanese banks were closed and their assets seized by the U.S. government after Pearl Harbor, and their officials were interned on the mainland for the duration of the war. None of these banks revived after the war.

The Japanese in Commerce and the Formation of the Chamber of Commerce

The Japanese immigrants obtained needed commodities from Chinese and Caucasian stores during the very early years. The earliest Japanese itinerant merchant in Hawaii was Kunizo Suzuki from Chiba-ken, known as Kuni of Hilo. He arrived in Hawaii in 1866 at the age of eighteen aboard a German whaler. After working on a plantation on Maui, he worked as a house servant and saved $150 with which he opened a small store in Hilo in 1885, selling Hawaiian fruits and serving meals to Japanese newcomers. He also sold Japanese foodstuffs and general merchandise to the outlying districts of the Big Island, transporting it on mules. Old-timers used to reminisce about the impressive, picturesque sight of Kuni's long mule team packed with goods silhouetted against the horizon. By 1898 he had become a very successful businessman and a trusted leader of the Japanese community. He had five daughters by two marriages. His first wife was a Hawaiian. After her death he married a Portuguese. Besides Kuni's, there were eighteen businesses operated by Japanese in Hilo in the 1890s, including a hotel, a restaurant, a bakery, and a watch repair shop.[13]

Three import-export companies from Yokohama opened branch stores in Honolulu in 1889. The first merchant who came to Hawaii on his own, however, was Sanshichi Ozaki from Shizuoka-ken, who arrived in December 1891 at the age of twenty-seven. He rented a room in Honolulu for $1.50 a month to live in and a chicken coop for 75 cents a month in which to store his merchandise, about $100 worth, which he brought from Japan. He carried his wares on his back and made the rounds of various plantations on foot. He opened a food and general merchandise store in Honolulu in 1892, but later he specialized in hardware.[14] About fifteen merchants arrived between 1892 and 1895.

Hidegoro Fujii of Tokyo, who came to Hawaii in 1897 as a special correspondent for the *Shimbun Nippon* and became editor of the *Hilo Shimbun,* observed at the turn of the century that the businesses operated by the Japanese catered mainly to Japanese customers. There were more than two hundred small stores that were started with small capital amounting to several hundred dollars saved or borrowed from tanomoshi. Noticeable among the trades started by the Japanese were barbershops in Honolulu and Hilo. Of the more than fifty barbershops in Honolulu, most were operated by the Japanese. Japanese barbershops charged 15 cents for a haircut and 5 cents for a shave while Caucasian barbers charged 50 cents for a haircut and 25 cents for a shave, too expensive for the average Japanese.[15]

The Commissioner of Labor reported that after annexation, an increasing number of Japanese and Chinese went into trade and skilled labor and that Caucasian enterprises such as the gourmet industry, tailoring firms, cobbler shops, bakeries, and hotels began to employ them. Plumbing, tinning, and the building trades, such as masonry, carpentry, plastering, and painting, became increasingly occupations of the Japanese. Thus, the small-scale businesses and industries fell into the hands of the Japanese and Chinese while the large-scale corporate organizations with large capital remained in the hands of the Caucasians.[16]

The Nihonjin Shonin Kumiai (Japanese Merchants Union) was organized in 1895 by those engaged in trade to protect and promote their common interests. This group was disbanded within two years, however, because of the constant clash of opinions and conflicting interests that resulted from the mixed membership, which included representatives of large Japanese import-export companies, combined wholesale-retail businesses with their own capital, and retailers with no capital. Moreover, because the members were from various prefectures of Japan with different customs and dialects, they were distrustful of each other and the prospects for cooperation were poor.[17] After the Honolulu fire of 1900 thirty-seven merchants who had helped the fire victims got together and organized the Nihonjin Shonin Doshikai (Japanese Merchants Association) of Honolulu with the manager of the Yokohama Specie Bank as its president. This organization changed its name to the Honolulu Japanese Chamber of Commerce in 1908. In 1916 it rented an upstairs room of the Yokohama Specie Bank as an office. In 1938 it merged with the Japanese Building Contractors' Association, which was founded in 1911, and became the Japanese Chamber of Commerce and Industry.[18]

The United Japanese Society

As the population increased in Hawaii, particularly in Honolulu, it became necessary to have an overall organization for activities that would require the large-scale participation of the Japanese as a group.[19] With the assistance of Acting Consul General Ichitaro Shibata, the United Japanese Society was organized in August 1932 by combining the Honolulu Japanese Chamber of Commerce, the Honolulu Japanese Building Contractors' Association, and more than forty large and small groups such as prefectural associations, village and town clubs, and others. Its office was located in the office of the Japanese Chamber of Commerce, whose president was also the president of the newly formed United Japanese Society.[20] Thus, prominent Japanese businessmen invariably became leaders of the Japanese community in Honolulu before World War II with respect to the larger community as well as to the Japanese residents. With this overall organization the Japanese community became more efficient in undertaking various activities and service projects for the larger community, such as fund-raising for the Red Cross and the Community Chest and welcoming celebrities from the mainland, and was also better able to sponsor activities within the Japanese community such as welcoming Japanese celebrities and naval training ships, establishing scholarships for Hawaii-born children, and collecting and sending relief material and money to Japan for disasters caused by earthquakes, floods, tidal waves, typhoons, and so on.

Japanese Vernacular Newspapers

The Japanese vernacular newspapers were a powerful organ in the Japanese community, influencing and forming public opinion among the readers on various issues concerning the Japanese immigrants. At times they even sponsored mass meetings to take action on important issues. There was also keen competition between the Japanese papers, which took different stands on important issues. Their editorials sometimes resulted in splitting the Japanese community. The first Japanese paper was a mimeographed weekly, the *Nippon Shuho*, published in Honolulu in 1892 by Bunichi Onome, a former immigration inspector, to expose the high-handed bureaucratic officialdom of the Japanese Section of the Immigration Bureau. Within a few months it became the *Honolulu Hochi*, with a new publisher. From 1894 this paper changed its name three times under three different publishers. Its last name was *Yamato Shinbun*. In 1906 Yasutarō Sōga bought this paper and completely reorganized the whole enterprise as a joint-stock company with a new editorial policy and a new name, *Nippu Jiji*.

Numerous weeklies and dailies appeared subsequently, changing ownership and editorial policies.[21] In 1894, *Hawaii Shinpō* was published in Honolulu by Chuzaburo Shiozawa, first as a weekly but soon as a daily. Shojiro Takahashi, Shiozawa's elder brother in Tokyo, was invited by Shiozawa to be its editor. Takahashi had spent three years in San Francisco. Upon his return to Japan he opened an English-language school in Tokyo. Sōga attended this school during his grade school years. Sōga came to Hawaii with Mr. and Mrs. Takahashi. Shiozawa went to San Francisco and from there he came to Hawaii. He established himself as a businessman. Shiozawa employed Sōga as the manager of his plantation stores in Waianae, Waipahu, and Molokai. Sometarō Shiba bought *Hawaii Shinpō* in 1908. Both Shiozawa and Takahashi returned to Japan eventually. Shiba was firmly against the 1909 plantation strike in which Sōga and the *Nippu Jiji* were completely involved.

The *Honolulu Shimbun* was started by Rev. Takie Okumura in 1901 as a weekly, which became *Hawaii Nichi Nichi Shimbun* daily. Together with *Shin Nippon,* which became a daily in 1901, and *Hawaii Shinpō* it organized the Reform Association that finally ousted the emigration companies and the Keihin Bank from Hawaii. Another vernacular paper was the *Hawaii Hochi* published by Kinzaburo Makino in 1912 to protect the civil rights of the Japanese immigrants.

In 1930 there were the following vernacular papers (table 2). In Honolulu, *Hawaii Hochi* and *Nippu Jiji;* on Maui, *Maui Shimbun,* triweekly; on Kauai, *Kauai Shinpō,* weekly, and *Yoen Jiho,* weekly; on Hawaii, *Hawaii Mainichi,* daily, *Kazan,* daily, *Kona Hankyo,* twice a week, and *Hawaii Asahi,* triweekly. In 1940, all but *Hawaii Asahi* were continuing. With the outbreak of World War II, all the vernacular papers were closed and their publishers and editors were interned on the mainland for the duration of the war. However, for the purpose of informing the Issei of directives from the military government, the *Nippu Jiji* and *Hawaii Hochi* were permitted to resume publication. The *Nippu Jiji* changed its name to *Hawaii Times* and Sōga's son Shigeo found an experienced journalist, Rinji Maeyama, to be its editor. *Hawaii Hochi* changed its name to *Hawaii Herald.* Makino was not interned and only four of his editorial staff were interned on the mainland. In 1941 the circulation of *Hawaii Times* was 10,000 and that of the *Hawaii Herald* was 9,843. After the war *Hawaii Times* continued to use the name, while the *Hawaii Herald* resumed its prewar name *Hawaii Hochi.*

Yasutarō Sōga described his earliest experiences as a reporter in Hawaii:

> As soon as I came back to Honolulu from Molokai in October 1899, I was persuaded by Mr. Shojiro Takahashi, the editor of a daily, *Hawaii Shinpō,* to become its reporter. *Hawaii Shinpō,* which had about a hundred subscribers, was a small paper of four pages. Its building was a two-storied wooden house on Nuuanu Street near Beretania. The downstairs was a printing shop while the upstairs had the editorial office and the living quarters of the Takahashis. Until I joined this paper, Mr. and Mrs. Takahashi did everything—editorials, reporting, advertisement, and management—with the help of three workers in the printing shop and a delivery boy. The printing machine was a primitive hand-manipulated one. In spite of such a small-scale paper,

Table 2. Major Japanese Vernacular Newspapers on All Islands before World War II

Name	Place of Publication	Date of First Issue
Nippu Jiji (Hawaii Times)	Honolulu	1906
Hawaii Hochi	Honolulu	1912
Maui Shimbun	Maui	1906
Record	Maui	1917
Kona Hankyo	Hawaii	1897
Hawaii Mainichi	Hawaii	1909
Kazan	Hawaii	1914
Hawaii Asahi	Hawaii	1917
Kauai Shinpō	Kauai	1904
Yoen Jiho	Kauai	1924

Source: *Hawaiian Japanese Annual and Directory* (1928), pp. 139–140, 208, 245, 246.

Editor Takahashi was an outstanding intellectual with strength of character, and because of his unflinching editorials, he was regarded as the fiercest critic of the Japanese consulate and the emigration companies, which exploited the immigrants. His wife, Masako, was a very capable businesswoman who, in spite of her inability to speak English, went not only to Japanese firms but also to American firms to get orders for advertisements and other printing orders so that she was known among the Americans as "Little Japanese Businesswoman." Two important incidents took place soon after I became a reporter, namely, the great fire of Honolulu, and the abolition of the contract labor system as the result of the annexation of Hawaii to the United States.

In addition to my work as a reporter, I took care of making drafts for the advertisements and various printing orders, proofreading, etc., and when the delivery boy was absent, Mrs. Takahashi and I delivered the paper, and at times I even collected money. On Sundays and holidays—American, Hawaiian, and Japanese—our paper was not published. So, I enjoyed complete relaxation.[22]

The Japanese vernacular papers were not completely isolated from the English papers during the early years if an occasion arose to call forth cooperation. One such occasion was the Russo-Japanese War of 1904–1905. Publisher Shiozawa of the *Hawaii Shinpō* and Walter G. Smith, chief editor of the *Pacific Commercial Advertiser,* decided to have the war news in Japanese inserted in the *Advertiser* for the benefit of the Japanese domestic servants in Caucasian homes. Sōga spent every night until after midnight in the *Advertiser*'s downtown office translating the telegrams coming in continuously and then sending the translated version to the *Hawai Shinpō* to be printed. After proofreading it, he returned home on his bicycle. Editor Smith had been a war correspondent for the *San Francisco Chronicle* during the Sino-Japanese War of 1894–1895 and had a sympathetic attitude toward the Japanese.[23]

Japan's war with Russia, one of the most formidable world powers, was of great concern to the Japanese in Hawaii. Many immigrants received draft calls from Japan by wireless after the mobilization order was issued on February 5, 1904, and the pier of Honolulu was crowded with their kin and friends to see them off. Normally, if men who reached the age of twenty-one were living abroad, their conscription was postponed. The fact that some Issei received draft calls reflected Japan's expectation of a fierce war with Russia. As anticipated, the loss of lives was very great. On the other hand, during the war many immigrants continued to come from Japan; 6,534 in 1904 and 6,091 in 1905.[24] When the news of the fall of Port Arthur, Russia's impregnable fortress in northeast China, reached Hawaii on January 2, 1905, it was celebrated in Hilo and Honolulu.[25] Ten weeks later, Mukden, another strategic stronghold, fell, leaving the Russian army in complete defeat. To achieve such victories, the Japanese army made untold sacrifices.

The *Yamato Shimbun* daily, dated May 8, 1905, published a statement to the effect that the victories on land and sea were a reflection of the illustrious virtue of the emperor, but without the brave and patriotic men of army and navy who fought so valiantly and gave their lives, such victories could never have been achieved. We Japanese subjects, it said, are overwhelmed with deep emotion and gratitude for these men.[26]

The Japanese immigrants during the Russo-Japanese war expressed their deep loyalty to their homeland by raising money to be used for the most needed work in Japan. About 60,000 Issei raised 378,347 yen and 20 sen ($189,173.60). The representatives of various organizations in Japan involved in relief work for bereaved families of men killed in action, for returned soldiers including the wounded, and for the Red Cross Society, among others, came to Hawaii to solicit help. Especially to assist the bereaved families of men killed in the war, Keisuke Mochizuki, later a cabinet member, came to Hawaii and visited all of the islands, raising money.[27]

The Japanese in Hawaii also celebrated the naval victory of the battle of the Sea of Japan. Russia's invincible Baltic Fleet was sighted in the East China Sea in May 1905 by reconnaissance ships as well as by fishermen of Miyako Island of Okinawa. It was immediately communicated to the Japanese Naval Headquarters from the wireless station in Ishigaki. Russia's Baltic Fleet was heading for Vladivostok, the only Russian port on the east edge of Siberia facing Japan. When the Baltic Fleet passed the Tsushima Strait, the entrance to the Sea of Japan, the Japanese navy was prepared to intercept it and determined to destroy it. It was a decisive battle for Japan's existence: Admiral Heihachiro Togo signaled from his flagship, "The rise or fall of our Empire depends on this one battle. Each of you is expected to redouble his effort." The fierce battle was fought on May 27 and 28, resulting in the complete annihilation of the Baltic Fleet. Most of the fleet, including the flagship, was sunk, with only three of the thirty-eight ships managing to escape to Vladivostok.[28]

The naval victory in the Sea of Japan was the end of the war with Russia. Juhei Ishizuka, vice president of the Central Japanese Association, sent a congratulatory message to the Minister of the Navy, requesting him to convey the message to Admiral Togo. The Secretary of the Territory of Hawaii, Alalau Leonard C. Atkinson, who happened to be in Washington, D.C., sent a telegram to Consul General Miki Saitō, congratulating him on the great victory of the Japanese navy. Non-Japanese seemed to express increased friendliness toward the Japanese.[29] The victories of their homeland in the Sino-Japanese and Russo-Japanese wars gave the Japanese immigrants as well as the people of Japan a new conception of themselves as the subjects of a first-rate nation of the world.

The Emergence of the *Nippu Jiji* and the *Hawaii Hochi*

In May 1905, Sōga became the managing editor of the *Yamato Shimbun,* and in 1906 he reorganized it as a joint-stock enterprise, made a complete change in editorial policy, and named it the *Nippu Jiji.* It was a six-page semiweekly, printed on a lithograph machine, with a circulation of about 350 and fewer than a half-dozen employees. In 1919, an English-language section was added, and the *Nippu Jiji* grew to become an influential bilingual daily of more than twelve pages with a daily circulation of 15,000, employing 200 workers. It was a member of the leading American news agencies such as the Associated Press and International News Service as well as the Domei News Agency of Japan.[30] After World War II when Sōga returned from internment on the mainland, he resumed editorial writing in the *Hawaii Times* as editor emeritus, sharply criticizing the social disorganization among the Issei in the postwar years. He died in March, 1957, at the age of eighty-five.

Kinzaburo Makino began publishing his *Hawaii Hochi* in 1912 for the sole purpose of protecting the civil rights of Japanese immigrants. Makino had the firm belief that under the American constitution the rights of everybody living in America were equally protected. He fought for the oppressed and disadvantaged, as exemplified by his participation in the 1909 plantation strike, when he was chairman of the Higher Wage Association. He was imprisoned along with three others for conspiracy. Through his newspaper as well as through personal social action Makino fought for and rescued individuals and organizations in trouble, particularly in cases involving the authorities. The circulation of *Hawaii Hochi* before World War II ranged from about 12,000 at its peak to less than 10,000.

In June 1917, Tatsukichi Kuwahara and his wife, invited by Honpa Hongwanji Japanese language school in Honolulu, and Futoshi Ohama, Kazuyuki Yamato, and Hatsune Tsutsumi, invited by the Japanese-language school in Hanapepe, Kauai, were detained by the Immigration Service, to be deported to Japan eventually. The Hawaii Office of Immigration Service held that coming to Hawaii with a promise of job constituted contract labor immigration and was therefore against the law. Having heard of this from Reverend Imamura of Honpa Hongwanji, Makino employed attorney Joseph Lightfoot, who instituted a lawsuit at the U.S. District Court in Honolulu against the Immigration Service on the grounds that these five language-school teachers were not contract labor immigrants and they should be treated like international merchants. Lightfoot was able to obtain permission for temporary landing, with Matsutarō Yamashiro of the Yamashiro Hotel and Kinjiro Kobayashi of the Kobayashi Hotel as bondsmen. The five teachers left the Immigration Service on September 14 after more than sixty days of detention.

In the meantime, the case was transferred to the Ninth Circuit

Court of Appeals in San Francisco, whose decision was that the language-school teachers were not contract labor immigrants and must be treated as nonlabor immigrants. Not satisfied with this decision, the Immigration Service in Honolulu and the Territorial Government of Hawaii appealed to the United States Supreme Court to review the case. The Supreme Court upheld the Ninth Circuit Court. It took three years, from June 1917 until November 1920, to resolve the legal status of Japanese-language school teachers. During this time, Makino, through the *Hawaii Hochi,* appealed to the PTAs of all the language schools for donations to help with the lawsuit.[31] The most spectacular of his fights was the Japanese-language school litigation, discussed below.

One of Makino's close friends observed that Makino was an exceptional fighter for social justice. He could not sit still when others were in trouble. It was his nature. He was born to fight and demonstrated his unusual strength in social struggle. His whole life was a continuous fight and no matter how hard the fight was, no matter what suffering and hardship he encountered, he never showed signs of retreating. The harder the fight and fiercer the battle, the more energetic he seemed to be.[32]

Makino was a heavy drinker who had a hot temper, but he was also quick to apologize when he realized that he was unreasonable. He liked children and was often a guest story-teller at the Manoa Language School when he lived in that area. He disliked any gathering at which formality prevailed and never attended official receptions at the Governor's mansion or Japanese consulate. Makino was born in Yokohama, Japan, in 1877, the younger son of an English merchant and his Japanese wife. He came to Hawaii in 1899 and went to Naalehu, on the island of Hawaii where his elder brother Jo had a store. He came to Honolulu in 1901 and operated a drug store. Makino died in February 1955 at the age of seventy-six.

Japanese Language Schools

As children of school age as well as preschool age increased in the Japanese community, there was a need for facilities to keep them off the streets after public school hours while both their fathers and mothers were still at work during the daytime. This need was met by Japanese-language schools. The first Japanese-language school was started in 1895 in Kohala on the island of Hawaii by the Rev. Shigehide Kanda, who employed Hideo Kawahara as the instructor for the school's thirty pupils. The second school was started in Kula, Maui, in 1895 by Seiji Fukuda, one of the first immigrants to arrive from Japan in 1885, who hired Tamaki Gomi, a Methodist minister, as the instructor. The school had more than thirty pupils. A third Japanese school was founded in 1896 in Honolulu by the Rev. Takie Okumura. Rev. Shiro Sokabe's boarding school, which he established in 1897 in Honomu, Hawaii, to take care of the children of the plantation laborers, also served as a language school. The children attended the public school daily and studied the Japanese language two afternoons a week. Thus, the earliest Japanese language schools were founded by Christians. Since most of the Japanese immigrants were Buddhists, they were hesitant at first to send their children to these schools, but after they found out that children were accepted regardless of their religious backgrounds, they sent their children to be enrolled.[33] Language schools increased as Buddhist priests began their ministry in Hawaii. Since the establishment of Japanese language schools helped to stabilize the Japanese immigrants in the plantation communities, the planters encouraged them by providing them with rent-free land, materials, and monetary subsidies. By 1900 there were ten Japanese language schools, run by Christian churches, by Buddhist temples, or by the parents of the pupils independently of religious affiliations, with 1,500 students throughout Hawaii. By 1910 the number of schools increased to 140, attended by 7,000 children. By 1916, although the number of schools had not increased much, the number of students had grown to 14,000. The schools had 360 instructors and annual operating costs of $120,000.[34]

Legislative Opposition

The Japanese language schools were criticized by the territorial government and the public at large on the grounds that they indoctrinated the children with such Japanese ideals as loyalty to the emperor and thereby hindered the Americanization of the children. After World War I strong nationalistic feelings swept over the United States, and in Hawaii the desire to get rid of foreign influence was manifested in efforts such as the introduction in 1919 of a bill in the Territorial Legislature to abolish all foreign-language schools. It was defeated, however, because of strong protest from the Oriental communities.[35] This defeat did not end the Territorial Legislature's concern about the language schools, however. The bill was only the first of many efforts to Americanize the Japanese language schools.

In a special session in 1920, the legislature enacted Act 30, the foreign language school law, requiring licensing of schools and their instructors and revision of the textbooks to make the content more suitable for Hawaii-born children. In pursuance of this, a committee of twenty-four Japanese businessmen, professionals, Christian ministers and Buddhist priests, and the editors of three Japanese vernacular papers had been formed to make suggestions for the prospective Act. The bill that the Senate and House passed and the governor signed into law was largely made up of the suggestions offered by the Japanese committee. The new law required the language-school teachers to pass examinations in speaking and writing English and in knowledge of the Constitution of the United States, its history, and the ideals of democracy.

The same Japanese committee also requested the Department of Public Instruction to secure instructors to prepare the language teachers for these examinations. Accordingly, Henry Butler Schwartz, superintendent of the Methodist Church in Hawaii, Karl Clayton Leebrick, professor of history and political science at the University of Hawaii, and W. E. Givens, principal of McKinley High School, were assigned to this task. The special classes for the Japanese language-school teachers began on January 4, 1921, at the Makiki Japanese Language School and were later moved to the public library, ending on May 19 of that year. The examinations took four days, from July 5 to 9. Approximately three hundred Japanese teachers along with teachers of other nationalities took the examinations and a large majority of them passed and were duly licensed. The American community was pleased with the sincerity of the language-school authorities, and the teachers themselves were appreciative of the opportunity to learn about America.[36]

In 1922 a bill was introduced calling for the elimination of the kindergarten and the first and second grades of the Japanese language schools. In those days the kindergarten and the lower grades were actually serving as day care centers for the children during the day when both fathers and mothers were working. The parents held a mass meeting protesting the new bill. Despite their objections, it was passed and signed by Governor Wallace R. Farrington. A large majority of the language-school authorities considered this legislative decision unconstitutional, and they acquired the services of attorney Joseph Lightfoot, who filed a brief with Governor Farrington on September 20 attacking the constitutionality of the language-school regulations.[37] In the meantime, Consul General Keichi Yamasaki, who had called a meeting of forty prominent leaders of the Japanese community to discuss the language-school situation, announced that the decision reached at this meeting was that the Japanese language schools should cooperate with the territorial government, and he advised against legal action, which would surely hurt the cordial feelings between the Japanese and American communities.[38]

Seven Japanese language schools in Honolulu sent a petition to the governor on December 26, 1922, requesting a delay in the application of the new regulations until they made some other arrangements to take care of the children already in the lower grades and kindergartens. The petition was rejected. Consequently, these schools decided to go to court and legally contest the regulations. Kinzaburo Makino, publisher of the *Hawaii Hochi,* spearheaded this action, while Yasutarō Sōga of the *Nippu Jiji,* came out against the litigation. The battle for and against the legal contest raged by way of the vernacular press. Sōga asserted that the language-school issue had already hurt relations between the Japanese and American communities and that legal action would make it worse and affect future generations. Makino insisted that the litigation was not anti-American but truly American by resorting to the courts to examine the legality of laws which seemed unduly restrictive.[39]

Palama Language School, joined by the Japanese Central Institute, Kalihi Language School, and Toyo Gakuin, with the seven other schools, instituted through Attorney Lightfoot in the Territorial Circuit Court a lawsuit to test the constitutionality of Act 30 and the regulations of the Department of Public Instruction on December 28, 1922. Subsequently, a temporary injunction against the enforcement of the regulations was granted by Seba C. Huber, former United States district attorney, Samuel B. Kemp, former associate justice of the Territorial Supreme Court, and James L. Coke, former chief justice of the Territorial Supreme Court, working jointly on behalf of the litigating school authorities.[40]

In 1923 the school commissioner announced that the licenses issued to the language schools were void, that the new license required payment of a fee at the rate of one dollar per pupil, and that the Department of Public Instruction would have full power to prescribe the subjects and courses of study as well as entrance and attendance qualifications covering age of students, education level, school attainment, mental capacity, and textbooks. Subsequently, sixteen schools filed suit in the Territorial Circuit Court, declaring that the payment of a license fee at the rate of one dollar per pupil for the school year was unreasonable, and that the absolute power of the Department of Public Instruction over language-school teaching was unconstitutional. Gradually, the number of litigating schools increased, and by August 1923, 87 of the 144 Japanese language schools in Hawaii had joined the suit.[41] On February 6, 1923, Circuit Court Judge James J. Banks ruled that Act 30 regulations relative to textbooks were valid but that the regulations on qualifications for attendance were not within the authority of the Department of Public Instruction. The case was sent to the Territorial Supreme Court.[42]

Stricter regulations were added by the legislature as Act 152 in April 1925 to prohibit the language schools from filing petitions against the government regulations. On May 10, when this new regulation became effective, all the litigating language schools closed their doors for several weeks and appealed to the U.S. District Court. Federal Court Judge De Bold granted a temporary injunction restraining the territorial government from enforcing Act 152 and advised that the whole case be sent to the Ninth Circuit Court of Appeals in San Francisco. The Appellate Court handed down its decision that the injunction granted by Judge De Bold was valid and declared Hawaii's foreign language school law unconstitutional. Not satisfied with this decision, the territorial government petitioned the United States Supreme Court on July 8, 1926, to review the decision by the Appellate Court. Having found no error in the judgment of the Appellate Court, the Supreme Court declared Hawaii's foreign language school laws unconstitutional on February 21, 1927.[43]

Legal Victory

On March 29, 1927, a mass meeting was held at the Japanese Central Institute on Nuuanu Street sponsored by the Foreign Language School Legal Contest Association, attended by a large audience of about 5,000.[44] The success of the victory was credited to the brilliant and untiring efforts of Joseph Lightfoot and the determined leaders of the litigating language schools, who never gave up their fight. The most fruitful experience for the Japanese in the course of this prolonged contest was in learning how the fundamental principle of democracy in America worked even in an unpopular case such as theirs in the eyes of the American public. As their case moved from Hawaii to San Francisco and finally to the Supreme Court of the nation in Washington, D.C., they travelled mentally and spiritually, acquiring a taste of the reality of American democracy in the process. In this sense, the language-school legal contest was a tremendous victory for the Japanese immigrants, whether they were for or against the litigation. What they affirmed at the mass meeting was actually a sincere pledge of loyalty to their newly discovered America, as they said,

> We assert our firm belief in the principles of justice which underlie the institutions of America as embodied in the Constitution of the United States and enforced by the decrees of its courts. . . . We reassert our pride in the fact that our children are American citizens. . . . We emphatically reaffirm our continued loyalty to America and our desire to rear our children as loyal, patriotic and useful citizens of the United States. . . . [45]

After this there was no supervision of the Japanese language schools by the Department of Public Instruction, except a requirement to fill out an annual report for statistical purposes. However, the adverse feeling of the larger community toward the Japanese language schools continued, and the schools were still seen as perpetuating the Japanese culture and way of thinking and detrimental to the Americanization of the children of Japanese parentage.[46] When the language schools reopened, children attended for one hour a day after public school hours as before. The tendency was, however, that the attendance decreased in the higher grades as older students developed other interests or began to work to assist in family income. On the other hand, in the world of employment, including Caucasian-owned firms, Nisei who were proficient in Japanese as well as in good English were preferred, especially for dealing with Japanese customers. By 1940 the number of Japanese language schools had increased to more than two hundred with over 40,000 students.[47]

The standard Japanese taught at the Japanese language schools was intended for formal communication, and the students who had an aptitude for it learned it very well while those who did not have much interest in language study dropped out. Actually, except for intellectuals and their families, the language used daily in the homes of the large majority of the Japanese immigrants was the familiar dialects of the Issei's old villages and towns, while their Hawaii-born children used pidgin Japanese in daily communication with their parents and other elders. Nevertheless, the schools made far-reaching contributions as was evidenced by Nisei Interpreters' Corps in the Pacific and Asian theaters during World War II and the postwar period.

Part IV
The Impact of War

12

World War I and Hawaii's Japanese

THREE weeks after England declared war on Germany at the beginning of August 1914, Japan followed suit, declaring war on Germany and severing diplomatic relations with Austria in compliance with the Anglo-Japanese alliance executed between Great Britain and Japan on January 30, 1902. Japan moved quickly to incapacitate German military bases in Asia and the Pacific and to patrol these areas to protect the ships of the Allied nations. Germans were already seizing and sinking British, French, and Russian passenger and cargo ships, and Japan reduced its shipping to minimum. Japan's efficient campaign resulted in the fall of the German fortress in Tsingtao in China and German-held bases on the Pacific islands within six months. The three weeks from October 15 to November 7, 1914, were full of apprehension for the residents of Hawaii, particularly the Japanese and the German communities.

The German cruiser *Geier*, which escaped from Chinese waters, came into Honolulu Harbor to have some repairs done, since the United States was still a neutral country. Anchored outside the harbor was a Japanese battleship, *Hizen*, to keep watch on the *Geier*. The *Shunyo Maru*, a Japanese passenger boat, was due to arrive at Honolulu from San Francisco about that time but was instructed to slow her speed and delay her arrival. In the meantime, the *Aeolus*, a German freighter, was captured by the *Hizen*, her crew was transferred to a neutral ship, and she was set afire. As a result of communications between the governments of Japan and the United States, the Navy Department in Washington instructed Captain Rashoff of the *Geier* to leave Hawaii or to be disarmed after the repair work was finished. Subsequently, by an order from the Navy Department, the ship was seized and its officers and crew were taken in the custody of the United States and later sent to Fort Douglas in Utah. The *Hizen* eventually departed to patrol the Pacific and Asian oceans with other Japanese warships.[1]

The indiscriminate attacks on and sinking of unarmed passenger boats of neutral countries by German submarines in the Atlantic made it impossible for the United States to remain neutral. Congress passed the resolution to go to war with Germany on April 5, 1917, and President Woodrow Wilson declared war on Germany the next day. In Hawaii all the newspapers including the vernaculars of various nationalities printed editorials strongly supporting the actions of Congress and the president. Accordingly, all German ships anchored in the vicinity of Hawaii were seized by the U.S. Navy and their crews and officers sent to the Immigration Service to be interned on the mainland.[2]

As the relentless war continued in Europe, the Selective Draft Act was passed by Congress on June 18, 1917, to increase the size of the U.S. military forces. This selective conscription allowed the nationals of allied countries, the so-called "friendly aliens," to enlist in the National Guard. To encourage their registration, the president's proclamation was translated into Japanese, Chinese, Korean, Portuguese, Spanish, Hawaiian, Bisayan, Ilocano, and Tagalog, with details explaining how to fill out the registration card, and advertised in every newspaper in the territory. Posters were put up on the walls of stores and businesses. July 27, the first registration day, was declared a holiday for all Hawaii. Registration booths were set up in plantation communities on all the islands and in various districts of Honolulu, and volunteers from the YMCA and YWCA as well as other organizations assisted. On the day of this first registration, more than 27,000 recruits between the ages of twenty-one and thirty registered. Of these, 11,000 were alien Japanese and 596 were Hawaii-born Nisei.[3] The large number of Japanese nationals enlisting was an indication that the Issei men in general, particularly those who came to Hawaii as infants or small children, were still young while the Nisei generation that had reached the draft age was small. Recognizing the enthusiastic response as a concrete demonstration of their loyalty to the United States, the authorities decided to form Company D, to be made up of Japanese nationals and Nisei, attached to the First Regiment of the National Guard of Hawaii.

This unit was described as the first Japanese unit under the American flag. Captain William G. Allen, its commander, stated that it was going to be one of the largest companies of the Guard in number and one of the crack organizations in point of efficiency.[4]

The response to the wartime enlistment of the Japanese on the island of Hawaii was observed by Kenpū Kawazoe:

> At this Ookala Plantation [where his father worked], every time a train left the small station, young Japanese men were sent off by voices of send-off cheers, leaving behind their familiar camp to join the army. They were to leave Hilo at 10:00 A.M. on June 14 [1918] on board the S.S. *Maunakea* for Honolulu. They left the armory [in Hilo] at 8:30, marched more than two miles, and at 9:30 they arrived at Kuhio Pier. The vicinity of the pier was crowded with hundreds of men and women to see off the enlistees. Fluttering in the wind were a huge American flag and a 20-foot-long banner proclaiming in large letters "Sending Off Enlistees of the Second Regiment of the National Guard by the Hilo Japanese Community and the Hilo Young Men's Association." At 10:00 A.M. as the *Maunakea* started to weigh anchor, a chorus of "Sending Off Enlistees," with "March on till the flag of liberty is hoisted in Berlin, till the banner of peace flutters in Europe,"[5] suddenly burst out from the crowd on the pier.

The second and third registrations took place on July 31 and October 26, 1918, with the age limit lowered to eighteen years and raised to forty-five years. Yasutarō Sōga recalled that he was forty-four years old when he received the questionnaire asking if he would join the United States Army. He went to the registration office at Punahou School with the answer "Yes."[6] In three registrations a total of 71,000 individuals registered, of whom 29,000 were Japanese nationals and Nisei. The total number of those selected for military service was 7,000, of whom 838 were Japanese nationals and Nisei.[7]

Japanese Participation in Civilian Wartime Services

The entire Japanese community in Hawaii participated vigorously in food production and conservation projects, victory bond and war savings stamp sales campaigns, relief fundraising, Red Cross activities, and other service programs.

When the United States entered the war, Hawaii was importing practically all its staple foodstuffs such as flour, wheat, meat, eggs, vegetables, and soy sauce, from the mainland. The major exception, rice, was imported from Japan. In the year preceding April 6, 1917, the day the United States declared war on Germany, Hawaii imported $10 million worth of foodstuffs. On the other hand, Hawaii exported $74 million worth of sugar and pineapple to the mainland, of which $63 million was sugar.[8] The federal government made it mandatory that Hawaii become self-sufficient in its food supply while at the same time increasing the production of sugar and pineapple to supply the needs of the mainland. Accordingly, in June 1917, the Territorial Legislature created the Food Commission to increase, conserve, regulate, and control the food supply. To serve on this commission, Governor Pinkham appointed James D. Dole, chairman, Charles G. Brockus, Frank E. Blake, Richard Ivers, Arthur K. Ozawa, and John Waterhouse. Ozawa died unexpectedly on June 22. Seven more men were added to the commission, but none was Oriental.[9] Ozawa was a son of a Gannen Mono couple from Yedo (Tokyo) and the first Nisei lawyer in Hawaii.

The Food Commission was responsible not only for increasing the production of staple foodstuffs but also for the control of the prices of these commodities. Hawaii consumed 60 million pounds of rice annually, most of which was imported from Japan; only one-fifth was raised in Hawaii. During the war years in Japan (1914–1918), young farmers were being drafted into the army and much of the rice produced was being diverted to Japanese troops stationed in the old German forts in north China and in the former German-held islands of the South Pacific, creating a shortage. Because of the shortage of rice in Japan, the Japanese government curtailed exportation of rice to Hawaii. After the rice-riot in Japan in 1917, which had to be put down by the army, Japan put an embargo on rice exportation. Consequently, the price of local rice in Hawaii rose so high that the Japanese residents complained to the Food Commission. As a result, a subcommittee of the Food Commission, made up of James Dole, John Waterhouse, Iga Mōri, Motoyuki Negoro, and Keikichi Ishida, was formed in September 1918 and given the authority to decide fair prices for staple foodstuffs such as rice, soy sauce, miso, and so on.[10]

Under the direction of Arthur L. Dean, president of the College of Hawaii, as executive officer, and consulting attorneys A. L. Castle and C. R. Hemenway, county agents on all islands, in order to expedite the program of the Food Commission, taught and supervised the raising of vegetables among all the ethnic groups. On the plantations, managers gave full cooperation for the raising of corn on unused lands for stock feed.[11] The acute shortage of food in the Allied countries and the United States required increased food rationing and rigid observance of conservation measures. Wheatless Day to encourage economizing of flour and bread, Meatless Day, Eggless Day, Porkless Day, and others were organized to help limit the consumption by individuals of specific food items. The Women's Committee of the Food Commission made special efforts to promote this nationwide program in Hawaii by speaking at schools, emphasizing the theme "Not Wasting Food," demonstrating food economy at the YWCA cafeteria, and introducing banana bread, which was adopted by the local bakeries and sold to the consumers.[12]

Liberty Bond sales among the Japanese in Hawaii were headed by Consul General Rokuro Moroi and the manager of the Yokohama Specie Bank, Seitaro Aoki. The War Savings Stamp campaign was promoted by four able men who made up the Japanese War Savings Stamp Committee. Adults and school children participated enthusiastically in these financial campaigns. The Honolulu Japanese Women's Association, founded in 1916, with the consul general's wife as its president, worked with other war service organizations of the larger community in war relief fundraising efforts as well as in the Liberty Bond campaign.[13] Japanese women also vigorously participated in Red Cross service units, making surgical dressings, hospital garments, and knitting sweaters and socks.[14] Such visible participation made them deeply conscious that they were part and parcel of the American community. The Issei women cherished their memories of participation in the wartime services of the Red Cross during World War I. This involvement was a strong underlying factor in their desire to be trusted and to participate in war service activities during World War II when their legal status became that of "enemy alien."

During and after the war, when the United States was engaged in major relief work in the war-devastated countries of Europe, the Hawaii Japanese community participated fully. For example, when the Chamber of Commerce of Honolulu sponsored fundrais-

ing for Belgian Relief, Bishop Emyo Imamura of Honpa Hongwanji Temple of Honolulu made December 18, 1918, Belgian Day
and raised $3,750 from the Buddhists in Hawaii. Such acts
demonstrated the eagerness of the Japanese immigrants to serve
the country of their adoption.[15]

Naturalization of Japanese Veterans

In May 1918, Congress enacted a special Naturalization Act to
permit any alien who served in the United States' armed forces
during World War I to acquire American citizenship by naturalization. Legal opinions were divided as to whether or not this
included Oriental veterans who were ineligible for naturalization
because of their racial background. Naturalization examiner
W. R. Ragsdale took a firm position that this special Naturalization Act was only for the benefit of those whose racial backgrounds were eligible for naturalization. He maintained that Oriental veterans were excluded from the act and that he had received
instruction from authorities in Washington to refuse the citizenship examination to those of Japanese background. However,
Judge W. Vaughan, United States district judge for the District of
Hawaii interpreted the term "any alien" in the act to include all
veterans of all races. Despite severe criticism against him for granting naturalization to nonwhite foreigners, approximately four
hundred Japanese and three hundred other Orientals were naturalized by November 14, 1919. After Judge Vaughan's six-year term
of office expired in May 1922, the territorial government announced that the naturalization of veterans who were ineligible for
naturalization because of racial background was void. In 1926,
the United States Supreme Court announced that the Naturalization Act of 1918 was inapplicable to alien Japanese. These experiences made the Japanese keenly aware of the discriminatory
nature of the naturalization law. As a result of untiring efforts by
many World War I veterans who wanted justice for all veterans of
the war, however, Congress reversed its earlier decision in 1935,
authorizing the naturalization of World War I veterans who had
been denied naturalization due to their racial backgrounds. Under
the revised act, 79 Japanese, 90 Filipinos, 19 Koreans, and 16
Chinese were naturalized again.[16]

13

Prelude to War with Japan

Rise of Militarism in Japan

THE early 1930s in Japan witnessed the rise of ultranationalism and increasing military control of the government. Using strategies that involved terrorism and the assassination of liberal statesmen, including the prime minister and several cabinet members, the military was eventually able to extend its influence over virtually all areas of government policy making. Plans were made to expand Japanese influence on the Asian mainland. In 1932, the Japanese army established the puppet state of Manchukuo in Manchuria in order to use it as a military base for the invasion of China. Yasutarō Sōga visited Manchukuo in 1934, observing that the capital, Shinkyo, was awesomely impressive but that more awesome was the enormous power of the Japanese army. He had the strange sensation that if that mighty power should be weakened, something underneath would immediately explode. There were in Manchukuo more than two thousand Japanese government officials, whose arrogance prevented them from getting along with Manchurian officials. Sōga found that from the time a visitor got to Korea, beyond Japan proper, until he left Manchukuo, he was under the surveillance of Japanese police. When Sōga arrived at the Yamato Hotel in Mukden, a member of the Tokkoka (gendarmes) called on him for interrogation.[1]

Calling its military aggression in East and later Southeast Asia a *Seisen* (holy war) to bring "co-prosperity" to the region under Japanese control, Japan justified its military expansion as a sacred mission. All means of communication—the press, radio, and even the theater and popular songs—were utilized to unite the nation to achieve this goal. Individuals and organizations with international connections or involved in the peace movement were kept under close surveillance and were later forced to suspend their activities. Anti-American and anti-British sentiments became synonymous with patriotism, because these two countries expressed the strongest opposition to Japan's military aggression in China and elsewhere. Foreigners, including Nisei, were watched closely on suspicion of being American spies. Visitors from Hawaii, even Issei, were subjected to surveillance. If they took snapshots of scenic shorelines they would be interrogated and their film confiscated. One such visitor was the Rev. Takie Okumura, who was in Japan in the early 1930s on a trip given to him by the members of the Makiki Christian Church in Honolulu in appreciation for his long ministry.[2]

The assassinations of liberal statesmen and businessmen who were anti-military continued with alarming frequency. The so-called 226 Incident (February 26 assassinations) was planned by young military officers to carry out the assassinations of liberal, anti-military government officials and political leaders. They invaded the residence of each of these people and killed him right in front of his family. Commuters to Tokyo that morning saw the extraordinary sight of a division of soldiers on the grounds outside the Imperial Palace and policemen directing the civilians to make a detour.[3] Because of the strict control of the press and other media, it took considerable time for people in Japan outside of Tokyo to learn about this incident. The *Nippu Jiji,* however, received a detailed account immediately from its correspondent in Tokyo. Soga later recalled:

> We published the news of this incident in detail and sent copies of our paper to our subscribers in various parts of Japan. This caused investigation of our subscribers by the police, and as a result a considerable number of our subscribers in Japan wrote, asking us to stop sending our paper to them. Since that time, any one of our staff who went to Japan even on private business such as visiting his ailing kin was subjected to interrogation by the police at the hotel in Yokohama.[4]

Japanese subjects visiting in America were also closely watched. For example, Miss Ikuko Koizumi, a well-known educator, who was attending the Third Pan Pacific Women's Conference in

Honolulu in August 1934, criticized militarism in Japan in her speech. Before landing in Yokohama, she received an alarming wireless message from her kin warning her about possible danger. Fortunately, she was able to slip off of the ship unnoticed because of the large crowd at the dock to welcome Prince and Princess Kayo, who were returning to Japan on the same ship, and the strict security measures taken to protect the entourage.[5]

The trouble experienced by Rev. Yasuzo Shimizu was mentioned in an earlier chapter. When in Hawaii and Los Angeles in 1940 to raise money for his school in Peking, China, Shimizu in his public speech had commented on the atrocities committed by Japanese troops in China. He was arrested by the military authorities when he returned to Japan. The funds he raised for his school were eventually turned over to the the military and he was released.

Americans in Japan, including a large number of missionaries most of whom had spent decades in Japan, were required to leave by the Japanese government. A few who had married Japanese took their spouses' family names and were "adopted." One adoption was that of Florence Denton who devoted fifty years in Japan to the education of Japanese women as a member of the Department of Home Economics of the Doshisha University in Kyoto. Miss Denton, then eighty-three years old, was very ill and in no condition to travel to the United States where she had no relatives to take care of her. The Mikimoto family, famous for its pearl industry, "adopted" her and thus she became legally a daughter of the Mikimoto family. Many returned missionaries were assigned to Hawaii. Their services were invaluable during World War II because of their fluency in the Japanese language as well as their intimate knowledge of the Japanese people.

The War News from Japan

The important news of Japan, which came by way of Domei News Agency in the 1930s, was on the military aggression in China by the Japanese army: bombing, destruction of cities and towns, killing of thousands of civilians, maiming and capturing many times more, pushing the governments of the eastern cities and towns to the remote western provinces. Millions of Chinese were forced to

evacuate from their homes to trek to unknown western provinces.[6] Reading the *Nippu Jiji,* one was shocked by accounts of the
massacres and other atrocities perpetrated by the invading Japanese troops. Each time the Japanese army destroyed a city, it
announced a victory. Since the atrocities had been reported in the
English-language papers whose sources were American correspondents stationed in China, the news that appeared in the *Nippu Jiji*
was not novel to the larger community. Sōga observed that the
Japanese army must have expected to be through with its China
campaign within a few months. But the resistance on the part of
the Chinese army was strong and the Chinese were determined to
fight back even if they had to retreat further into the interior. The
Japanese army was dragged farther and farther inland.[7]

On September 23, 1937, Dr. Hu Shih of the Nanking government, a philosopher and former president of Peking University,
stopped in Honolulu on his way to Washington, D.C., as the
ambassador from China. That evening the Institute of Pacific
Relations gave a dinner party in his honor at the Oahu Country
club. In his greeting he said,

> In the United States, both the government and the people under-
> stand the situation in China fully well. Therefore, there is no need for
> me to explain it. The Chinese people, different from the earlier years,
> are deeply aware of their country as a nation and are confident that
> they would never yield to any foreign enemy. We take advantage of our
> superior geographical situation. No matter how hard Japan attacks
> us, it will be a waste of energy for them. . . .[8]

The majority of the Issei never believed that their old country
would ever engage in acts of atrocity in China or anywhere. All of
the Issei who came to Hawaii before July 1, 1924, had memories
of peaceful villages and towns. Although the Japanese vernacular
papers published the news of the military coup d'état and the 226
Incident, such political upheavals were beyond their grasp. Their
relatives in Japan could not write to them because of the censorship of all mail outgoing to and incoming from foreign countries.
That the new nation Manchukuo was a creation of the Japanese
military clique and why it was created was little known or understood by the Issei. They knew nothing about the fact that the presence of the Japanese army in Manchuria was a provocation to the
Chinese army guarding the borders with China, which resulted in

armed conflict in 1931 and provided a good excuse for the Japanese invasion of China proper. All that the Issei were aware of was that their old country was at war with China and in need of help from them. The Issei bought Japan's patriotic bonds, sent money, sent *imon bukuro* or comfort kits containing candies, cookies, medicine, thread and needles, soap, toothpaste, pencils, paper, and other items to soldiers or civilians by way of the Japanese consulate. The popular war songs such as "Shina no Yoru" ("A Night in China") and "Shanghai Musume" ("Maidens of Shanghai") that blasted daily from music stores on North King Street and other Japanese areas implied that Japan's military expansion in China was successful. The war in China was still a far away affair for the Issei in Hawaii.

Naval Training Ships

Japanese naval vessels had called regularly at Honolulu since 1876. From October 18 to 23, 1939, two training ships, *Iwate* and *Yakumo,* each with about two hundred aboard, called at Honolulu. The *Star-Bulletin* reported the activities of the visiting officers, cadets and crews: sightseeing in Honolulu on October 19; a military review in honor of the visiting officers and cadets at Schofield Barracks on October 20; an all day around-the-island trip on October 21; a reception honoring the visiting crews and officers at the Japanese consulate from 11:00 A.M. to 6:00 P.M. on Sunday. None of the above events was mentioned in the *Nippu Jiji* except the Schofield review. Acting Consul General Binjiro Kudo asked the nineteen prefectural groups or Kenjin-kai to welcome the crews of the visiting ships. Each Kenjin-kai decided to welcome those of the same prefectural background. As early as October 10 each Kenjin-kai published its plan along with its members' names and even pictures in the vernacular papers. When the training ships arrived, the Japanese in rural communities disregarded their prefectural differences. Waialua Japanese gave a luncheon at the sugar plantation's gymnasium, and Waipahu Japanese gave a community welcome party. In Honolulu, different prefectural groups gave a similar program, including a Sumo tournament between the guests and the Issei hosts. The training ships left for Hilo late on October 23.

On the last day, October 29, a serious incident took place in Hilo. Crew member Mario Sato of the *Yakumo* deserted his ship. Sato was born in Peru and was a Peruvian citizen. His father was born in Gunma-ken, Japan. Sato had not given up his Japanese citizenship but had dual citizenship. He could speak Spanish and English very well, but his Japanese was poor. In 1937, while he was studying in Japan, he was drafted into the Japanese navy. When the *Yakumo* was about to sail from Hilo to the South Pacific and Japan, Sato left the ship. The *Yakumo* sailed without him. After several days, he was found in the home of a Caucasian. The Japanese consulate in Honolulu referred his case to the Japanese Embassy in Washington, D.C., which requested Sato's extradition. After repeated negotiations, the American government decided to treat this case simply as a violation of the immigration law of the United States and notified him that he was permitted to return to Peru by paying his own passage. Some Caucasians in Hilo raised money for his fare, and he returned to Peru via the United States mainland.[9]

Participation in Japan's 2600th Anniversary

In November 1940, Japan commemorated the 2600th anniversary of the founding of the Japanese nation. To mark this occasion, Japan decided to hold an overseas Japanese convention and invited Japanese in twenty-eight countries, including North and South America, Asia, Southeast Asia, and the Pacific to participate in an exhibition of items of the countries in which they resided from November 1 to 15 on the 8th floor of Takashimaya Department Store in Tokyo. Hawaii agreed to participate and through the Honolulu Japanese Chamber of Commerce, twenty-five items from groups and individuals were sent to Japan. The most popular display from Hawaii was that of the Honolulu Japanese Contractors' Association, which was made up of 130 members. They sent large pictures of the buildings they had built such as the Makiki Christian Church (a replica of Himeji Castle), Honpa Hongwanji Temple, the Makiki Jodo Sect Temple, the Japanese Hospital (Kuakini), the Japanese consulate, moving picture theaters, and residential houses for Caucasians and Japanese. In addition, the Contractors' Association sent samples of Hawaiian trees such as

milo, koa, ohia, monkey pod, and kamani, along with a description of each tree. Besides exhibits, there were evening lectures and
movies of different countries where overseas Japanese lived. There
were also sightseeing, Kabuki theater parties, a memorial service
for those who had passed away at Tsukiji Hongwanji Temple, a
reception by the mayor of Tokyo, and other activities. Of about
2,000 overseas Japanese attending this commemorative affair,
about 300 went from Hawaii.[10]

Strained Relations with Japan

After Manchukuo was created by Japan as an independent nation,
the League of Nations dispatched in 1932 a commission headed by
Victor A. G. R. Lytton to investigate the situation and to advise
Japan to place Manchukuo under an international commission.
Japan rejected the League of Nations' advice and all efforts by the
United States, Great Britain, Canada, and other nations to stop its
invasion of China as foreign interference, while at the same time
increasing its war activities in China. In March 1933, Japan
resigned from the League of Nations. In the meantime, there was
an increased exchange of good will among Japan, Germany, and
Italy, resulting in the signing of the Triple Alliance in Berlin on September 27, 1940. During these years of tense relations between the
West and Japan, individual Americans and British continued to
visit Japan. Among such individuals were Charles S. Chaplin in
1932, George Bernard Shaw in 1933, and Helen A. Keller in
1937. These famous people were eagerly received by the Japanese
people and Japanese government. The Japan Amateur Athletic
Association participated in the International Olympic Games at
Los Angeles in 1932, and in 1936, it was decided that the next
Olympic Games would be held in Tokyo. Thus, peacetime activities continued regardless of the political atmosphere.

Fiftieth Anniversary of Contract Labor Immigration

The most significant celebration of the Japanese community was
the fiftieth anniversary of the arrival of the first government contract immigrants in 1935. A total of 1,928 arrived in 1885,

namely, 945 aboard the *City of Tokyo* arrived on February 8 and 983 aboard the *Yamashiro Maru* arrived on June 17. Sixty-seven of them were still living on Hawaii, Maui, Molokai, Lanai, and Kauai as well as Oahu. In Honolulu a grand celebration was held on February 17 on the big grounds of the Japanese Consulate on Nuuanu Street. Hoisted high above the Consulate building were the American and Japanese flags. About 10,000 people filled the grounds. Before 10 A.M., 31 first contract immigrants were led by kimono-clad Nisei girls to the platform and were seated and given leis. They were followed by Consul General Teijiro Tamura, Governor Joseph B. Poindexter, B. H. Wells of the Hawaii Sugar Planters' Association, and Wilfred C. Tsukiyama, attorney for the City and County of Honolulu, representing Nisei. At 10 A.M. Miyozuchi Komeya, the chairman of the celebration committee, opened the ceremony with "Hawaii Ponoi" played by the band.

After greetings by the Consul General and Governor Poindexter, the Consul General presented the 31 first government contract immigrants silver wine mugs and Shichinosuke Miki thanked them on behalf of the recipients. Three cheers of *banzai* were followed by the national anthems of the United States and Japan played by the band. From 11:30 to 3:15 P.M. those present enjoyed all kinds of entertainment.

Nippu Jiji published a special edition, and its editor, Soga, noted:

> All over the Hawaiian Islands there are small Japanese cemeteries with a large number of old grave-posts. In many cases even the grave-posts have disappeared. . . . That the Japanese in Hawaii assisted vastly in the development of the industries of all the islands and made a great contribution to the community is attested by the facts and admitted by everyone. . . . They withstood every difficulty and made every sacrifice. There may be many failures and mistakes in what they have done, but on the whole they have overcome all their disadvantages and brought up the second generation the way they are today. . . . The first generation is passing and the second generation is coming to the fore.

Nisei as Members of the Larger Community

By the 1930s there was already a growing number of mature Nisei involved in business and professional activities. They operated as members of the larger community. Beginning in 1922, Nisei regularly ran for political office and depended on votes from people of all racial and ethnic backgrounds. They competed as Republicans and Democrats for seats in the Territorial Legislature and county councils.

In 1935 when the Japanese community observed the fiftieth anniversary of the arrival of the first contract immigrants to Hawaii, Governor Joseph B. Poindexter commented on the civic participation of the descendants of those pioneers, stating, "They are a very part and parcel of our community . . . our government, our institutions."[11] Because of their intimate participation in the larger community, Nisei tended to hold the same critical view of Japan's increasing military aggression as that of the general public.

In Hawaii the antagonism toward the Japanese and suspicion of the loyalty of the American citizens of Japanese ancestry existed as an undercurrent rather than as publicly sanctioned hostility. There was no solid collective attitude toward the Japanese. Those who had less contact with the Japanese as employees or friends had a stereotyped image of them. It happened that those who knew the Japanese more intimately were the more numerous and politically and socially influential segments of the dominant white community. They defended the loyalty of the Hawaii-born Nisei.

As relations between Japan and the United States became increasingly strained, the issue of the loyalty of the Japanese in Hawaii became one of national importance in terms of defense. Many community leaders as well as Hawaii's delegate to Congress were swamped with such questions as: "What about the Japanese in case of war with Japan?" The *Honolulu Advertiser,* March 23, 1941, published a long statement by Samuel W. King, Hawaii's delegate to Congress, defending the local Japanese. In confronting the so-called "Japanese problem in Hawaii," King pointed out that only about 35,000 people of both sexes, some 8 percent of the total population, whose ages ranged from fifty years up, were "Japanese" in the sense of being aliens. And they were "aliens," he noted, because the United States had denied them the privilege of naturalization. He went on to say that of the "122,000 citizens of Japanese race in Hawaii, . . . at least 50,000 are children in age range from infancy to about sixteen years, of both sexes, most of whom are attending school. They are native-born citizens of native-born parents, being in fact third-generation residents of

Hawaii." He asserted that anyone who could believe that Japanese-Americans could retain any loyalty to Japan after having been brought up in an American environment belittled the value of American institutions and the benefits American democracy offers to the individual. He ended with an exhortation: "I sincerely believe our newspapers and our leaders in public affairs would be rendering a patriotic service if they would join together in a definite change of front toward these citizens, think of them as one would men of Italian, or German, or any other European ancestry, and treat them as individuals, according to their merit, without continually harping on race."

Preparation for War with Japan

As war with Japan became imminent, apprehension grew in the larger community concerning the Japanese residents. It was of particular importance for those responsible for internal security to have some means of assessing the conduct of the Japanese as well as the rest of Hawaii's cosmopolitan population in the event of war. As early as eighteen months prior to the Pearl Harbor attack, Robert L. Shivers, the newly arrived chief of the Hawaii office of the Federal Bureau of Investigation, began to make plan to determine if there was any reason for suspicion concerning the loyalty of the local Japanese. He observed the situation in Hawaii in 1939 as being very complex, with

> one-third of the total population being of Japanese extraction, the presence of people (Filipinos, Koreans, and Chinese) whose homeland had long been or would surely come under the heels of the Japanese Army, in the event of a war in the Pacific, and the undercurrent of suspicion and growing fear of the behavior of the Japanese population in Hawaii. It was readily apparent that unless all the racial groups were held together and worked together as a united community in a common effort . . . it would be most difficult . . . to maintain the internal security of these islands and free the Army and Navy for their main task of prosecuting the war against the enemy without the necessity of using a part of their forces in maintaining order behind the lines among the civilian populace. A united front in this complex, cosmopolitan community was vitally necessary for the successful prosecution of the war in this theater.[12]

Shivers secured first the cooperation of the leaders of the larger community who knew the local Japanese intimately. Through their assistance, leading Nisei whose loyalty to the United States was unquestioned were carefully selected to form two advisory groups in April and June 1940, one meeting with him, the other meeting with his agent. In meetings held weekly or oftener at his residence, he and his Nisei group together thrashed out controversial matters, including the religious and secular institutions and organizations and business enterprises, and evaluated the leaders among the Japanese. They discussed the loyalty of both the Issei and Nisei as well as the Kibei and how to best maintain the morale of the Japanese community in case of war.[13] Shivers reported the findings of these meetings: "As these surveys progressed, it became increasingly apparent that there was no reason to question the loyalty of the citizens of Japanese ancestry, except for a small number of Kibeis who constituted about one-third of one percent of the citizen population. It was also very clear after these surveys had been completed that a very small percentage of the alien Japanese in the Hawaiian Islands would be actively disloyal to the United States in the event of war between this country and Japan."[14]

Other precautionary efforts were aimed at the Filipinos who were living in close proximity with the Japanese in the plantation communities, because their homeland would surely be invaded by Japan. Special consideration was also given to the Koreans whose homeland had been under the yoke of Japan since 1910, and the Chinese whose homeland had been ravaged by the Japanese army for the past ten years. These groups were apprised of the loyalty of the majority of the Japanese and were advised not to take the law into their own hands but to trust the authorities to handle all subversive activities. Leaders from all the ethnic groups were asked to cooperate with the authorities in effecting these policies and to help their respective groups to remain calm in case of war. There was also an organized effort for interracial cooperation in the form of the Committee for Interracial Unity.

The Committee for Interracial Unity

This committee was the outgrowth of a meeting of representatives of various ethnic groups called by an American of Chinese ancestry, Hung Wai Ching, in December 1940, almost a year before Pearl Harbor, to discuss how to combat the growing resentment against those of Japanese background because of Japan's expanding military aggression. Since a war with Japan, which was beginning to seem inevitable, would severely strain the pattern of racial harmony traditional in Hawaii, the committee wanted to prepare the community for that eventuality. Following a series of preliminary organizational meetings, an interracial steering committee was set up that included key civilian leaders from the business and professional community as well as the heads of the military intelligence services and the local branch of the FBI. Robert L. Shivers was selected chairman of the committee.[15]

The committee, according to Shivers, was interested not only in the immediate problems of defense in the event of war, but also in what would happen after the war. If the people of various ethnic backgrounds could live harmoniously during the war, it was reasoned, then a basis for a good relationships would have been established for the future.[16] The committee formulated a set of guiding principles by which to achieve a united citizenry and the preservation of Hawaii's human relationships. The committee agreed to:

1. Feel that Hawaii has something unique and worthwhile to preserve in the way of human relationships.
2. Accept the idea that a united citizenry is essential to our defense.
3. Have faith in the American way of life and be willing to protect it.
4. Place absolute reliance in our constituted authorities, confident that they will treat everyone with equal fairness and see to it that he is so treated by his fellow citizens, and that everyone acting in any way inimical to the general welfare will be promptly and severely dealt with. There is no need for and there must not be any vigilanteism on the part of any group.
5. Overcome fear—fear on the part of the nationals of those countries with which we might become involved in a war that they will be mistreated and persecuted, and fear on the part of the rest of the people that these particular aliens might actively assist our enemies.
6. Develop a sense of personal responsibility to do everything

possible to make Hawaii and the entire nation strong militarily and otherwise. This includes the aliens who must accept the fact that they owe a certain obligation to the land in which they are now living and that they will be protected and allowed to enjoy all normal privileges only as long as they obey our laws and conduct themselves constructively.

7. Be willing to give every loyal citizen, regardless of race, a place in the scheme of national defense. No group should be denied the opportunity to do its share merely because of racial considerations.

8. Remember that loyalty grows only when it is given a chance to grow. It does not flourish in an atmosphere of suspicion, discrimination, and denial of opportunities to practice that loyalty.[17]

The members of the Steering Committee contacted the governor of the Territory of Hawaii and the mayor of the City and County of Honolulu as well as civic, business, and leaders of various ethnic groups on Oahu and the other islands to implement these principles. The meetings, which were held throughout the islands, were announced in the vernacular as well as the English-language papers.[18] Thus, the civilian population of Hawaii was well-prepared for the eventuality of war with Japan.

The Oahu Citizens for Home Defense

Another committee, the Oahu Citizens for Home Defense, was organized by Shivers early in 1941 with a wider range of trusted Nisei leaders. Its purposes were:

1. To work with the constituted authorities in continuing the task of evaluating what went on in the Japanese community.

2. To plan for and carry out the task of bringing out more positively the inherent loyalty of the Americans of Japanese ancestry to the United States.

3. To prepare the Japanese community psychologically for their responsibilities toward the United States in the event of war and for the difficult position in which the war would place them in their relationship with the rest of the community.[19]

This committee sponsored a "Patriotic Rally" in the McKinley High School auditorium in Honolulu on June 13, 1941, with some two thousand citizens and aliens of Japanese ancestry and two-hundred invited guests of other national or ethnic groups present to hear Colonel M. W. Marston, then assistant chief of staff for Military Intelligence, deliver a message on behalf of Lt. General Walter C. Short, then commanding general of the Hawaiian Department, U.S. Army. The importance of this gathering was described by Shivers:

> He enunciated publicly for the first time the official attitude of the U.S. Army toward those of Japanese ancestry, both citizens and aliens, in the event of war, and urged people of all races to place their trust in the constituted authorities and refrain from any acts which might disrupt the united citizenry and place the Army in the position of having to enforce peace and order in the civilian community. He promised just treatment for all citizens, regardless of racial ancestry; swift and severe punishment for any and all those acts which are detrimental to the welfare of the United States; and fair treatment to the aliens of Japanese ancestry in the event of war so long as they conducted themselves in a manner uninimical to the United States. This meeting helped immeasurably to allay much of the fear and insecurity which were then developing in this community as the war clouds gathered more ominously over the Pacific. It also provided some definite and clear-cut criteria to guide the behavior of the Japanese as well as the rest of the community in event of war.[20]

14

The Japanese Community during World War II

ON December 7, 1941, the residents of Oahu, both Honolulu and rural areas, were awakened from their Sunday morning slumber by the terrific sound of explosives at about 7:00 A.M. The usual Sunday morning Hawaiian melodies on the radio were suddenly interrupted by the announcement that Oahu was under attack. To convince the listeners who began to call up the radio stations, the announcer repeated such statements as "This is no maneuver. This is the real McCoy"; "Do not use your telephone"; "Keep calm"; "The United States Army Intelligence has ordered that all civilians stay off the streets"; "Take cover"; and "Keep your radio turned on for further instructions," along with a number of urgent official announcements. Finally, the announcer indicated that a rising sun insignia had been sighted on the enemy planes attacking Pearl Harbor. Dr. Forrest J. Pinkerton, director of the Blood Bank at the Queen's Hospital, appealed to the citizenry to donate blood. All doctors, including those of Japanese ancestry, were requested by name to report to various hospitals. The University of Hawaii and high school ROTC units were called to active duty immediately. Later that day they were formed into the new Hawaii Territorial Guard with 35 officers and 370 men and sent to guard strategic locations and important installations. Older Boy Scouts were assembled to assist various rescue operations. At 4:25 P.M. it was announced that martial law had been established, with Major General Walter C. Short, commanding general of the Hawaiian Department, as military governor of Hawaii. General Short's proclamation was repeated twice, once in English and once in Japanese for the benefit of the alien Japanese residents.[1]

General Order no. 5, issued on December 8, was specifically directed to the alien Japanese, ordering them to refrain from active

215

hostility or giving information or comfort to the enemy; forbidding them to possess or to use contraband such as firearms, weapons, or explosives of any sort, radio transmitting sets, signal devices, codes or ciphers, cameras, or graphic representations of any United States military installation or equipment; and prohibiting them to travel by air, change their residence or occupation, or move from place to place without permission. At the same time they were assured that:

> So long as they [the Japanese] shall conduct themselves in accordance with law, they shall be undisturbed in the peaceful pursuit of their lives and occupations and be accorded the consideration due to all peaceful and law-abiding persons, except so far as restrictions may be necessary for their own protection and for the safety of the United States. All citizens of the United States are enjoined to preserve the peace and to treat them with all such friendliness as may be compatible with loyalty and allegiance to the United States.[2]

A few days later the assistant chief of staff for Military Intelligence, Col. Kendall G. Fielder, spoke on behalf of the military governor, stressing the importance of unity among the citizenry, urging residents to trust the constituted authorities to handle all subversive cases and not to take the law into their own hands, and at the same time indicating that there would be just and humane treatment of the Japanese.[3]

Subsequent restrictions prohibited aliens to buy or sell liquor, to be employed in restricted areas without permission, or to be at large during the blackout. Foreign-language broadcasts were discontinued and the Japanese vernacular press was temporarily suspended; it was resumed on January 8, 1942, to inform the alien Japanese of the news and military orders. Also, gatherings of aliens were forbidden and all foreign institutions such as the language schools, including the Chinese language schools as well as the Buddhist and Shinto temples, were closed.[4] The newspapers carried the official announcement on December 8 that all unidentified boats approaching Oahu would be fired upon. Fishermen who had been at sea for several days knew nothing of the Pearl Harbor attack and were unaware of this announcement. Several of them were killed or seriously wounded or picked up and taken for internment.[5]

The Reactions of the Japanese Residents to the Attack

The Japanese population, both the Issei and the Nisei, were completely stunned by the sneak attack on Hawaii by Japan. Keenly aware of being identified racially with the enemy who had committed this unpardonable crime, the Japanese were afraid of reprisals from the other residents and punishment from the authorities. The first and foremost reaction of every resident of Japanese extraction was "What an awful mess they [Japanese planes] have made for us!" They expressed disgust and dismay, as the following examples of their reactions indicate:

"Of all places, why did they come to Hawaii? What an awful mess they made for us! I am simply disgusted."
"I don't care which way they go, but I don't want them to come to Hawaii. I just don't want them here."
"How on earth did they get here? Why didn't the American planes chase them away or destroy them right away? I can't understand. They shouldn't have been allowed to linger around so long as they did."[6]

Yasutarō Sōga recalled his immediate reaction to the attack:

The Japanese attack on Pearl Harbor was utterly unexpected. Although the relation between Japan and the United States was increasingly strained toward the end of 1941, all of us Japanese in Hawaii thought that there would be some way out ultimately, never dreaming that it would lead to war. . . . Therefore, on the morning of December 7, I was relaxed in my kimono and reading magazines on the porch of our house, as I used to do on Sundays. I think it was shortly after 9:00 A.M. that one of our staff called me up, telling me that Japanese planes attacked Pearl Harbor and that a war seemed to have started. I told him, "How could there be such utter nonsense! It must be a maneuver." Thus, I completely ignored what he said. Feeling somehow uneasy, however, I turned on the radio. Already both KGU and KGMB were broadcasting the war news. . . .

I listened to the radio as if I were sucked toward it in spite of my disbelief of the news. Numerous orders were being issued one after another by the announcer. Among them was the order calling the names of each individual doctor, including the names of several Nisei doctors, to report immediately to such and such hospital. . . . It was also announced that the authorities had apprehended some Japanese. . . . In the meantime, a telephone call came from the head of a surgical dressing unit of the American Red Cross to my wife, telling her that the surgical dressing units would meet oftener instead of once a week and that she must report tomorrow. The instruction included an order that no other language but English was to be used in the surgical dressing room. . . .[7]

Ted Tsukiyama, a Nisei, wrote about his memories of that day many years later:

We couldn't sleep that fateful Sunday morning because of the constant rumbling of thunder. Going outside, we saw the sky black with smoke punctuated by puffs of aerial bursts. I thought that they're sure making this maneuver look real. Turning on the radio we heard the announcer screaming "Take cover, get off the streets! This is the real thing!" I was benumbed. I could not comprehend. Suddenly I clearly heard the announcer say, "All members of the University ROTC report to your campus units immediately!" I jumped into my ROTC uniform and rushed up to the university campus to the ROTC barracks . . . as we were trained to do, just like any other soldier or sailor reporting to his battle station. . . .

There were reports that Japanese paratroopers had landed on St. Louis Heights. Our orders were to deploy and meet the enemy and delay their advance into the city. . . . As we thought of the sneak attack that morning, a wave of fury and anger swept over us. There was no doubt or indecision as we advanced. It was going to be either them or us. But fortunately, the enemy never showed.[8]

Hideo Naito, an alien, then a cook at the Royal Hawaiian Hotel kitchen, remembered:

Since I worked in every kind of food preparation, I became the head cook, although I was the only Japanese. When the war started, we could not get what we wanted. So, we fed our hotel guests with hamburger sandwiches. It was blackout at night. We had only one candle light in the kitchen. We were only three, so we got helpers from the other departments of the Royal Hawaiian Hotel. The hotel administration gave our names to the Red Cross. So, as soon as the war started, the Red Cross gave each of us an armband with the Red Cross mark. The first night of the war we worked until about two after midnight. It was blackout and there was no bus to go home on. I walked from the hotel in Waikiki to my home in Liliha at that hour. There were guards posted along the streets. As I walked, the guard would shout "Halt" and stop me. Then, I would shout, "Red Cross Emergency Aid!" Then, he passed me, shouting to the next guard, "Red Cross Emergency Aid!" That was how I returned home that first night.[9]

The Detention of Leaders of the Japanese Community

The apprehension of potentially dangerous Japanese started immediately. Included in this group were the Japanese consular staff and agents, Shinto and Buddhist priests, Japanese language school principals, and prominent leaders in the Japanese community, who were mostly successful businessmen and professional men such as physicians, journalists, and publishers. Less important but active members of various Japanese organizations were also taken into custody. Some Christian ministers in the rural communities were considered agents of the Japanese consulate because of their assistance to rural residents in such matters as filling out the forms for expatriation of Japanese citizenship for Nisei who had dual citizenship or in obtaining passports when the Issei wanted to visit Japan, and they, too, were detained.

By the end of the first day 482 persons were in custody on Oahu; 370 Japanese as well as 98 Germans and 14 Italians.[10] The chief of the Honolulu office of FBI, Robert L. Shivers, reported that 1,441 persons of Japanese ancestry were eventually detained. Of this number, 879 were aliens, of whom 301 were subsequently released or paroled. The number of American citizens taken into custody came to 534, of whom 160 were later released. Of this group, 468 were Kibei and 28 were expatriated citizens. Altogether 980 Japanese were sent to internment camps on the U.S. mainland, and later about 1,000 dependents, mostly their wives and teenage and younger children, joined them.[11] Shivers reported that the overwhelming majority of the citizen group was loyal to the United States, and if there was disloyalty among the alien Japanese who remained at large, that disloyalty was never translated into action against the United States.

In February 1942, Swedish Vice-Consul Gustaf W. Olsen took over the Japanese consulate to transact the affairs of the Japanese government in Hawaii. He visited the internees and also made periodic inspections of the prisoner-of-war compounds and of hospitals where wounded Japanese prisoners were being treated. He notified relatives in Japan of the deaths of Japanese nationals and made arrangements for care of their estates. The Territorial Department of Public Welfare gave financial assistance to five hundred to six hundred dependents of the internees during the early part of 1942. After August 1942, the federal funds of the War Assistance Program became available to enemy aliens and others who had been affected by government actions. This program spent $75,290 for the care of 1,020 individuals. Also, the American Red Cross and the American Friends Service Committee assisted the internees' dependents in solving various pressing problems, including employment.[12]

Rumors

During the very early stage of the war, because of the immediate danger confronting everybody, the Issei and the Nisei did their part along with the general population of Hawaii. They answered every call of emergency. They donated blood. Nisei defense workers actually fought the enemy during the attack, helped to take care of the victims, fought fires, and cleared damaged areas. Nisei women as well as some of the Issei women went to work in their respective Red Cross units on December 7. The danger of enemy raids was so overwhelming that everybody participated in whatever way he could in defense of the islands. As one Issei said, "When the ship is on fire, all those on it forget race and blood and pull together to extinguish it, or else they would all perish." After the first hectic week was over, however, the Hawaiian community found itself infested with rumors purporting to explain the suddenness and ease with which the enemy inflicted such major damage on the Hawaiian defense and throwing suspicion on the Japanese residents of Hawaii. The following are examples of the kind of talk circulating in the community:

"One of the Japanese fliers shot down on December 7 had a McKinley High School ring on his finger."
"Japanese residents waved their kimono and signaled to the Japanese fliers."
"An arrow-shaped sign was cut in the cane fields to direct the Japanese fliers to Pearl Harbor."

"Some Japanese sent radio signals to the Japanese fleet and assisted their attack on Hawaii."

"A barber in Wahiawa was a Japanese spy and he got all the military information from his army customers and sent it to Japan on his secret transmitter. He was shot to death by MPs at his home on December 7."

A big headline in the *Honolulu Advertiser* on December 8, "Saboteurs Land Here," and the statement by secretary of the navy Frank Knox after his brief investigation in Hawaii that Hawaii had been subjected to the most effective fifth column activities since the invasion of Norway by Germany reinforced the suspicion on the part of the general public toward the Japanese and intensified the uneasiness on the part of both the Issei and the Nisei. Every rumor, however, was checked by the army's Intelligence Office and the FBI and officially denied by way of radio and the press; in general these denials were accepted by the public. However, the widespread distrust of the Japanese resulted in the dismissal of Nisei defense workers in strategic areas. When the reports of their dismissal from nonmilitary employment circulated, however, both the Issei and the Nisei became deeply apprehensive about their fate.

The Official Policy of the War Years

Regardless of the rumors and suspicion and antagonism toward the Japanese on the part of the larger community, the official policy of the military government as well as that of the civilian leaders was to maintain the traditional Hawaiian race relations intact throughout the war years. Their directives and administrative actions were in accordance with this policy. The fact that this policy was consistently followed was exceedingly reassuring to the Issei as well as the Nisei, who were in no less a precarious position than the Issei because of their racial kinship with the enemy. The official policy of interracial unity was stressed in the first greeting to the people of Hawaii by Lt. General Delos C. Emmons, who succeeded General Short as military governor of Hawaii and commander of the Hawaiian Department after he arrived in the islands around mid-December. *The Honolulu Star-Bulletin* published it on December 22, 1941, in part as follows:

Fellow citizens of Hawaii: The past two weeks have been eventful ones. We have seen these beautiful islands transformed . . . into a powerful military base which is throwing its complete strength into this war. Hawaii has always been an American outpost of friendliness and good will and now has calmly accepted its responsibility as an American outpost of war. In accepting these responsibilities it is important that Hawaii prove that her traditional confidence in her cosmopolitan population has not been misplaced. . . . This message . . . is not intended as a morale booster, for such is not necessary. Morale is high and it will remain so if we will continue, as nearly as practicable, with our normal activities. . . .

There should be no unnecessary curtailment of normal activities in these islands. The work of the community must go on. There must not be indiscriminate displacement of labor. In this connection, it has come to our attention that many people have been dismissed from private employment because of fear and suspicion on the part of their employers. I wish to emphasize the fact that if the courage of the people of these islands is to be maintained and the morale of the entire population sustained, we cannot afford to unnecessarily and indiscriminately keep a number of loyal workers from useful employment. Let me suggest to you that if there is any doubt concerning any individual who may be employed by you at this time, that you check with the constituted authorities before taking action. It is gratifying to learn that some who were summarily discharged have been reemployed.

Additional investigation and apprehensions will be made and possibly additional suspects will be placed in custodial detention, but their friends and relatives need have no fear that they are mistreated. These people are not prisoners of war and will not be treated as such. I intend, very shortly, to permit an inspection of detained aliens to be made by representative citizens and aliens in order that the public may be reassured as to the treatment those detained are receiving. . . . There is no intention or desire on the part of the Federal authorities to operate mass concentration camps. No person, be he citizen or alien, need worry, provided he is not connected with subversive elements.

Let me reiterate the necessity for pulling together. While we have been subjected to a serious attack by a ruthless and treacherous enemy, we must remember that this is America and we must do things the American way. We must distinguish between loyalty and disloyalty among our people. Sometimes this is difficult to do, especially under the stress of war. However, we must not knowingly and deliberately deny any loyal citizen the opportunity to exercise or demonstrate his loyalty in a concrete way.

The Territory of Hawaii is not new to me for I have lived here for over two years, and have a wide acquaintanceship among the various races. I feel that I know the people here, their loyalty to the American way of life and the extent to which they can be counted on to help our mutual defense.

Yasutarō Sōga recalled how the treatment of the detainees changed after General Emmons took command:

When going to the toilet at night the guard standing in the pitch dark always challenged us, shouting, "Halt." We were required to respond instantly, saying "Prisoner," otherwise we would be shot to death. . . . Newly appointed commander of the Hawaiian Department Lt. General Delos C. Emmons came to Sand Island for an inspection about December 20, 1941, soon after his arrival. . . . On December 22 his subordinate officer came and spoke to us all. He said, "You are neither criminals nor prisoners. You are merely detainees. Consequently, there is no need for you to be controlled by military rules. It will be sufficient if you show your respect when our national flag is being lowered at sunset. . . ."[13]

The actions of the Department of Public Instruction gave Japanese residents further official reassurance. The public schools were reopened a month after the Pearl Harbor attack. The superintendent of the Department of Public Instruction, Oren E. Long, wrote a letter on January 10, 1942, instructing all the principals and teachers about their responsibilities in wartime.

We are opening school under conditions that are different from any we have ever before experienced. In the first place, we are at war with Japan, another world power of the Pacific area. We live in a combat zone of that war. This means that everything we do and say—even our very thinking—will be affected by war conditions. . . . For the consideration and possible guidance of each of you, the following criteria are set forth:
1. *You are primarily a teacher.* Your relationships and contacts throughout the community must be those of an *American teacher.* In addition to your other responsibilities, you must assume that of building understanding and morale. Everything you do and say must more than ever be ruled by reason and logic. *All* prejudices *must* be submerged and under no circumstances appear in action or speech.
2. The children of the community are your major responsibility. To calm and reassure them is both your privilege and duty. Of necessity, your contacts with children will mean also contacts with their homes. In all of these contacts, you must be a *builder of morale.*

224 The Impact of War

3. You face the greatest challenge you have ever faced—a challenge to constructive and helpful leadership. Teachers not only *can* do more than any other group to bolster the morale of children and parents, but they *must* do more. There is no place for negative influence. Any act of a teacher which disturbs children and parents at this critical time, which breaks down their confidence in themselves, must be considered hostile to vital interests of the community and of the nation. This is true, regardless of the intention.

War is always terrible. As teachers, we must be sensitive to its possible effect upon those whom we teach. Let us be perfectly frank in recognizing the fact that most helpless victims, emotionally and psychologically, of the present situation in Hawaii will be the children of Japanese ancestry and their parents. The position of loyal American citizens of Japanese ancestry and of aliens who are unable to become naturalized but who are nonetheless loyal to the land of their adoption is certainly not enviable. Teachers must do everything to help the morale of these people. Let us keep constantly in mind that America is not making war on citizens of the United States or on law-abiding aliens within America.

As teachers, we are not a group apart; we are members of this community, reflecting the morale of the community and helping to build it. . . . In so far as we allow personal prejudices and intolerance to guide our actions, we break down community solidarity at a time when civilian and military leaders are almost prayerfully pleading that unity be maintained. . . .[14]

On January 12, 1942, Arthur L. Dean, chairman of the Commissioners of Public Instruction, also wrote to all principals and teachers with the following message:

A person is not born to speak one language or another; he is not born with adherence to any set of principles; he is not born with loyalty to one country as against another; his language, his principles and his loyalty are determined by his environment. You are one of the most important of such environmental factors. Your treatment of the children entrusted to you, and your conduct, will in no small degree influence the children toward or away from the American way of life and all that America stands for.

This is no time to entertain prejudices against children or your fellow teachers because their ancestry is different from yours; they did not select their ancestors. They certainly have no responsibility for the conduct of the axis powers. . . . Let's all pull together and prove that *this is America.*[15]

The Impact of the War on the Issei

With the war with Japan, the Issei became enemy aliens while their Hawaii-born children were American citizens. This often meant changed parent-child roles and the loss of parental authority over children. Since public use of the Japanese language was prohibited, the Issei had to depend on their children's interpretations of the regulations concerning enemy aliens. The Issei who knew no other language kept silent even at home, and when they needed to talk they whispered. They were filled with fear and chose to remain inside their homes. In addition, the arrest of almost all the Issei leaders and the closing of all the Japanese institutions stopped the functioning of their society, making the Issei the most desolate and isolated element of the island population. The freezing of Japanese assets, including bank accounts, and the loss of livelihood due to wartime regulations added to the atmosphere of insecurity, although the shortage of manpower absorbed most of those unemployed aliens later.

Their fear of arrest was so predominant that they did not even dare to go to console their intimate friends if any member of the latter's families had been arrested. For this reason, for the first few months after the Pearl Harbor attack, the homes of the internees were the most deserted households in the Japanese community. This was in great contrast to the traditional Japanese custom of mutual helpfulness in time of crisis. The Issei felt that any form of identification with the internees would likely cause suspicion and endanger their own security. In such an extreme crisis the Issei disregarded their cultural definition of conduct completely and behaved on the basis of speculation derived from the immediate situation.

In their effort to eliminate anything that would identify them with the enemy, they destroyed even cultural objects such as brocaded *obi* (kimono sashes), letters and photographs of their relatives, and old books, along with the Japanese flags and portraits of the emperor and empress. In their desperate effort to be identified with the United States, they placed portraits of George Washington, Abraham Lincoln, and President Roosevelt as well as American flags in their homes as well as their restaurants, barbershops and other business establishments. The Issei chose these American figures as legitimate representations of America with the symbolic value of protection.

Issei accepted from the beginning the role of their children as American citizens. This sentiment was strongly expressed by the letters of the internees, instructing their wives to conduct themselves solely as the mothers of American citizens or instructing their sons not to let their fathers' internment interfere with their duty to their native land and to conduct themselves as loyal Americans. The following are the examples of such sentiments.

> My first and foremost concern was how my internment affected my children. I did not want them to feel humiliated by my internment. I wanted them to understand that my internment was due to the war and not to any subversive activities on my part. I wanted them to think and behave as proud American citizens. I did not want them to feel mortified and behave in a cowardly way because of my internment. That was my greatest concern.[16]

> When my son came home my husband had already been taken away. My son had been guarding somewhere ever since December 7. He was a member of the ROTC. I told him that his father was taken because he had been one of the leaders of the Japanese community and not because he had done anything against the government. I told him that he must bear in mind always that he was an American and conduct himself as such. His duty was to defend his country with his utmost. My son said that he knew all that and that he would never disappoint me.[17]

> My husband sent me a note from the Immigration Detention Quarter where he was interned, telling me that from that time on I must forget completely that I was the wife of an enemy alien and concentrate on being the mother of American children. He wanted me to sever all my connection with him and Japan and devote myself to helping our children to serve their country. He sounded very stubborn but I can understand how he felt about the position of our children. One of our sons was already in the Army, stationed at Schofield, when the war broke out.[18]

The Issei's Participation in the Larger Community

While the Japanese attack was still going on, individuals connected with various community groups reported to the office of the Chief of FBI to implement the plans they helped to set up before the war. The Honolulu Police Contact Group was organized among the Americans of Japanese ancestry under the leadership of Captain John A. Burns, the head of the Espionage Division of the Honolulu Police Department. This group helped to allay the fears of the alien Japanese as well as the citizens and to channel their efforts to an American victory. Indirectly, this program helped to alleviate the fears of other ethnic groups and contributed to the unity of the community. Another group, the Citizens' Council, composed of many leading professional men and businessmen, worked to keep the community united in purpose and action and did much to avert friction and tension in the Territory's multiracial communities.[19]

A Morale Section was created on December 18 as part of the military government to work under the assistant chief of staff for Military Intelligence, in close liaison with the FBI, and in cooperation with and often through the civilian leaders and organizations in the community. Under this Morale Section were several ethnic or national subcommittees, which were to work among their respective groups to disseminate military orders and to alleviate the problems arising from the war situation.[20]

The Japanese subcommittee of the Morale Section was organized as the Emergency Service Committee in February 1942 on Oahu, and similar groups were organized subsequently on Kauai, Maui, and Hawaii. In addition to thirteen Nisei men, Charles F. Loomis and Hung Wai Ching of the Morale Section served as ex-officio members. There was also an advisory board made up of about fifty men of Japanese ancestry who were leaders of their respective districts. Among the purposes of the Emergency Service Committee were (1) to help both citizens and aliens demonstrate their loyalty in concrete ways to speed the defeat of Japan and all other enemies; (2) to help them face realistically and cooperatively the difficult situation in which the war had placed them; and (3) to work with the leaders and organizations of other racial groups for the preservation of Hawaii's traditional harmony between all races and the promotion of a united home front in cooperation with the army, the Red Cross, and other local, federal, and territorial agencies. This group assisted the army in its recruiting drives "to bring out positively . . . the inherent loyalty of the Americans of Japanese ancestry as well as to keep the aliens on our side."[21] The services of the Emergency Service Committee were directed by the following principle:

While the Emergency Service Committee functions primarily on behalf of and among the Americans and aliens of Japanese ancestry, it has always placed the welfare of the Territory and the nation before that of any racial group. Every task it has undertaken has first been evaluated in terms of the community. It is not and never has been an organization for the protection of the rights of one racial group and the enhancement of its participation in the war effort at the expense of the rights and privileges of other racial groups. . . .[22]

The Emergency Service Committee sponsored more than two hundred meetings in the Japanese communities to alleviate confusion and bewilderment by explaining the wartime restrictions and at the same time urging the Japanese to participate actively in the war effort of the larger community. Under their encouragement the "Kiawe Corps" was formed among Issei men on all the islands to clear the kiawe thickets that might be used by possible enemy invaders. During January and February 1942, more than 1,200 men participated in clearing areas for military camps; burning rubbish; stringing barbed wire; constructing trails; doing repair work, demolition, and clearance; and building evacuation centers for women and children in case of enemy invasion. During the Christmas seasons of 1942 and 1943, the Emergency Service Committee raised money to be used for Nisei units in the army and wounded servicemen of all races in the hospitals in Hawaii. Later, aroused by the news of the inhumane execution of American fliers in Tokyo, this committee sponsored the "Bombs on Tokyo" campaign and raised over $10,000 from the residents of Japanese ancestry. The money was presented to Lt. General Robert C. Richardson, Jr., who succeeded General Emmons.[23]

In spite of the numerous rumors inciting the general suspicion of the Japanese, there were no incidents of violence against the Japanese physically or in terms of property damage. The Issei who had to report to their employers or to their Red Cross units the day after Pearl Harbor had expected to be stared at on the bus or on the streets, but no one seemed to pay any attention to them. As a result, they were deeply impressed by the absence of reprisals and expressed their appreciation mixed with admiration with such statements as "America is a big-hearted country," or "Americans are big-hearted people." The equal treatment of the Japanese in distribution of gas masks, in precautionary health measures such as administration of typhoid and dengue fever shots, the assignment of evacuation centers in the event of enemy raids, rationing of food, gasoline and tires, and so on made the Issei extremely grateful. There was nothing in terms of necessities and protection from which the Japanese were excluded. Their reaction to such an unexpected degree of generosity and fairness was utmost gratitude and unreserved willingness to offer everything they had. They felt that they owed their lives to the American government. Many Issei expressed their feeling of gratitude by saying, "If we Issei were all to be punished to death, we are in no position to protest. But we are given everything which is given to other people. We owe our lives to this country."[24]

Along with official reassurances, the Issei were helped to feel that they were included as part of the larger community by such organizations as the Emergency Service Committee, the Friends Service Committee, and the International Institute of the YWCA. Because of their strong desire to be trusted and included in the war effort, and citing their participation in relief efforts during World War I, over seven hundred women, mostly Issei, were organized in war service clubs in March 1942 by the International Institute of the YWCA in twenty Japanese neighborhoods in Honolulu. They used the halls of the Buddhist temples, Shinto shrines, Japanese language schools, and teahouses, all of which were closed for the duration of the war, as well as private homes, to work for the Red Cross and Office of Civil Defense (OCD). In rural communities, similar groups were organized under the leadership of the wives of the plantation managers. Thus, while Issei men worked with the Kiawe Corps and other labor service groups on Sundays, Issei women worked vigorously on weekdays, one day a week, for the Red Cross and OCD, making bandages, sewing surgical gowns, hospital gowns, making hospital slippers, knitting socks and sweaters for the armed forces, and sewing hundreds of quilts for the evacuation centers for women and children in case of enemy invasion.

The wartime regulations prohibited enemy aliens from holding gatherings, but special permission was given for the service groups to meet on the condition that a non-Japanese leader be present. For most of the Issei women, participation in these groups marked the first time in their lives that they worked directly under the leadership of Caucasian women. In terms of human relations this experience gave them new horizons beyond the confines of Japanese groups. A fisherman's wife from Kakaako recalled:

> Until the war I had always been afraid to go near haoles [Caucasians], although there was no particular reason for that. Because of the war, we came to know such wonderful people as Mrs. Cox and Dr. Bowles as well as other fine Americans. Once I told Mrs. Cox in my pidgin English, "I can't speak English. So, I can't convey directly how I feel. But one thing I am sure is that you and I feel and think exactly the same way. We share our deep feelings very intimately and there is no barrier between us. I can't think of you except as someone very intimate to me. All of us in this group feel the same way." Mrs. Cox told me that she felt exactly the same way as I felt. War is a brutal thing and we hate it, but this war did one good thing for us and that is that we Japanese came to know such fine Americans.

The wife of a Japanese language school principal in Kalihi-Kai said:

> I have lived in Hawaii for more than thirty years but I never thought that there was a chance in my life to get acquainted with Americans. Since the war started I have had a direct contact with them. Americans are very kind people and America is a wonderful country. Now I am learning English although I am old.

Some of the service groups had a chance to see how their service products were being used. For example, the Service Club working at Kakaako Japanese language school was invited to the Navy Hospital (St. Louis High School), which the club had helped to equip by sewing surgical gowns, hospital gowns, bed covers, and curtains. Their transportation was furnished by the army. In spite of the fact that most of the patients had come back recently from bitter engagements in the South Pacific, these Issei women did not encounter any kind of hostility. Instead, they were treated as guests. Some of the patients who were in advanced stages of recovery decorated the platform of the auditorium with the seventy exquisite Bon lanterns the women presented to them and told the women that they were going to have a party that evening. The women found these young men similar to their own sons and understood the feelings of their parents. Such experiences were a great encouragement for them not only in terms of the war effort but also in terms of positive identification with the American community. Through participation in the war effort of the United States, they explained that as Issei they considered themselves adopted children of the United States, which meant that their primary obligation was to the United States. In the Japanese tradition, the adopted son or daughter is expected to side with his or her adopted family in case of a feud between the two families. To them their service work was in compliance with the Japanese tradition also.

There were also other experiences which contributed to the Issei's increased America-oriented consciousness. Many of the GIs who guarded the beaches or remote areas often found the Japanese the only civilians living in the vicinity and received hospitality from them such as home-cooked meals and hot baths. In Honolulu also many Japanese families came to know servicemen from the U. S. mainland as family friends.

While the Issei vigorously participated in the war effort, they were still sensitive to any report that hinted at removal of the Japanese from Hawaii. When the rumor of mass evacuation of the Japanese to the mainland circulated widely, many Issei actually bought trunks, suitcases, and warm clothing in preparation. Only an official denial of such a plan stopped their stampede. In January 1943, when a high-ranking official of the telephone company in Honolulu advocated mass evacuation of the Japanese and distributed pamphlets on downtown streets, the authorities paid little attention to him, viewing him an isolated case. He even consulted powerful officials of the California Joint Immigration Committee, who were among the foremost advocates of removal of the Japanese, citizens and aliens, for mass detention. These officials, however, told him that they completely opposed the removal of any Japanese in Hawaii to the West Coast or to any part of the mainland.[25]

In April 1943, the military authorities again announced that it was a military necessity to keep most of the Japanese in Hawaii, indicating that mass removal of the Japanese population would create extreme labor shortages and that the shipping situation would make impossible such large-scale transportation. The army's position regarding the Japanese was reiterated by Colonel Fielder in a University of Hawaii convocation address entitled "Democracy and Military Necessity in Hawaii" on April 15, 1943:

We did not impugn, because of race, the good name of the rest of them, alien or citizen. . . . It has not been the intention of the authorities to toss over all good democratic doctrine and deport all of them merely because of their physical kinship to the enemy. Mass evacuation was never planned. . . . This must not be construed as sentimentality, or hands-off for business reasons or anything else of a negative nature. But rather as a sane, reasonable, democratic and safe judgment. It is simply felt that the Japanese element of the population, if accepted and united in purpose and action, is an asset to the community. Yet rejected and treated as potential enemies they would constitute a burden, even a danger to our security. . . .

VVV, the Varsity Victory Volunteers

Because of their legal status as enemy aliens, the Issei derived much of their sense of security from their position of being the parents of American citizens. As long as their children were trusted by the authorities and included in the activities of the larger community, they felt that they were identified with America and their security was guaranteed. Therefore, when the news that the Nisei draftees who had actually defended the islands during the the Japanese attack were being disarmed began to circulate, an atmosphere of insecurity and distress mounted both among the Issei and the Nisei. The whole Japanese population suffered the heaviest blow when all the members of the Hawaii Territorial Guard of Japanese ancestry were discharged on January 19, 1942, after having served for six weeks, on orders from Washington. It appeared as if the last means they had to prove their loyalty was gone. Ted Tsukiyama recalled the feelings of the Nisei guardsmen:

We made the long truck journey back to the university armory and we were honorably discharged. When we parted, our officers cried. Our fellow guardsmen, our classmates and friends for many years, they cried. And of course, we cried. . . . To have our own country, in its most extreme time of need and danger, repudiate us, that was something more than we could take. . . . I have difficulty in grasping words in the English language that can adequately and sufficiently describe our feelings that day when we were dismissed from the service of our own country because our faces and our names resemble that of the enemy. There was no depth to which our emotions sank. The very bottom had dropped out of our existence![26]

These discharged, disheartened Nisei Guardsmen had the good fortune of having Hung Wai Ching, then the secretary of the University of Hawaii YMCA who was also one of the three members of the Morale Committee of the military governor, to counsel them. His constructive and inspiring challenge was the beginning of a new course of action for the AJAs in Hawaii. Tsukiyama recalled what Hung Wai Ching said:

> OK, you had a bum deal. I agree, you had a bum deal. But what are you going to do about it? Are you going to sit on your butts and feel sorry for yourselves for the rest of the war? Are you going to lie down and be quitters? . . . You think the only thing you can do is to hold gun. Don't you think there are other ways in which you can serve your country, especially when they are crying for manpower for defense?[27]

Hung Wai Ching opened their minds to other options they might take to be of service to the country and to demonstrate their loyalty. The young men held a meeting and decided to offer themselves as a noncombat labor battalion. They sent a petition to General Emmons, signed by 169 men:

> We, the undersigned, were members of Hawaii Territorial Guard until its recent inactivation. We joined the guard voluntarily with the hope that this was one way to serve our country in her time of need.
> Needless to say, we were deeply disappointed when we were told that our services in the Guard were no longer needed. Hawaii is our home, the United States, our country. We know but one loyalty and that is to the Stars and Stripes. We wish to do our part as loyal Americans in every way possible and we hereby offer ourselves for whatever service you may see fit to use us.[28]

Their petition was accepted on February 23, 1942, and they were formed into a labor battalion as the Corps of Engineers Auxiliary attached to the 34th Combat Engineers Regiment at Schofield. They called themselves the VVV, the Varsity Victory Volunteers. They did rock quarrying, they strung barbed wire and built military installations, roads, warehouses, dumps, and so on. Tsukiyama said, "We felt trusted, accepted, useful and productive." He also noted Hung Wai Ching's continued effort to help them: "One day the quarry gang looked up from their work and there was Secretary of the Army John J. McCloy with Hung Wai Ching inspecting the quality of their quarrying work. The War Department was soon convinced. In June, 1942, all Niseis then in service were assembled for combat training in Wisconsin and the 100th Battalion was born."[29]

The VVV was inactivated at their request after eleven months to permit them to volunteer for the all-Nisei combat unit. The formation of the VVV marked the turning point in the position of the Japanese in Hawaii, boosting their morale and restoring their sense of belonging to the larger American community.

The 100th Battalion

There was already in the regular army an engineer battalion composed entirely of Nisei, numbering nine hundred men and officers. This unit was attached to the 1399th Engineer Construction Battalion, handling all kinds of construction facilities, water systems, sewage, and drainage installations. This unit remained in Hawaii throughout the war years.[30]

In the meantime, 1,406 Nisei inductees, some former members of the Territorial Guard and some pre-Pearl Harbor volunteers, were temporarily formed into the Hawaiian Provisional Battalion and shipped to the mainland on June 5, 1942. Their departure was secret, but their immediate families had a chance to see them before their departure. In September they were activated as the 100th Infantry Battalion under Lt. Colonel Farrant L. Turner, former resident of Hawaii, who had utmost confidence in them. They were to train at Camp McCoy in Wisconsin for eventual combat in the European theater. This unit was initiated as the first test of national significance regarding the loyalty of the Americans of Japanese ancestry.[31]

The hospitality the young men were accorded by the citizenry of Wisconsin appeared in the local press in Hawaii and the Nisei's activities at Camp McCoy were shown in a newsreel in the local movie theaters. The hospitality according to Nisei prompted their parents and friends to reciprocate to the servicemen from Wisconsin stationed in Hawaii. The term "Camp McCoy" called forth the deepest sentiments of the parents and family members and friends of the 100th Battalion. For the first time the whole Japanese community became keenly mainland-conscious.

The 100th Battalion moved to Camp Shelby, Mississippi, for final training in January 1943. While there they met Earl M. Finch, a rancher, who became a "one man USO," devoting his time and money to the Nisei soldiers, taking care of their furlough arrangments and entertainment, and shielding them from the Southern race prejudice. The news about him made the Issei exceedingly grateful. The 100th Battalion moved to Camp Kilmer, New Jersey, in August 1943 for staging and then sailing from New York for action in the Mediterranean and European theaters. [32]

Beginning late in September 1943, headlines such as "Killed in Action," "Missing," "Wounded," with Japanese names began to appear in the local press, along with the news of the distinguished exploits and citations of the 100th Battalion. The local Japanese community accepted the news with mingled feelings of pride and sadness. From this time on the record of the 100th Battalion was so prominently highlighted that the legal status of their Issei parents enemy aliens became almost completely obscured. From this time on, there were frequent questions from the Issei as to when or how soon they would be able to get American citizenship themselves.

The 442nd Regimental Combat Team

In January 1943, the War Department issued a call for 1,500 volunteers from among the Americans of Japanese ancestry in Hawaii for a combat team for the European theater. In announcing this call, General Emmons stated:

> Open to distrust because of their racial origin, and discriminated against in certain fields of the defense effort, they nevertheless have borne their burdens without complaint and have added materially to the strength of the Hawaii area. They have behaved themselves admirably under the most trying conditions, have bought great quantities of war bonds, and by the labor of their hands have added to the common defense. Their representatives in the 100th Infantry Battalion, a combat unit now in training on the mainland; the Varsity Victory Volunteers; and other men of Japanese extraction in our armed forces have also established a fine record.
>
> In view of these facts, and by War Department authority, I have been designated to offer the Americans of Japanese ancestry an addi-

tional opportunity to serve their country. This opportunity is in the form of voluntary combat service in the armed forces. I have been directed to induct 1,500 of them as volunteers into the army of the United States. This call for volunteers affords an excellent opportunity to demonstrate the faith that the army has in their loyalty and fighting qualities. I believe that the response to this call will be sincere and generous and that it will have the hearty support of the parents concerned and of the community as a whole. The manner of response and the record these men will establish as fighting soldiers will be one of the best answers to those who question the loyalty of American citizens of Japanese ancestry in Hawaii.[33]

To this call 9,507, about one-third of the Nisei men between the ages of eighteen and thirty-eight years, responded. Because of this large number, the original quota was increased to 2,600. They were inducted on March 28 and, after a big official send-off on the Iolani Palace grounds, they left Hawaii for Camp Shelby, Mississippi, for training. Arriving there, they were joined by 1,200 mainland Nisei volunteers to become the 442nd Regimental Combat Team. They left Shelby in April 1944 for Camp Patrick Henry, Virginia, and on May 1 they sailed from Hampton Roads for Europe. With the 100th absorbed into the 442nd, they carried on many major campaigns. Their exploits were widely publicized in Hawaii. The *Honolulu Star-Bulletin* pointed out that from the beginning the army followed the policy of publicizing the AJA units in order to boost morale and at the same time to show to a suspicious world what democracy could do.[34]

The Issei's sentiments were expressed by the women of the service clubs:

"I am prepared to nurse my son if he comes back crippled. That is a small part I can share with him in his service to his country."

"My son is in Europe, in the thick of fighting. I feel that I am fighting with him. That's why I work for the Red Cross with my utmost."

"My daughter-in-law and I decided not to let my son know about the death of his father now. My son is in Europe and has just begun fighting. He needs courage. We must not weaken his spirit at this time."[35]

Issei parents of the men killed in action spoke proudly of the citations and presentation of medals in recognition of their sons' service. They developed a new conception of themselves and at the same time formed an exceedingly sentimental attachment to the United States. Their Japanese features, the color of their skin, or their humble lodgings now mattered very little when officers of the army visited them. The observance of Veterans Day and Memorial Day became the most important events for the Issei, and they began to participate proudly in the public services along with the parents of the GIs of other ethnic groups.

The first Buddhist memorial service for AJAs was observed on October 21, 1943, for Joseph Shigeo Takada, killed in action in Italy on September 29, 1943. After that, most of the Buddhist memorial services held were for AJAs killed in action. Of necessity, Buddhist temples had the American flag in the place of honor near the altar. The Buddhist temples, which had been Japan-oriented with ancestor worship, became America-oriented to honor those who died in service to America, their native land. The Buddhist temples were officially closed until the end of the war but there were no restrictions against using the temple halls for funerals. There was only one Nisei priest who was not interned. He was assisting the Army's intelligence service most of the time, but at the same time, being the only Buddhist priest on Oahu, he was in great demand. Sometimes the nuns of different sects officiated at funeral services. On the other islands where all of the Buddhist priests were interned Christian ministers took care of all the funeral services.

AJAs in the Pacific Theater

As early as May 1943, Japanese interpreters were recruited in Hawaii for service in the Pacific. AJAs in the other army units were also transferred to the interpreters' corps. About half of some 5,000 interpreters trained by the army were from Hawaii. They served in every engagement in the Pacific—Guadalcanal to the Indo-China-Burma theaters, the Philippines, Okinawa, and finally to Japan—some working at the headquarters while some worked at the front or even penetrated the enemy's lines. Their work included intercepting transmissions and cracking the enemy's codes, translating, and interrogating. They were described as one of America's superb secret weapons.[36]

Women were recruited for the WACs in October 1944. Twenty-six of the fifty-nine who were accepted were of Japanese ancestry. Since most of the eligible women were already in the essential jobs many of them were advised not to enlist.[37]

Toward the End of the War

With special encouragement from the army authorities the Women's War Service Association was organized by the wives, widows, sisters, and mothers of Nisei servicemen in July 1944. These women had been participating actively in the war effort of the larger community. Among numerous activities were USO Day dinner and entertainment for 25,000 servicemen from the mainland; clothes drives for the Philippines, Okinawa, and Korea; hospital visitations to the wounded veterans; and assistance in the adjustment process of AJAs with medical discharges, who began to arrive in 1944, and their families.[38]

In the meantime, Americanization of the Issei Japanese by community leaders continued and English classes were held for them. For the middle-aged Issei learning a new language was very difficult, but they had a taste of it and their Nisei children encouraged their efforts. As the theater of war moved westward, farther away from Hawaii, one of the major industries in Hawaii, the pineapple companies, began to recruit workers in Japanese neighborhoods more positively by sending their agents to visit them. A large number of Issei women worked in the pineapple canning factories in the prewar days, and this recruiting merely meant resumption of their prewar jobs.

Inconsistency in Wartime Regulations

While there was strict censorship of the local mail and outgoing mail from Hawaii, the incoming mail from the mainland entered Hawaii freely, as in the case of certain Japanese vernacular papers, the *Colorado Times, Rocky Shimpo,* and *Utah Nippo,* all of which published the war news from Japan's standpoint. These vernaculars began to come to Hawaii by way of internment camps or relocation camps on the mainland. The Issei who read these papers compared the war news with that in the local vernaculars and concluded that if the mainland vernaculars were permitted to circulate in Hawaii, their war news must be true, and many stopped their subscription to the *Hawaii Times* and *Hawaii Hochi (Hawaii Herald)* and began to subscribe to these mainland vernaculars. According to the chief editor of the *Colorado Times* who visited Hawaii from January till April 1947, there were approximately one thousand subscribers in Hawaii. He also estimated that the number of subscribers to the *Utah Nippo* and the *Rocky Shimpo* to be about a half that number each.[39]

These biweekly vernaculars of the mid-Rocky Mountain area were insignificant papers before the war. During the war when all the well-established West Coast Japanese dailies were closed and all their subscribers were moved to the relocation camps or internment camps, those who could not read English began to subscribe to these papers for the news of the outside world. On the other hand, without strict censorship in these Rocky Mountain states, the publishers had access to the war news broadcasts aimed primarily at the people in Japan, which were monitored by the news agencies of the United States. All the war news in those mainland vernaculars was under the headline "Tokyo Hoso" (Tokyo Broadcast) or "Daihonei Happyo" (Imperial Headquarters Communique) with the occasional accompaniment of parenthesized identifications such as FCC, UP, AP, San Francisco, Washington, or New York in very small print. The large headlines and captions, however, gave the Issei readers an impression that the news was directly from Tokyo. These papers consistently justified Japan's military aggression and criticized American weakness. When the Japanese forces were successively defeated in the battles the news directed to their own people was always "a victory." Japan's devastating defeat in the decisive naval engagement off the Philippines was reported as a phenomenal victory and the people in Japan celebrated it by sipping sake. While the military leaders of Japan needed to prevent the weakening of the morale of their people by bad news, in reality the people were deceived until the end. In the same way, these mainland vernaculars prepared their Issei readers for an ultimate victory of Japan instead of preparing them to face the reality of Japan's defeat. Consequently, when even those vernaculars published the news of the surrender of Japan, the Issei readers concluded that these papers were bribed by the local Japa-

nese papers, and started condemning all the newspapers, expressing their determination not to believe anything in the papers.
Thus, these mainland vernaculars contributed to maladjustment
and disorganization among certain portions of the Issei after V-J
Day.

Another inconsistency was the issuing of special permission to
one alien Japanese group, Seicho-no Ie, to have its gatherings
while all the other alien Japanese groups, religious or secular, were
prohibited to gather, with their priests and leaders interned, for
the duration of the war. The special permission was obtained by
way of a prominent Caucasian doctor whose household servants,
an Issei couple, were members of the Seicho-no Ie group in Honolulu. This couple explained that the Issei were all feeling lost in a
spiritual vacuum without the gatherings of their traditional religions—Buddhism or Shinto—since the outbreak of the war, and
they felt that the Seicho-no Ie gatherings would be of great help to
them. Special permission was given to this group, however, strictly
on the basis that it would confine its activities to memorial services
of Nisei killed in action.[40]

15

The Issei Community in Postwar Years

WITH the coming of V-J Day on August 14, 1945, the wartime leaders and the agencies that had been taking care of the Issei were abruptly inactivated, leaving the Issei in a complete social and psychological vacuum. The end of the war brought numerous new problems of adjustment for the Issei, particularly because it involved the defeat of their old country. For the limited number of Issei who were quite detached from Japan, intellectuals, Christians, and some businessmen, the adjustment was not terribly difficult. Even before the war these individuals had been critical of the military clique in Japan. In general, they were able to read English newspapers and, therefore, their sources of information were not exclusively Japanese. Psychologically they were part of the American public, and they participated in the life of the larger interracial community in Hawaii, having personal friends among various ethnic groups. They believed from the outset that the military in Japan was a menace to that country, as well as to the peace of the world, and that defeat was the only way to end military dictatorship in Japan.

The bulk of the Issei who were able to make a positive adjustment, however, had a somewhat different background. They had not been critical of prewar Japan, but they had followed the war news in the local papers realistically and had expected the defeat of Japan as the inevitable consequence. Although they felt sad for their old country, the news of Japan's defeat did not constitute a shock to them. They had made a commitment to Hawaii as their home and they identified their future with their children and grandchildren.

Regardless of the fact that the Issei generally accepted Japan's defeat as a fact, most of them suffered a deep sense of disgrace and

241

humiliation and avoided public appearances as much as possible for the first few weeks after V-J Day. They compared themselves with other Orientals and felt that the latter would look down upon them with contempt. As an elderly shoemaker observed, "Now I notice that all Japanese walk on the street with their heads drooped in humiliation while the Koreans, Chinese, and Filipinos go about proudly and jubilantly."[1]

A similar sentiment was expressed when a group of Issei women who had participated actively in the Red Cross Surgical Units were asked to take part in a victory parade on September 3, 1945. "How can we take part in the parade celebrating the defeat of Japan?" they asked. "It would show our disgrace publicly and be too humiliating for us. The Koreans, Chinese, and Filipinos can proudly participate in the parade, because for them it is the occasion to celebrate the liberation of their homelands from the Japanese."[2]

Many readers of the *Colorado Times* and other mainland Japanese vernacular papers accepted Japan's defeat as a fact, although they suffered extreme shock to the extent that they "could not eat or sleep for days." These newspapers had been publishing what the Japanese government wanted people to believe—that Japan was winning the war.

With the Issei's realization of Japan's defeat came disillusionment about prewar Japan's social and political system and leaders. This disillusionment was expressed in criticisms of Japan. The widow of a fishing boat carpenter, a staunch Buddhist, said:

> Of course, the defeat is hard for the people in Japan. But, I hope that those at the top, such as Mitsui and Mitsubishi, will share their wealth with the common people of Japan from now on. The common people were always willing to sacrifice everything when their services were asked for in the name of the emperor or patriotism. . . . The militarists and Mitsui, Mitsubishi, and others who started the war for their own gain at the cost of the common people must redeem their crime by sharing all they have with others. The defeat of Japan must have awakened the people of Japan to realize the fact that they have been cheated all these years. . . . If Japan had won the war, the fate of the common people would have become unbearable, because the militarists and rich people would have become more arrogant and more powerful than ever. We hear that the people in Japan welcome the American soldiers [of the Occupation Army]. I don't blame them.

They know they can't depend on their own leaders who led the country to disaster.[3]

The wife of a Buddhist priest said:

Ever since they were born, the Japanese people were taught to believe that Japan was a country to win wars. Their minds were soaked in this idea so that it is very difficult for them to change, especially when they are old. In this sense, even the military leaders are the products of this ideology. So, I don't think they really consider that they misled their country. My husband went to Japan for a few months in 1940. He hated the way the Japanese army men were behaving. They were arrogant and looked down upon the civilians. He did not like the Japanese government officials either. The life in Japan was so regimented that the people did not know how to be natural. It is good for Japan to have so many American soldiers stationed there. The Japanese people cannot help but learning some of the American informality and friendliness. . . .[4]

A newspaper editor's wife said:

I always noticed that those so-called liberal people from Japan who visited the United States and who advocated vigorously international friendship and cooperation between America and Japan while in America never spoke loudly enough and enthusiastically enough when they returned to Japan. . . . Of course, they had their families and they could not sacrifice them in the rising tide of ultranationalism and militarism. I recall visiting merchant marines used to say such careless things as "Oh, we can destroy your islands in two hours; Pearl Harbor is nothing." When we visited Japan fifteen years ago, the people there were already warlike and made no effort to understand America. . . . Japan lost the war. So, the people there must accept this fact and make up their minds to cooperate with America to rebuild peace-loving Japan which will contribute to the peace of the world.[5]

Social Disorganization among the Issei: The Katta-gumi

There was a small portion of the Issei population on the island of Oahu, 3 percent or so at the peak, dwindling to 1 percent in the course of eight months, who insisted that Japan had won the war.[6] They were the "Katta-gumi" (the Japan-Won-the-War groups).

These Issei had relied on the mainland Japanese vernaculars for war news, which they got from Japanese sources and which was intended to keep morale high in Japan. When the mainland papers also reported the defeat of Japan, these Issei readers stopped reading all newspapers. Completely isolating themselves from any news, they began to circulate their own beliefs concerning the war results. Although the circulation of rumors of Japanese victory was confined to the Issei community, not everyone living in the same neighborhood was Katta-gumi. For this reason there were arguments and even fistfights over the issue of the war results wherever the Issei gathered—be it at stores, meetings, parties— between the hardcore Katta-gumi individuals and those who accepted the fact of Japan's defeat.

Rumors were rampant among those who believed in Japan's victory. As they came together in the course of repeating the rumors, there was mutual reinforcement of the emotional state they had in common. In the process of such interaction, they built up a certain image which furnished a common orientation for them. Various forms of symptomatic, elementary collective behavior manifested itself, such as gathering on the hills to watch for an approaching Japanese fleet; soliciting $10 from each house for a welcome party for Prince Takamatsu aboard a vessel of that fleet; visiting the former Japanese consulate to greet a new consul general in ceremonial Japanese kimono, only to be told that there was no Japanese consul general. (The Japanese consulate building was occupied by the Swedish vice-consul, who transacted the affairs of Japanese nationals until April 1950, when the Japanese Government Overseas Agency was established. Only in April 1952, after the Peace Treaty of San Francisco, did the Japanese consulate resume its functions.)

A young Buddhist priest of the Zen sect, the Rev. Y., who was interned for part of the war years in a camp on Oahu and part of the time worked in a pineapple factory, was a ready-made leader for the fanatical Katta-gumi groups. With him as the central figure, they held large gatherings in the areas where the Japanese population was concentrated, such as Palama and Moiliili, attracting individuals who considered him a hero who dared to speak on "Japanese victory." The same individuals attended all the gatherings where Reverend Y. spoke. The Katta-gumi Issei also had area organizations called "Dōshi-kai" (Association of Persons with Common Objectives). Some individuals belonged to two or more Dōshi-kai with different group leaders who were responsible for their respective area gatherings. Such multiple participation gave the impression that Katta-gumi was a formidable movement, accompanied by a bloated self-image and sense of mission on the part of the local area Dōshi-kai leaders.

Closely associated with the Katta-gumi was Seicho-no Ie, which furnished its members with an image of Japanese victory as part of its dogma. Seicho-no Ie was founded in Japan in the 1930s at a time when military aggression overseas had become Japan's national goal. Some of the Katta-gumi leaders were former Seicho-no Ie members who had broken away from it. According to the Seicho-no Ie doctrine, the only real thing in the world is the spirit. The world of substance does not actually exist. The pain or sickness the human body suffers does not exist. All the occurrences in the world of substance do not actually take place. Interpreting the defeat of Japan in the light of this belief, Seicho-no Ie contributed to the extreme maladjustment and disorganization among some of the Issei population after V-J Day. Seicho-no Ie was introduced to Hawaii in 1935 by a small group of Issei who read its sacred book *Seimei no Jisso* [The reality of life]. They began to meet regularly to share their experiences of faith healing and enlightenment. The number who attended these gatherings averaged twenty in Honolulu. Seicho-no Ie was very little known in Hawaii before World War II. During the war, since there were no Buddhist or Shinto gatherings, the household servants of a well-known doctor who were Seicho-no Ie followers asked their employer to get permission for Seicho-no Ie to meet. He was successful, and Seicho-no Ie was granted a permit to hold meetings in November 1944 from the Foreign Funds Control. Thus, it became the only Japanese group to gather during the war. According to the Foreign Funds Control, the membership of Seicho-no Ie in Honolulu in March 1946 was four hundred and in the whole Territory it was more than one thousand and steadily increasing.[7] During the war, Seicho-no Ie used the Higashi Hongwanji Temple in Palama for its large gatherings, but after the war when its priest returned from an internment camp on the mainland, it used the Palama Settlement gymnasium. After the war its activities became more aggressive, with seventy small neighborhood groups holding daily gatherings.

Seicho-no Ie's most powerful leader, Mrs. M., was its official head. She was known to be able to foresee events. She claimed that she saved the lives of several hundred Nisei in the battlefields through her spiritual intervention. At the daily gatherings at her residence she administered faith healing, which was mainly talking on her part on the basis of the Seicho-no Ie belief. Most of the healing sessions consisted of exhortations, which included an assertion of her authority: "Everything I say is absolutely true. You may think I am starting a rumor, but what I say now will be proved when the 'Dawn' comes and everything becomes clear." Her exhortations were mostly statements suggestive of Japanese victory, such as the following:

> The American bombing did not do much damage in Japan. There might be a few places which suffered a fire. But that was from the burning oil spread from the burning American airplanes shot down by Japanese anti-aircraft guns. Tokyo is almost intact. . . . As a matter of fact, the widest streets in the world are under construction now. Mind you, it is not MacArthur who is giving direction. . . .
>
> When the commission sent by the Japanese government arrives here, it will investigate all the Japanese to determine who remained loyal to Japan and who were traitors during the war. . . .
>
> It is true that an atomic bomb was dropped on Hiroshima, but the damage was limited to a small area. It has been publicized too much. Actually, we don't even know whether the atomic bombs were developed in America. We know that science was far more advanced in Japan than in America and that Japan had much more superior bombs. But Japan is a moral country. That's why she did not use them.[8]

At the end of the gathering several mimeographed pamphlets, all concerned with Japan's divine mission and invincibility, were circulated. They must have reached Hawaii's Seicho-no Ie by way of the internment camps on the mainland to which the International Red Cross delivered gifts from Japan, including food and books and magazines, during the war. One of the pamphlets was an article entitled "The War We Cannot Lose," by Toshio Shiratori.[9] Throughout the article the dominant sentiment was Japan's divine mission and invincibility:

> Our Empire of Japan alone is without any experience of defeat in wars with foreign nations and she should never lose in any war. No matter what happens, this country must fight out to win. This is as

revealed in the holy commandment [of Amaterasu]. . . . As Premier Koiso broadcast the other day to commemorate the anniversary of the Imperial Rescript,[10] Great Goddess Amaterasu is the sole divine being in the universe and the Emperor reigns the world as her heir. We reverently acknowledge the holy proclamation that the Imperial reign is as eternal as the heaven and earth. This being the fundamental principle of the national polity of Japan, it is the absolute and supreme duty of Japanese subjects to protect this national polity. Therefore, to the barbarians who dare to attempt to destroy this national polity and to wage war against the Imperial throne of Japan, there is only one answer, namely, their complete annihilation. . . .[11]

The lay leaders under Mrs. M. assumed the status of officers and directors, introducing each other to their audiences as *sensei* ("honorable teacher") when they presided over meetings or as they bore testimony to their healing experiences, which were combined with exhortations similar to those of Mrs. M. For lay leaders who were household servants, restaurant workers, laundry workers, or small shopkeepers, the title *sensei* up-graded and elevated them in the eyes of their audiences. These lay leaders as well as the general membership expressed sentiments similar to Mrs. M.'s in their casual conversation after the meetings:

> I hate America for using atomic bombs so cruelly. But I don't think Japan lost the war. General MacArthur is in Japan to carry out reparations by America. America bombed Japanese cities. So she has to rebuild them. That's why many carpenters were sent there from Hawaii.
> I am not going to send clothes and food to Japan, because Japan did not lose the war and it is not necessary to send such a help to Japan. Besides, I don't believe in material help. Japanese people live better with spiritual help. Japan is the only country strong enough to save the world now.[12]

Seicho-no Ie became less aggressive than it was immediately after the war as time passed, for the following reasons: (1) Mrs. M. returned to Japan to join her husband who was interned on the mainland and returned to Japan without stopping in Hawaii; (2) Japanese victory was not credible when the people realized Japan's defeat was a fact and began to send food and clothes to their relatives; (3) many young men from Hawaii including Nisei were serving as members of the American occupation army in Japan; and

(4) two postwar religious sects with entirely fresh outlooks and approaches came to Hawaii.

Seicho-no Ie moved its headquarters church to Matlock Avenue about 1957. Rev. Sento Yasushi came from Japan about 1967 to head the ministry in Hawaii. There is a church in Kaneohe also, and one church on each of the other islands. The number of members in Hawaii is about 2,500 of which 2,000 are on Oahu. Seicho-no Ie has put out a new volume of its sacred book, compiled by its founder Masaharu Taniguchi. He died in 1985 at the age of ninety. He was succeeded by his son-in-law, Seicho Taniguchi.

Most of the Japanese interned on the mainland returned to the islands in the fall of 1946, at the time the Katta-gumi were flourishing in the Japanese community. The professional people among the internees—the businessmen, newspaper editors, physicians— were well aware of the outcome of the war. However, many of the internees who had relied for war news on the mainland vernaculars as well as magazines and other publications sent from Japan by way of the International Red Cross had ideas about the war results similar to those of the Katta-gumi. Within a few days, however, their families and relatives had helped them to understand the situation. As they began to settle down, they were appalled by the fanaticism of the Katta-gumi. Only one returned Buddhist priest, of the Shin sect, actively participated in the Katta-gumi gatherings, where he gave his version of the testimony on Japan's victory. Many Buddhist priests when they returned found their temples being used by the Katta-gumi groups, with their own members declaring that they no longer needed their former priests because they had better leaders. The returned priests were described as "Communists," "Red," "Pro-American," "No-backbone," and as "Having succumbed to American propaganda," "Having forgotten the 'On' [grace] of their homeland and that of the emperor." It took several months for these priests to remove the fanatical groups from their temples and restore normal relationships with their parishioners.[13]

The Decline of the Katta-gumi

For those Issei who had made the adjustment to the reality of the postwar situation, the Katta-gumi were a source of frustration and embarrassment. Joined by the prewar leaders of the Japanese community who had returned from the mainland, they harshly criticized the leaders of the Katta-gumi for taking advantage of the ignorance of their followers, indicating that their presence in Hawaii was injurious to the reputation of the Japanese as a whole and that they were spoiling things for which the AJAs had fought and sacrificed their lives. The critics were also impatient with the leniency shown to Katta-gumi leaders by the authorities and expressed the view that the only satisfactory solution to the problem was their deportation to Japan, where they claimed to belong.

An indirect but significant contributing factor to the decline of the prestige of the Katta-gumi was the visit to Hawaii of Earl M. Finch, known as the godfather of the Nisei soldiers while they were training on the mainland. His visit put the Katta-gumi in an embarrassing position. Articles concerning his generosity and kindness to AJAs appeared in the local papers, both English and Japanese, almost daily, and the whole Japanese community, particularly the Issei parents, relatives, and friends of the AJAs, were preoccupied with his visit, making it impossible for the Katta-gumi leaders to remain indifferent. For this reason, at their large weekly gathering in the hall of the Kotohira Shrine in Palama on February 14, 1946, the presiding leader announced their intention to donate a sum of money toward Mr. Finch's work for the wounded Nisei veterans in the hospitals on the mainland. The hearty applause after this announcement indicated the general sentiment of the audience. The words of praise and appreciation for Mr. Finch expressed and exchanged between Issei in the audience showed their satisfaction about this announcement.[14] Their donation was rejected by the AJA committee, however, as not representing a sincere motive and therefore unacceptable.

The Rev. Y. was charged with violation of the loyalty law in the First Circuit Court. A year later, in May 1947, however, his case was dismissed by Judge John Albert Matthewman. Yasutarō Sōga of the *Hawaii Times* commented in his editorial of May 10 that this decision did not mean that the defendant was right, but it merely meant that he did not violate the law. The Issei population reacted with disfavor to the court's decision.

> It may be all right to arrest and punish those who raised the Japanese flag on the Japanese emperor's birthday, but the flag-raising hurts only those who raised it. I can't understand why the authorities punish

those who don't do much harm while allowing those who are actually doing harm, misleading the ignorant Japanese, to continue unpunished.

Maybe the authorities don't care. Those fanatical pro-Japanese groups and their leaders are not worth their attention.

It is too costly to excuse these leaders in the name of democracy. The freedom of speech should be for the benefit of the majority and not for the few who do the damage.[15]

Because of official admonitions, the Rev. Y. limited his public appearances to small gatherings. This resulted in the discontinuation of the large gatherings that were so spectacular and impressive. In time, Katta-gumi leaders shifted their work from the local Japanese to the prisoners-of-war on Oahu.[16] Their projects included sending home-cooked Japanese food and providing Japanese entertainment. After the departure of the Japanese prisoners, however, the Katta-gumi leaders had no concrete projects convincing enough to keep their members together. This led them to concentrate on the differences and disagreements among themselves, which caused them to split into numerous rival groups with names such as "Hissho-kai" (Sure Victory Association) and "Shosei-kai" (Association of the Faithful), among others. By April 1947, there were at least eight known Katta-gumi groups, bitterly critical of each other.[17] Moreover, the rivalry among the various groups meant that none of them could monopolize Reverend Y. as its exclusive leader. As a result, the lay leaders began to criticize him as being more favorably disposed to this or that group, and he thus ceased to be the central, unifying figure for the whole movement.[18]

The fundamental cause of disintegration of the Katta-gumi came from within its rank and file, because of the fact that the basis of the organization was in the nature of unrealizable expectations, as these statements by ex-Katta-gumi members indicate:

> The representatives of Dōshi-kai collected $10 from each house in this neighborhood for a welcome party in honor of Prince Takamatsu who was to arrive with the Japanese fleet. I was among the very few around here who refused to donate for such a silly thing. Prince Takamatsu never came and now the people are wondering what happened to that money. Some say that they are going to give it to Red Cross to be used for the tidal wave victims in Hilo.

> My husband says now that it is no use to go to hear Reverend Y. It is only a waste of time. What he said has never come true.

I gradually quit believing rumors, because none of them came true, while everything published in the newspapers proved to be true. . . . Now whenever I hear anyone say Japan won the war, I make every effort to convince him about Japan's defeat. Many people call me "Haisen-gumi" (defeat group) and "pro-American." I don't care. I am telling them the truth.

Almost all of these men used to be fanatical believers in Japan's victory. But now, they appear as if they had no part in such a thing. They criticize those who still say Japan won the war. They show great appreciation of America and try to do their best to learn about it. Well, it's a wholesome adjustment on their part any way. So, we try not to embarrass them by mentioning what they used to be earlier.[19]

The Katta-gumi eventually shifted their program to one of helping disabled Japanese soldiers in Japan. In 1950, Katta-gumi groups comprised of 470 members sent $10,000 to *Yūai Juji-kai,* a service organization in Japan under the Department of Welfare, to assist disabled Japanese soldiers. The Rev. Y. returned to Japan and became a member of the board of directors of this organization. The Katta-gumi groups organized themselves as the Hawaii Branch of *Yūai Juji-kai.* They sent gifts amounting to almost $4,500 to help over 4,000 former Japanese soldiers in Japan. When the minister of welfare of Japan stopped in Hawaii on his way to the United States, the Hawaii *Yūai Juji-kai* gave him a grand welcome party. In May 1951, the leaders of Katta-gumi published a statement announcing that they now recognized Japan's defeat and apologizing for having caused much trouble in the local community.[20]

Normalization of the Issei Community

The temporary upsurge of fanaticism notwithstanding, the Issei community began to resume its prewar stability. As they realized the successful administration of General MacArthur's Occupation Army and the willingness of the Japanese people to cooperate in reorganization and democratization of Japan, the Issei's confidence in the leadership of the United States profoundly increased. They began to see the merits of democratization of their old country in contrast to its previous rigid social system through the observations of their sons and relatives in the Occupation Army, and at the same time their earlier feelings of humiliation stemming from the defeat of their old country disappeared. The presence of Nisei veterans and their active participation in the life of the larger community also helped the Issei to enjoy an increased sense of belonging to America and stabilized their position.

Another change for the Issei was the aggressive unionization of plantation laborers undertaken by the ILWU (International Longshoremen's and Warehousemen's Union) immediately after the war. Issei laborers who were used to the paternalism of the plantation system expressed mixed feelings concerning their changed status, contrasting the former warm relationship with the personnel of the plantation management to the present cold, formal relationship as well as their former inferior position to their present role as defined by Union membership and more clear-cut labor classifications. Those who had large families seemed to miss the former perquisites, including free housing, which they lost after unionization.[21] Regardless of whether they liked it or not, the Issei on the plantations became part of the American labor movement.

The Japanese Chamber of Commerce

In March 1947, the prewar Japanese Chamber of Commerce was reorganized by businessmen returned from mainland internment camps under a new name, the Honolulu Businessmen's Association. There was strong opposition to maintaining an exclusively Japanese group from some of its prewar officers, who insisted that the time for Japanese organizations had gone and the Japanese must operate as part of the American community through institutions such as Honolulu Chamber of Commerce. The majority of Issei businessmen felt, however, that the Issei as a whole were still unable to participate fully in American organizations because of their inability to speak English freely. The first president of this new Businessmen's Association, Daizo Sumida, indicated that it would cooperate closely with the Honolulu Chamber of Commerce not only in matters related to trade but also in translating and circulating materials issued by the latter for the non-English-speaking Japanese businessmen to help them get acquainted with the latter's work. He also indicated that the Issei still needed some kind of organization in order to participate in community-wide projects such as the Community Chest drive. Also, having an organization, the Issei were in a better position to control un-

American activities in the Issei community such as those manifested by the Katta-gumi. The leaders of the Businessmen's Association declared that they would have no connection with Japan except in trade and that they would operate as an organization of the permanent residents of the United States. Sumida articulated the feelings of the Issei business leaders as follows:

> We revived this businessmen's organization for the definite purpose of contributing to the Territory of Hawaii as permanent residents of the United States. Our interest is in Hawaii and not in Japan. In fact we don't want to be considered as Japanese. Legally, we are not eligible for naturalization, but that does not change our attitude. We consider ourselves permanent American residents. Personally, I don't like to have even such distinctions as Issei and Nisei. As a matter of fact, we invite Nisei businessmen not as the younger generation but as our equals or even someone from whom we Issei can get advice and at the same time save the Issei from becoming isolated from the mainstream of American life.[22]

The executive secretary of the Honolulu Chamber of Commerce expressed disappointment, since the Caucasian business circle had generally desired the Japanese businessmen to operate as part of the Chamber of Commerce of Honolulu, although he understood the language difficulty of the Issei.[23] Very close cooperation between the two organizations developed, however, as evidenced by the fact that all the directors of the Japanese Businessmen's Association became members of the Honolulu Chamber of Commerce and the general members were also urged to join the latter. By 1946, the number of Japanese members of the Chamber of Commerce rose to 500 or so, one-fourth of its total membership of 2,000. In the meantime, at the annual meeting of the Honolulu Businessmen's Association on February 22, 1948, it was decided that the association would resume its former name, the Honolulu Japanese Chamber of Commerce.

Reopening of Japanese Language Schools and Other Japanese Institutions

The Japanese language schools were reopened after the Chinese language schools won a test case to reopen their schools in October 1947. In the spring of 1948, fifteen Japanese language schools were open with forty-five teachers and about 3,000 students. By August 1950, seventy-one Japanese language schools were open in the whole Territory—twenty-seven in Honolulu, fifteen in rural Oahu, six on Kauai, six on Maui, sixteen on Hawaii, and one on Lanai—all of which were under the supervision of the Territorial Board of Education as in the prewar days, giving lessons one hour a day after public school hours.

Buddhist temples and Shinto shrines were reopened with their prewar priests in charge. Especially noticeable was the active participation of the Nisei in the Buddhist temples. For the Memorial Day service at Honpa Hongwanji Temple in 1947, Nisei members invited Earl M. Finch and Mayor John Henry Wilson as the main speakers. Also, the Young Men's Buddhist Association, through the Joint Memorial Day Committee of Honolulu, sent a large floral wreath to Paris by Pan American Airways to honor those from Hawaii who died in Europe. Thus, the important affairs of the Buddhist temples became increasingly part of the affairs of the larger community.

Preparation for the Naturalization of the Issei

The Issei businessmen as well as Issei newspaper editors resumed their position of leadership in the community. In spite of their internment during the war, they became the spearhead of Americanization of the Issei. As various bills for granting naturalization to ineligible aliens were introduced to Congress after World War II, including those introduced by Hawaii's delegate to Congress, Joseph R. Farrington, the efforts among the Issei for Americanization became more positive. Among such efforts was the formation of the American-Way Program Committee to prepare the Issei for their eventual naturalization. This movement became territory-wide with branches on all the islands. Their program included translating the opinions of scientists, critics, and politicians that appeared in American books and magazines and publishing them in the Japanese vernaculars. They were reprinted and circulated among the Issei. Also, as part of the regular projects, this committee sponsored 15-minute programs called "Beikoku-shugi Kyokai" (Americanism-Promotion Association), broadcast over the radio station KULA every Sunday. Independent of this committee but reflecting the general trend among the Issei were the English classes held in some of the Japanese language schools and churches. Thus, the Issei population was looking forward to their eventual naturalization.

The bill extending the privilege of naturalization to aliens ineligible for naturalization, introduced by Senator Patrick A. McCarran of Nevada and Representative Francis E. Walter of Pennsylvania, was passed by the 80th Session of Congress. It was vetoed by President Truman, however. The amended bill, which included provisions to allow the immigration of an annual quota of 185 individuals from Japan and 100 from each of the other countries in the vast Asian-Pacific area east of Iran and west of Hawaii and north of Australia, was passed by the 82nd Session of Congress. President Truman vetoed this bill as discriminatory. Both Houses, however, overrode Truman's veto on June 27, 1952, and the McCarran Act became law on December 24 of that year. Thus, freed from the yoke of legal restrictions, the Issei at long last became eligible for American citizenship. In the following year, under the Department of Education, the adult education evening classes for preparing the aliens for naturalization tests, were opened at thirteen county high schools on Oahu, and similar classes were organized on the neighbor islands. Among many who were naturalized within a couple of years were fourteen elderly Issei men and women, ranging in age from seventy to ninety years.[24]

Conclusion

Collectively and individually the Issei came through a long, eventful, and at times rugged, journey. Since they came to Hawaii because they were needed for Hawaii's sugar production, their problems were invariably the concern of the dominant white community that controlled Hawaii's sugar industry and its social, economic, and political systems. Even when the Issei struck, they still belonged to Hawaii's economic system. When such a strike was prolonged, influential segments of the leading Caucasian citizens took the initiative to seek a solution. Moreover, these leaders invited the leaders of the Japanese community to discuss the issues together to find a workable proposal. The Issei were never outsiders.

As the Issei began to move to the city, principally Honolulu, they chose to live in the same areas, resulting in the concentration of the Japanese in what might be called ghettos. These settlements were for convenience, however, and never for self-protection from a hostile outgroup or as a result of racial discrimination. Many professional Isseis, merchants, bankers, physicians, and so on resided in the areas of their choice outside the Japanese ethnic settlements. Although there were residential areas where only wealthy Caucasians lived, such exclusiveness was similar to the residential areas of wealthy or upper-class people in Japan. It was taken for granted and never became a social issue among the Issei.

The ownership of real property by the Issei was encouraged in Hawaii as the proof of permanent residence. In 1928 the tax the Japanese paid on real property exceeded $10,000, showing for the first time a larger amount than the tax paid by them for interest on savings and personal effects, according to the Territorial Department of Taxation. Since that year this trend continued and the Japanese began to take pride in land and homeownership, a great contrast to the situation in California where the alien land laws of 1913 and 1920 forced Issei farmers either out of business or to continue farming as either the employees of their Nisei children, who were eligible to be the legal owners of their farmlands, or by paying Caucasians to be the nominal owners of their lands.

In a time of extreme crisis, the quality of leadership becomes of paramount importance. Fortunately for Hawaii during World War II, its leaders, both military and civilian, were individuals of unusual caliber and unwavering faith in American democracy. Foreseeing the predicament of both the Issei and Nisei in the event of war with Japan, the authorities prepared the civilian population including the Japanese for the united front and interracial cooperation necessary to win the war. The experience of the Japanese in Hawaii during the war was complete ingroup participation as part of the larger community.

Robert L. Shivers, Chief of FBI during World War II, declared:

> Hawaii has something unique and worthwhile to preserve in the way of human relationships. If the people of various ethnic backgrounds could live harmoniously during the war, then a basis for good relationships would have been established for the future.

Notes

Chapter 1

1. Ralph S. Kuykendall, *The Earliest Japanese Labor Immigration to Hawaii*, pp. 4–14, 17, 23–26; Ralph S. Kuykendall, *The Hawaiian Kingdom*, Vol. 2, *1854–1874, Twenty Critical Years*, pp. 183, 235.

2. Kuykendall, *Hawaiian Kingdom*, Vol. 3, 1874–1893, *The Kalakaua Dynasty*, pp. 154–162.

3. Ibid., pp. 165–166.

4. *Hawaii Nihonjin Iminshi* [A history of Hawaii's Japanese immigration], pp. 91–96.

5. Kenpū Z. Kawazoe, *Ishoku no Hana Hiraku* [Blossoming of transplanted trees], pp. 190–191. *Dekasegi* means to go abroad to work to earn money.

6. *Hawaii Nihonjin Iminshi*, pp. 98, 101; Kuykendall, *Hawaiian Kingdom*, vol. 3, p. 167.

7. Kuykendall, *Hawaiian Kingdom*, vol. 3, pp. 165–166.

8. *Hawaii Nihonjin Iminshi*, p. 106.

9. Ibid., pp. 98–99.

10. Ibid., pp. 108, 111, 151. In 1894, a year after the overthrow of the Hawaiian monarchy, the governments of Japan and the Republic of Hawaii agreed to annul the Immigration Convention signed in 1886 between Japan and the Kingdom of Hawaii. Chief Inspector Nakayama and all of the Japanese inspectors and physicians on his staff resigned in 1895, and the separate Japanese section of the Immigration Bureau was closed in 1896.

11. Kuykendall, *Hawaiian Kingdom*, vol. 3, p. 169.

12. Ibid., pp. 170–171; Harris Methodist Church, *88th Anniversary: 1888–1976*, pp. 3, 5.

13. *The Rainbow: A History of the Honolulu Japanese Chamber of Commerce*, Japanese section, p. 234; Ryūkichi Kihara, *Hawaii Nihonjinshi* [A history of the Japanese in Hawaii], pp. 466–470.

14. Keihō Yasutarō Sōga, *Gojūnen no Hawaii Kaiko* [My memoir of fifty years in Hawaii], pp. 27, 28.

15. Ibid., p. 18.

16. *Report of the Bureau of Immigration for the Year Ending December 31, 1898*, pp. 13, 14.

17. *A History of Japanese in Hawaii,* pp. 127–129.
18. Ibid., pp. 114, 115; Kawazoe, *Ishoku no Hana Hiraku,* pp. 138–143.
19. *A History of Japanese in Hawaii,* pp. 114–115.
20. Ibid., p. 115; Kawazoe, *Ishoku no Hana Hiraku,* pp. 139, 140.
21. Kawazoe, *Ishoku no Hana Hiraku,* pp. 140–141.
22. Ibid., pp. 142–143.
23. *A History of Japanese in Hawaii,* pp. 115–116.
24. Sōga, *Gojūnen no Hawaii Kaiko,* pp. 4, 6–8.
25. Ibid., pp. 11, 20–21.
26. *History of Japanese in Hawaii,* p. 172; *Report of the President of the Bureau of Immigration to the Governor of Hawaii for the Period 1888–1890,* pp. 13, 14.
27. Kihara, *Hawaii Nihonjinshi,* pp. 573, 574; *History of Japanese in Hawaii,* pp. 161, 162.
28. Interview, 1979. The Fukuoka Hotel was one of eleven Japanese hotels in Honolulu that took care of those going to the West Coast.
29. Carey McWilliams, *Prejudice: Japanese Americans, Symbol of Racial Intolerance,* pp. 28, 32–33.
30. Ibid., pp. 66–68; *Hawaii Nihonjin Iminshi,* p. 175.
31. Ernest Wakukawa, *A History of the Japanese People in Hawaii,* pp. 245, 351.
32. Ibid., p. 11.
33. Sōga, *Gojūnen no Hawaii Kaiko,* pp. 391–393; Kihara, *Hawaii Nihonjinshi,* pp. 648, 650.
34. Sōga, *Gojūnen no Hawaii Kaiko,* p. 392; interview with Kiyomi Suzuki, Katsunuma's daughter, in 1980.
35. Interview with Kiyomi Suzuki.
36. *Hawaii Nihonjin Iminshi,* p. 241; Sōga, *Gojūnen no Hawaii Kaiko,* p. 393; Kihara, *Hawaii Nihonjinshi,* pp. 651–652, 654, 656.
37. Sōga, *Gojūnen no Hawaii Kaiko,* p. 10.
38. *The Friend,* p. 133; Kihara, *Hawaii Nihonjinshi,* pp. 655, 656. The June 1913 issue of *The Friend* carried the full text of Dr. Scudder's Peace Sunday sermon on pp. 130–132.
39. The bill promptly passed both Houses of the California legislature and was signed by the governor. The reaction in Japan to this first official anti-Japanese act was widespread resentment and anti-American demonstrations.
40. Government of Hawaii, *House Journal,* Seventh Legislature, Regular Session, 1913, pp. 959, 1000; Kihara, *Hawaii Nihonjinshi,* pp. 656–657.
41. Ernest Wakukawa, pp. 310, 311, 312.

Chapter 2

1. Japan is made up of eight geographical regions called Chiho. Each of Chiho has several Ken or prefectures with their respective local governments. *Hokkaido,* the northernmost island is a Chiho by itself with its local government like a Ken. The Chihos on Honshu (Main Island) are *Tohoku, Kanto, Chubu, Kinki,*

and *Chugoku.* The area of Chubu Chiho facing the Sea of Japan is also called *Hokuriku Chiho.* The area of Chugoku Chiho facing the Sea of Japan is called *Sanin Chiho* while the area facing the Inland Sea is called *Sanyo Chiho. Shikoku* which has four prefectures is an island in the Inland Sea. *Kyushu Chiho* includes a large island extending from the southwest of Honshu to Okinawa-ken, the southernmost prefecture of Japan.

2. *Hawaii Nihonjin Iminshi,* p. 314.

3. *The Rainbow,* Japanese section, p. 109.

4. Interviews with Okayamans (1978, 1980). Despite such a small number of Okayamans in Hawaii, one successful Okayaman must be mentioned. Masayuki Tokioka came to Hawaii in 1909 at the age of 12 to join his parents. He went to public schools, including McKinley High School and University of Hawaii. He did his postgraduate work at Harvard University, majoring in business administration, receiving an M.A. In 1925 he founded International Savings & Loan Association, Ltd. and in 1929 he founded National Mortgage & Finance Co. Ltd. Both these financial organizations have grown without interruption and are flourishing in the 1980s.

5. Kenji Takahashi, *Fukushima Iminshi: Hawaii Kikansha no Maki* [A history of overseas emigration of Fukushimans: Returnees from Hawaii], p. 312; *Fukushima Isseiki* [The century of Fukushima], Preface, p. 12.

6. *Hawaii Nihonjin Iminshi,* p. 314.

7. *Golden Jubilee of the Government Contract Japanese Immigration to Hawaii: 1885–1935,* p. 116. Hotels operated by Okinawans were the Hawaii Ryokan by Kameichi Kakazu, Honolulu Ryokan by Kiyoshi Shimabukuro, and Kyushuya Ryokan by Seishin Gushiken. Tohoku Ryokan was operated by Jinshichi Tokairin of Fukushima-ken, catering principally to those from Tohoku Chiho and Niigata-ken and others from Hokuriku Chiho.

8. Interview (1979).

9. *Golden Jubilee,* p. 41.

10. Takahashi, *Fukushima Iminshi,* p. 266.

11. Interview (1979).

12. Interview (1980).

13. Interview (1980).

14. Interview (1979).

15. Interview (1979).

16. Sōga, p. 145.

17. *The Rainbow,* Japanese Section, p. 41.

18. *Fukushima Isseiki,* p. 489.

19. Sōga, p. 143.

20. Ibid.

21. Ibid., pp. 144, 145.

22. Tomizō Katsunuma, *Kansho no Shiborikasu* [Bagasse of sugar cane], Katsunuma Kinen Publishing Society, Honolulu, 1924, pp. 120–121.

23. Yukuo Uyehara, personal communication, 1980.

24. Sōga, p. 146.

25. Ibid., p. 144.

26. Interview (1980).

27. Interview with Chukichi Furuyama, 1979.
28. Interview (1979).
29. Interview (1980).
30. Interview (1979). Pumpkin in standard Japanese is Kabocha. The word "Tonasu" is used also.
31. The term "Chorinbo" was not used by non-Chūgokuans. Some informed persons of Chūgoku background agree that the people identified by this term were originally from Korea. According to the Rev. Hirai of Todaiji Buddhist Temple, Kiyomasa Kato, Commanding General of Hideyoshi Toyotomi's invading army of Korea in 1596–97, brought back servile Koreans to do the tasks which the Japanese considered unclean such as skinning of dead animals, tanning, manufacture of leather instruments and footgears, disposition of corpses on the highways, etc. Some elderly people from Kyushu recall the term "Chorinbo" used for those originally from Korea, but when they were growing up the use of this term was prohibited by law.

Also, the feudal lords of Kyushu and Chūgoku who participated in Hideyoshi's invasion of Korea brought back with them Korean ceramic artisans. They were assigned to manufacture of ceramics in the Nagato area of Chūgoku Chiho and Hizen area of Kyushu. Their ceramic products were the forerunners of the beautiful Hagiyaki of Yamaguchi-ken and Imariyaki and Aritayaki of Saga-ken of Kyushu. These Koreans were naturalized in 1598. Although they came from Korea at the same time, they were treated honorably.

The belief in "Inugami" (Dog-god), the evil spirit which causes curse to human beings, persisted among the immigrants from Chūgoku Chiho long after World War II. The less used word is "Hebigami" (Snake-god) with the same evil power. The individual who is suffering from sickness caused by the intense hatred of a person whose family strain has "Inugami", that hatred does not stop its curse until the victim is destroyed, according to the Rev. Hirai. The victims afflicted by Inugami come to her temple to be extricated from the curse by prayer. After the evil spirit has left the body, the victim starts regaining the normal health. According to the Rev. Hirai, the family which has the "Inugami" strain or "Hebigami" strain can extricate itself from it, if its members do not hate anybody for three generations, but it takes a tremendous effort on their part. (Interviews in 1980)

Chapter 3

1. Kanji Takahashi, *Fukushima Iminshi: Hawaii Kikansha no Maki* [A history of overseas emigration of Fukushimans: volume on returned former emigrants to Hawaii], p. 5.
2. Ibid., p. 12; *Fukushima Isseiki* [The century of Fukushima], p. 226.
3. Takahashi, *Fukushima Iminshi,* pp. 14, 15.
4. Ibid., p. 316.
5. Ibid.
6. Ibid., p. 91. Hapaiko was mechanized in 1925 according to the Oahu Sugar Company.
7. Ibid., p. 268.

8. Ibid., pp. 37, 38.

9. *Ko Okazaki Nihei-Oh Tsuitō Kinenshi* [The memorial booklet honoring the late venerable Nihei Okazaki], p. 40.

10. Ibid.

11. Takahashi, *Fukushima Iminshi*, p. 8.

12. Kiyoshi Ōkubo, *Hawaitō Nihonjin Iminshi* [A history of Japanese immigrants on the Island of Hawaii], pp. 527–666.

13. Takahashi, *Fukushima Iminshi*, p. 268.

14. *Ko Okazaki*, pp. 38, 92.

15. Ibid., pp. 1, 2.

16. Ibid., pp. 40, 41.

17. Ibid., pp. 38, 39, 92.

18. Ibid., pp. 2–5, 18; Takahashi, *Fukushima Iminshi*, pp. 11, 12.

19. Takahashi, *Fukushima Iminshi*, p. 12.

20. Yakichi Watanabe, *Hawaii Zaijū Fukushima Kenjin Ryakureki Shashinchō* [Album of pictures and personal records of Fukushimans in Hawaii], p. 129; interview with Mrs. Fumiko Kamada, 1980, daughter of the late Jinshichi Tōkairin and proprietor of Nuuanu Onsen Restaurant in Honolulu.

21. Ōkubo, *Hawaitō Nihonjin Iminshi*, pp. 77, 193–194, 210.

22. Tahakashi, *Fukushima Iminshi*, pp. 14, 15.

23. Interview with Mrs. Mariko Sumida, 1979, Dr. Takahashi's daughter.

24. Takahashi, *Fukushima Iminshi*, pp. 3, 4, 5, 6.

25. Tomizō Katsunuma, *Kansho no Shiborikasu* [Bagasse of Sugar Cane], pp. 101–105.

26. Takahashi, *Fukushima Iminshi*, p. 5.

27. Kenpū Kawazoe, *Ishoku no Hana Hiraku* [Blossoming of transplanted trees], pp. 348, 349.

28. Katsunuma, *Kansho no Shiborikasu*, pp. 109–110. Japanese neighborhoods usually had regular, licensed peddlers, whose vehicles were specially equipped with an ice box for fish and vegetables and compartments for food and other household commodities, who made their rounds twice a week. These mobile supermarkets were indispensable to Issei housewives. Dr. Katsunuma could never compete with them.

29. Ibid., pp. 74, 76.

30. Takahashi, *Fukushima Iminshi*, p. 171.

31. Interview, 1979.

32. Interview, 1979. Instead of showing his displeasure directly, he made a sarcastic remark implying the Fukushimans did not lie while Chūgokujins, with their smooth-talking, might. The Ainu are the aboriginal people of Hokkaido. Asking the Chūgokujins if they were of mixed blood with Koreans was his way of insulting them, suggesting they were part of the servile class of Koreans derogatorily called "Chorinbo" who were brought to western Japan by Hideyoshi's army in 1591–1592.

33. Interview with Charlie S., 1980. I was also a regular listerner of his weekly radio broadcast. The term "Chorinbo" is explained above, in note 32. "Eta" refers to a group of people in Japan whose traditional occupations were what the Japanese considered degrading or unclean, such as slaughtering and butchering,

tanning and leather work, including the manufacture of shoes and other leather goods. Consequently they were treated as outcastes. The date of their emergence is unknown. In 1871, the fourth year of Meiji, the use of the term "Eta-Hinin" (Eta nonhuman) was abolished by law. The Eta are still ostracized and live in residential districts called "Buraku" mostly in Osaka and Kyoto, where they operate an extensive leather manufacturing industry. The former Eta community is now called *Suiheisha* (Society of Demanding Equality). The prefectural government has a special bureau to help with their assimilation.

34. Ibid.

35. Ibid. Charlie S is referring to the religious sect called Tensho Kodaijingu-kyo, which was founded in Japan after World War II by Sayo Kitamura, the widow of a farmer in Tabuse, Kumage County, Yamaguchi-ken. She was called by her followers Ō-gamisama, Great Goddess, but she was generally known as the Dancing Goddess, because her religion involved spontaneous dancing and chanting. She died in 1967, but her granddaughter succeeded her and is called Hime-Gamisama, Princess Goddess. Charlie S. died in August 1981.

36. Takahashi, *Fukushima Iminshi*, p. 20.

37. Ibid., pp. 119–120.

38. Ibid., p. 13.

39. Interview with Toshio Tanji, 1980.

40. Takahashi, *Fukushima Iminshi*, pp. 225–261, 271–275; interview, 1980.

41. Interview, 1980.

42. Interview with Toshio Tanji, 1980.

Chapter 4

1. Kōei Ōzato, *Taira Shinsuke Den* [A biography of Shinsuke Taira], pp. 31–32, 35, 40, 47, 50–51.

2. Seiyei Wakukawa, *The Life and Times of Kyūzō Tōyama*, pp. 45, 46, 47, 121–122, 124.

3. Ibid., pp. 126–135.

4. *Hawaii Times*, January 1, 1959.

5. Wakukawa, *Life and Times*, pp. 136–137.

6. Ibid., pp. 135–136, 148, 252–253.

7. Ibid., pp. 150–153.

8. Ibid., pp. 153, 156–157, 160, 165.

9. Ibid., pp. 162–164, 254–257.

10. Ibid., p. 164.

11. Ibid., pp. 165–169, 178.

12. Seiyei Wakukawa, "Hawaii Okinawa Kenjin Shishō" [Excerpts from the history of the Okinawan Kenjin in Hawaii], *Okinawa, Hawaii Special Edition*, p. 17; Wakukawa, *Life and Times*, pp. 176–177.

13. These statements were recorded at a meeting of Issei members of the Okinawa Kenjin-kai in Hilo at Dr. Zenko Matayoshi's residence in 1960.

14. *Hawaiian Japanese Annual and Directory*, 1915.

15. Ibid., 1940.

16. Interview with Kiman Kaneshiro, 1961.

17. Ibid.
18. Interview with Taru Chinen, 1961.
19. Statistical data were provided by the U.S. Department of Agriculture Statistical Service and the State of Hawaii Department of Agriculture. I was allowed to have access to the original reports of the individual farmers whose names were available. I also interviewed hog farmers as well as the personnel of the Planning Department of the City and County of Honolulu, of Bishop Estate's Management Division, and of Kaiser Land Development Co., all of whom were responsible for the removal and closing of most of the Okinawan piggeries (1961).
20. An account of the 1935 *Osaka Mainichi Daily* meeting was published by Yasutarō Sōga in his *Gojūnen no Hawaii Kaiko.*
21. Interview with Makari Goya, 1957. Examples of Okinawan enterprises include Shoshin Steven Nagamine's Flamingo restaurants with six locations on Oahu (four in Honolulu), Agnes Asato's Wisteria in Honolulu, and Albert and Wallen Teruya's Times Supermarkets with fifteen locations on Oahu.
22. According to Onaga, good steak cost 10 cents a pound in those days. On Oahu, as well as Hawaii and Maui, the Okinawans were also active in the wholesale and distribution of fruits and vegetables. In the field of poultry, Chokichi Ige, Gensuke Nakama, Mankichi Shimabukuro, and Seisho Kakazu operated large-scale chicken farms with twenty to thirty thousand birds for meat and eggs in the 1960s. State Poultry, a large-scale hatchery founded by Anyu Uezu in 1960, continues to do a successful business in the 1980s.
23. Interview with Mrs. Shinyu Gima, 1960.
24. Interview with Kame Nakamura, 1960. *Tanomoshi* was a mini-savings and loan club organized among friends to meet emergencies. Friends who loaned money to another person collected the interest in a period of several months to a year or longer. See chapter 12.
25. Interview with Mrs. Umeno Goto, 1980.
26. Sōga, *Gojūnen no Hawaii Kaiko,* pp. 372–373. The term *dekasegi* means "making money away from the homeland," usually in reference to overseas emigration.
27. Interview with Ushisuke Taira, 1957. Taira was a realtor and had received an education on the U.S. Mainland.
28. Interview with Harry S. Uehara, 1957.
29. Interview with Dr. Henry S. Gima, 1957.
30. *Hawaii Times,* January 1, 1975, "Okinawa Imin no Zadan-kai on 75 Years of Kuto" [Discussion meeting on the 75 years of the fight to overcome hardship], p. 2.
31. Interview with Fujio Abe, former president of Kumamoto Kenjin-Kai, 1980.
32. Interview, 1980.
33. Interview, 1980.
34. Mitsugu Sakihara, *Gajimaru no Tsudoi: Stories of the Okinawan Immigrants to Hawaii,* p. 193.
35. Interview, 1980.
36. Interview, 1980.
37. Series of interviews with Thomas Taro Higa, 1977–1981.
38. Interview with Mrs. Taro Higa, 1980.

39. Sakihara, *Gajimaru no Tsudoi,* p. 197.

40. Interview with Mrs. Shimpuku Gima, 1980.

41. *Hawaii Pacific Press,* June 1980, p. 13.

42. Interviews with Hiroshiman and Okinawan residents of Waianae, 1980.

43. Interviews, 1978.

44. Interviews, 1979.

45. Interview with Sadao Asato, 1980.

46. Interview, 1981.

47. Interview, 1965.

48. Shigemori Tamaki, "Memories of Hawaii," *Hawaii Pacific Press,* July 1980, p. 7.

49. Sakihara, *Gajimaru no Tsudoi,* p. 44.

50. Interview with Sadao Asato, 1980; Sakihara, *Gajimaru no Tsudoi,* p. 45.

51. Interview, 1979.

52. Interview, 1980.

53. Interview, 1980.

54. Interview, 1980.

55. Interviews, 1979, 1980, 1981.

56. Interviews with Buddhist priests of Jodo-shu temple and Hongwanji temple on Kauai in 1960.

57. Ibid. Ancestor worship was the traditional religion of Okinawa, and for this reason they built spacious, elaborate graves, the interior of which was like a storeroom to keep the containers of the bones of deceased members of the family. The custom of "Senkotsu" was part of this ancestor worship.

58. Interviews and participation by the author in meetings during research trips to Hawaii, Maui, Molokai, and Lanai in 1960s.

59. Interviews and casual conversation, 1978–1980.

60. Sakihara, *Gajimaru no Tsudoi,* pp. 45, 46.

61. Interview, 1957.

Chapter 5

1. Ernest K. Wakukawa, *A History of the Japanese People in Hawaii,* p. 169.

2. William L. Abbott, "Labor in Hawaii," *Honolulu Star-Bulletin,* September 4, 1967. Abbott was the educational director of the United Rubber Workers, AFL-CIO.

3. Wakukawa, *History of the Japanese People in Hawaii,* pp. 187–189. The Board of Immigration, in cooperation with the HSPA, decided to bring Europeans such as Portuguese, Spaniards, and Russians to Hawaii as plantation laborers, and they offered a higher wage than what was offered to Asian workers. This plan was in response to concern that there were too many Japanese laborers.

4. Ibid., pp. 170, 172–173, 175.

5. Ibid., pp. 172–173. Fred K. Makino was then a proprietor of a drugstore and later became publisher of the *Hawaii Hochi* daily. Matsutaro Yamashiro was a proprietor of the Yamashiro Hotel in Honolulu.

6. Yasutarō Sōga, *Gojūnen no Hawaii Kaiko* [My memoir of fifty years in Hawaii], pp. 193–195.

7. Ibid., p. 207.

8. Ibid., p. 197.

9. Ibid., pp. 199–200.

10. *A History of Japanese in Hawaii,* p. 177.

11. Wakukawa, *History of Japanese in Hawaii,* p. 180.

12. Sōga, *Gojūnen no Hawaii Kaiko,* p. 227; Wakukawa, *History of Japanese in Hawaii,* p. 190.

13. Wakukawa, *History of Japanese in Hawaii,* pp. 179, 186; Sōga, *Gojūnen no Hawaii Kaiko,* pp. 207–208, 229.

14. Sōga, *Gojūnen no Hawaii Kaiko,* pp. 211–213.

15. Ibid., p. 214.

16. Ibid., pp. 215–216, 213–214.

17. Ibid., pp. 219–220.

18. Ibid., pp. 220–221.

19. Ibid., pp. 220, 224.

20. Interview, 1979.

21. Sōga, *Gojūnen no Hawaii Kaiko,* pp. 11–12.

22. Wakukawa, *History of Japanese in Hawaii,* pp. 248–249.

23. Romanzo Adams, *The Peoples of Hawaii,* p. 33. The total number of Japanese employed on sugar plantations in Hawaii in 1920 was 19,474 and that of Filipinos was 13,061. See also Wakukawa, *History of Japanese in Hawaii,* p. 246.

24. Wakukawa, *History of Japanese in Hawaii,* pp. 249–250.

25. Ibid., pp. 251, 252.

26. Ibid., pp. 252–253.

27. Albertine Loomis, *To All People: A History of the Hawaii Conference of the United Church of Christ,* pp. 296, 297, 298.

28. *Hawaii Nihonjin Iminshi,* p. 277.

29. Loomis, *To All People,* pp. 299–301; Wakukawa, *History of Japanese in Hawaii,* pp. 254–259.

30. Loomis, *To All People,* p. 300.

31. Sōga, *Gojūnen no Hawaii Kaiko,* pp. 470–471.

32. Adams, *Peoples of Hawaii,* p. 36.

33. Sōga, *Gojūnen no Hawaii Kaiko,* p. 499.

34. Wakukawa, *History of Japanese in Hawaii,* pp. 188–189; Annual Report of the Commissioner-General of Immigration to the Secretary of Commerce and Labor, 1911, pp. 122–123.

35. Loomis, *To All People,* pp. 299.

36. *Hawaii Nihonjin Iminshi,* p. 185.

Chapter 6

1. *Pineapple in Hawaii Today,* pp. 14–15; telephone interviews with staff of the Pineapple Growers Association of Hawaii, Dole Pineapple Division of Castle and Cooke, Inc., and the Del Monte Corporation, in August and September, 1986.

2. *The Rainbow: A History of the Honolulu Japanese Chamber of Commerce,* Japanese section, pp. 98–99; *Hawaii Nihonjin Iminshi,* pp. 205, 206.

3. *Hawaii Nihonjin Iminshi.*

4. Yasutarō Sōga, *Gojūnen no Hawaii Kaiko,* p. 126.

5. *Ko Okazaki Nihei-Oh Tsuitō Kinenshi* [The memorial booklet honoring the late venerable Nihei Okazaki], pp. 1–3, 39–40.

6. *The Story of Pineapple in Hawaii.*

7. Russ and Peg Apple, "Tales of Old Hawaii," *Honolulu Star-Bulletin,* May 15, 1977.

8. Telephone interview with staff members of each of the pineapple companies and with a staff member of the Pineapple Growers Association of Hawaii, September and October 1986; *Pineapple in Hawaii Today,* pp. 14–17, 20–21.

9. Telephone interview with a staff member of the ILWU, September 1986.

10. Sōga, *Gojūnen no Hawaii Kaiko,* pp. 504, 505.

11. *A History of Japanese in Hawaii,* pp. 206, 207; John F. Embree, *Acculturation among the Japanese of Kona, Hawaii,* pp. 20–22, 26, 27.

12. Helen Oyakawa, "Coffee Picking Was Lots of Work," *Honolulu Star-Bulletin,* May 28, 1977.

13. Special Message on the Coffee Situation from Governor William F. Quinn to the First Legislature, State of Hawaii, April 3, 1961.

14. Yukiko Kimura, "Okinawans and the Hog Industry in Hawaii," *Honolulu Star-Bulletin,* August 2, 1975.

15. *A History of Japanese in Hawaii,* pp. 207, 208; interview in 1980 with Sannosuke Ōnishi, a retired fisherman and skipper of his own fishing boat until World War II.

16. *Tuna: Hawaii's Harvest of the Sea.*

17. *Nihon Rekishi Daijiten* [Encyclopedia of Japanese history], vol. 12, p. 189.

18. *The Rainbow,* English section, p. 108.

19. Matsujiro Ōtani, *Waga Hito to Narishi Ashiato: Hachijūnen no Kaiko* [My memoir of eighty years of my footsteps], p. 1.

20. Ibid., pp. 2, 12.

21. Ibid., p. 3.

22. Ibid., pp. 5, 6.

23. Ibid., pp. 6, 7.

24. Ibid., pp. 10–13.

25. Ibid., p. 15; the Japanese government did not allow anyone with trachoma, a contagious eye disease, to leave the country, nor did the U.S. Immigration Service permit entry to anyone with the disease.

26. Ibid., p. 16.

27. Ibid., p. 17.

28. Ibid., pp. 18–20.

29. Ibid., pp. 22, 23.

30. Ibid., p. 34.

31. Ibid., pp. 33, 34.

32. Ibid., pp. 36–38, 39–45.

33. Ibid., pp. 48, 53, 54.

34. Ibid., Attorney William Heen's statement in Preface.

35. Ibid., pp. 56–57.

36. Ibid., pp. 58–61.
37. Okinawa (the Ryukyus) was under the jurisdiction of the U.S. Army from 1949 until its reversion to Japan in 1971.
38. Ōtani, *Waga Hito to Narishi Ashiato,* pp. 142, 143.

Chapter 7

1. *Hawaii Nihonjin Iminshi,* pp. 108, 111, 151.
2. Ryūkichi Kihara, *Hawaii Nihonjinshi,* p. 449.
3. Kenpū Kawazoe, *Ishoku no Hana Hiraku,* pp. 179, 180; Kenpū Kawazoe, *Imin Hyakunen no Nenrin,* p. 119.
4. Yasutarō Sōga, *Gojūnen no Hawaii Kaiko,* pp. 59, 61, 62; Kihara, *Hawaii Nihonjinshi,* p. 476; telephone interview November 5, 1978 with Dr. Ira D. Hirschy, who was the resident physician at Kalaupapa Settlement from 1936 to 1940. There were no Japanese among the 1,100 patients at Kalaupapa in 1897 according to the settlements' records. The number of Japanese patients gradually increased at an average of about fifteen a year; at times there were more than forty Issei and Nisei men and women at the settlement. According to Dr. Hirschy, cases of leprosy among the Japanese have become almost nonexistent since the late 1960s.
5. Sōga, *Gojūnen no Hawaii Kaiko,* pp. 126, 127.
6. Kawazoe, *Ishoku no Hana Hiraku,* pp. 276, 277; "Dr. Katsuki, Dean of Medical Profession in Isles, Dies at 101," *Honolulu Star-Bulletin,* January 19, 1967.
7. *Hawaiian Japanese Annual and Directory,* 1928, p. 59; ibid., 1934–1935, pp. 81, 82; ibid., 1939–1940, pp. 137, 138.
8. Kawazoe, *Ishoku no Hana Hiraku,* pp. 142–144; *Honolulu Star-Bulletin,* January 13, 1978.
9. *Hawaiian Japanese Annual and Directory,* 1928, p. 58; ibid., 1934–1935, pp. 81–82; ibid., 1939–1940, pp. 137, 138.
10. Interview, August 1, 1959.
11. *Hawaiian Japanese Annual and Directory,* 1928, p. 58; ibid., 1939–1940, p. 138.

Chapter 8

1. *Hawaii Nihonjin Iminshi,* pp. 89–90, 105.
2. Kenpū Kawazoe, *Ishoku no Hana Hiraku,* pp. 159–160.
3. Kenpū Kawazoe, *Imin Hyakunen no Nenrin,* p. 124; *Hawaii Nihonjin Iminshi,* p. 108.
4. Ryūkichi Kihara, *Hawaii Nihonjinshi,* pp. 441–442, 451–453.
5. Ibid.
6. *Hawaii Nihonjin Iminshi,* pp. 159–160.
7. Ibid., pp. 160–161; *A History of Japanese in Hawaii,* pp. 143–144.
8. Ernest Wakukawa, *A History of the Japanese People in Hawaii,* pp. 156–157, 158.

9. *Reports of the Commissioner of Labor on Hawaii, 1900–1905,* p. 143.
10. Wakukawa, *History of the Japanese People,* p. 180.
11. Kihara, *Hawaii Nihonjinshi,* pp. 723–724.
12. Interview, 1939.
13. Suikei Kumaji Furuya, *Imin no Rakugaki* [An immigrant's scribbling], pp. 152–153.
14. Yasutarō Sōga, *Gojūnen no Hawaii Kaiko,* pp. 199–200.
15. Ibid., pp. 601–603; *Nippu Jiji,* January 5–27, February 1940, 5, 10.
16. Sōga, *Gojūnen no Hawaii Kaiko,* p. 602. Quite likely, Shimizu was charged with treason. Kudo must have reported to the Japanese government about Shimizu's activities in Hawaii.
17. Furuya, *Imin no Rakugaki,* pp. 160–161; Sōga, *Gojūnen no Hawaii Kaiko,* p. 611.

Chapter 9

1. Carey McWilliams, *Prejudice: Japanese Americans, Symbol of Racial Intolerance,* pp. 26, 28, 31–33, 66–68.
2. Romanzo Adams, *The Japanese in Hawaii,* p. 16.
3. Ernest K. Wakukawa, *A History of the Japanese People in Hawaii,* p. 341.
4. Kenpū Kawazoe, *Ishoku no Hana Hiraku,* pp. 315–316; Harris United Methodist Church, *88th Anniversary: 1888–1976,* pp. 35, 37, 38; Yasutarō Sōga, *Gojūnen no Hawaii Kaiko,* pp. 182, 193.
5. Sōga, *Gojūnen no Hawaii Kaiko,* pp. 183–185; Wakukawa, *History of Japanese People in Hawaii,* pp. 339–341.
6. Sōga, *Gojūnen no Hawaii Kaiko,* pp. 183–185; Harris, *88th Anniversary,* p. 37; interviews, 1943.
7. Ryūichi Kihara, *Hawaii Nihonjinshi,* pp. 286–287; Sōga, *Gojūnen no Hawaii Kaiko,* p. 366.
8. Wakukawa, *History of Japanese People in Hawaii,* pp. 341–342; Romanzo Adams, *The Peoples of Hawaii,* pp. 21–23; Adams, *Japanese in Hawaii,* pp. 17–18.
9. Kihara, *Hawaii Nihonjinshi,* pp. 505–509.
10. Sōga, *Gojūnen no Hawaii Kaiko,* pp. 120–121.
11. Kihara, *Hawaii Nihonjinshi,* pp. 489, 490.
12. Sōga, *Gojūnen no Hawaii Kaiko,* pp. 322–325.
13. Ibid., p. 263; interviews, 1959, 1980.
14. Tomizō Katsunuma, *Kansho no Shiborikasu,* p. 53.
15. Sōga, *Gojūnen no Hawaii Kaiko,* pp. 435–438.
16. Ibid., pp. 435–438; Tsuneichi Yamamoto, ed., *Life of Kinzaburo Makino,* p. 66. The Fukunaga affair shocked the entire Japanese community, and it took many years to get over the shock. When I stopped in Hawaii in 1930, the local Japanese were still talking about the incident.
17. Adams, *Peoples of Hawaii,* p. 52.
18. Ibid., pp. 49, 54–57.
19. Ralph S. Kuykendall, *The Hawaiian Kingdom,* vol. 1, p. 329. Three hun-

dred Chinese coolies were imported from Amoy in 1852. It was the beginning of the importation of foreigners to work as contract laborers on the plantations in Hawaii. They were on five-year contracts with a monthly wage of $3 with food, clothing, and housing provided in addition to free transportation from China to Hawaii.

20. Wakukawa, *History of Japanese People in Hawaii*, pp. 112–118, 123; Sōga, *Gojūnen no Hawaii Kaiko*, pp. 82–83.

21. Wakukawa, *History of Japanese People in Hawaii*, pp. 118–123; Sōga, *Gojūnen no Hawaii Kaiko*, pp. 86–93.

22. Interviews and informal communications and personal observations from 1938 to 1944.

23. Adams, The *People of Hawaii*, pp. 8, 9. In the 1872 census of the Hawaiian monarchy, the Portuguese were separately classified from "Other Caucasians." In 1900, in the first census after Hawaii became a United States territory, Hawaii continued to use the separate classification for the Portuguese in order to obtain a figure comparable with the earlier census.

24. Interviews with high school teachers in 1947. Also, see Yukiko Kimura, "A Sociological Notes on the Preservation of the Portuguese Folk Dance," *Social Process in Hawaii* 19 (1955): pp. 45–50.

Chapter 10

1. The presence of a Buddhist priest was suggestive of a funeral. It was a Japanese custom to throw salt after ominous or unclean events.

2. *Chōshōin Ibunsho* [Collection of writings of Chōshōin, the late Bishop Yemyō Imamura], pp. 35–37.

3. *Chōshōin Ibunsho*, pp. 35–37.

4. Ibid.

5. Ibid. p. 160.

6. *Hawaii Nihonjin Iminshi*, pp. 227–230, 475–477; interviews with priests of major Buddhist sects, 1946.

7. *Hawaii Nihonjin Iminshi*, pp. 477–480; interviews with priests of major Shinto shrines and their wives or widows, 1946.

8. Albertine Loomis, *To All People*, pp. 251, 252.

9. Kenpū Kawazoe, *Ishoku no Hana Hiraku*, p. 171; Harris United Methodist Church, *88th Anniversary*, p. 3.

10. *Hawaii Nihonjin Iminshi*, pp. 139, 224, 225.

11. Ibid., pp. 137, 139. In Tokyo, the *Jiji Shinpo Daily*, reported Ando's temperance under the headline "Consul General Andō Stopped Drinking Sake." Enomoto, the sender of the sake barrels, wrote him, congratulating him for his courage, and sent him boxes of cake and dried fish.

12. Ibid., pp. 138–139.

13. Ibid., p. 139; Harris, *88th Anniversary*, p. 5.

14. Loomis, *To All People*, p. 255; Harris, *88th Anniversary*, pp. 1, 5, 6, 8.

15. Loomis, *To All People*, pp. 253–259, 268. Queen Emma Hall, one of the residences of the queen, was at the corner of Beretania and Bethel streets.

16. Ibid., pp. 291, 282.
17. Ibid., pp. 282, 283.
18. Ibid., p. 297; Sōga, *Gojūnen no Hawaii Kaiko,* p. 219.
19. Sōga, *Gojūnen no Hawaii Kaiko,* p. 406.
20. Ibid., pp. 406–407.
21. Interviews with Nisei businessmen.
22. Sōga, *Gojūnen no Hawaii Kaiko,* p. 409.
23. Ibid., pp. 408–409.
24. Loomis, *To All People,* pp. 269, 270–272, 273, 276, 278. I had the privilege of staying in the Sokabe Home for a couple of days in 1930 and observed the work of the Home personally as well as the plantation life of Honomu.
25. Sōga, *Gojūnen no Hawaii Kaiko,* pp. 138–140.
26. Loomis, To All People, p. 278.
27. Interviews with Mrs. Aiko Reinecke and Miss Edith Tokimasa, 1980.
28. Interviews with Mrs. Chimpei Goto, 1980, 1981, 1982.
29. Ibid.
30. Ibid.
31. Harris, *88th Anniversary,* p. 13; interview with Mrs. Chimpei Goto, 1982.
32. Interview with Mrs. Chimpei Goto, 1982.
33. Ibid.
34. Ibid.

Chapter 11

1. *Hawaii Nihonjin Iminshi,* pp. 135, 136.
2. Seidō Hidegorō Fujii, *Shin Hawaii* [New Hawaii], pp. 640–642.
3. Yasutarō Sōga, *Gojūnen no Hawaii Kaiko,* pp. 510–518.
4. Fujii, *Shin Hawaii,* pp. 475–480.
5. Ibid., pp. 484–491.
6. Ryūkichi Kihara, *Hawaii Nihonjinshi,* pp. 620–622.
7. Kenpū Kawazoe, *Ishoku no Hana Hiraku,* p. 368; *Hawaii Pacific Press,* March 1985, p. 19; Choki Kanetake, *Mokuyo Gosankai Rokujugo-shunen Ko-Moroi Soryoji Tsuito Kinenshi* [Book commemorating the 65th anniversary of the Thursday Luncheon Club in memory of the late Consul General Moroi, its founder].
8. Interviews, 1939, 1981.
9. Kihara, *Hawaii Nihonjinshi,* pp. 175, 177, 179, 181, 182; *Hawaii Nihonjin Iminshi,* p. 217.
10. Ibid.
11. Kihara, *Hawaii Nihonjinshi,* pp. 558–562, 564.
12. *A History of the Japanese in Hawaii,* pp. 213–214; *Hawaii Nihonjin Iminshi,* p. 217.
13. Kawazoe, *Ishoku no Hana Hiraku,* pp. 113, 114–115.
14. Ibid., pp. 188, 189.
15. Fujii, *Shin Hawaii,* pp. 544, 570–572.

16. *Report of the Commissioner of Labor on Hawaii, 1900–1905,* pp. 26, 27.

17. *The Rainbow: A History of the Honolulu Japanese Chamber of Commerce,* Japanese section, pp. 40–41.

18. Ibid., pp. 47, 48.

19. *Hawaii Nihonjin Iminshi,* p. 316.

20. Ibid., pp. 297, 462.

21. *A History of Japanese in Hawaii,* pp. 231–232.

22. Sōga, *Gojūnen no Hawaii Kaiko,* pp. 79, 80, 81.

23. Ibid., pp. 166–167.

24. *A History of Japanese in Hawaii,* p. 111.

25. Ernest Wakukawa, *A History of the Japanese People in Hawaii,* pp. 163–164.

26. Kenpū Kawazoe, *Imin Hyakunen no Nenrin,* pp. 221, 222.

27. Sōga, *Gojūnen no Hawaii Kaiko,* p. 165; Kawazoe, *Imin Hyakunen,* pp. 221, 222.

28. The people in Japan were familiar with the Russo-Japanese War because it was part of history and taught in the schools.

29. Kawazoe, *Imin Hyakunen no Nenrin,* pp. 223, 224.

30. Wakukawa, *History of Japanese People in Hawaii,* pp. 327–329.

31. Tsuneichi Yamamoto, ed., *Life of Kinzaburo Makino,* pp. 29–31.

32. Ibid., pp. 83–84.

33. *Hawaii Times,* January 1, 1976; Albertine Loomis, *To All People,* pp. 270–271; Wakukawa, *History of Japanese People in Hawaii,* pp. 265, 266.

34. *A History of Japanese in Hawaii,* p. 216.

35. *Hawaii Nihonjin Iminshi,* pp. 236–237.

36. Ibid., p. 238; Wakukawa, *History of Japanese People in Hawaii,* pp. 277, 278.

37. Wakukawa, *History of Japanese People in Hawaii,* p. 286.

38. Ibid., p. 288.

39. Sōga, *Gojūnen no Hawaii Kaiko,* p. 350; Yamamoto, *Life of Kinzaburo Makino,* pp. 51–52.

40. Wakukawa, *History of Japanese People in Hawaii,* pp. 289, 290.

41. Ibid., pp. 291, 292.

42. *A History of Japanese in Hawaii,* p. 222.

43. Wakukawa, *History of Japanese People in Hawaii,* pp. 223, 293, 295, 296.

44. Ibid., pp. 298–300.

45. Ibid., p. 299.

46. Ibid., p. 302.

47. *Hawaii Nihonjin Iminshi,* p. 468.

Chapter 12

1. Ralph S. Kuykendall, *Hawaii in the World War,* vol. 2, pp. 3–6; Ernest Wakukawa, *A History of the Japanese People in Hawaii,* pp. 192–196, 198–200.

2. Kuykendall, *Hawaii in the World War,* vol. 2, pp. 16–19.

3. Ibid., pp. 22, 49, 50, 54–56; Wakukawa, *History of Japanese People in Hawaii*, p. 205.

4. Wakukawa, *History of Japanese People in Hawaii*, pp. 205, 206.

5. Kenpū Kawazoe, *Imin Hyakunen no Nenrin*, pp. 283–286.

6. Yasutarō Sōga, *Gojūnen no Hawaii Kaiko*, pp. 300, 303; Kuykendall, *Hawaii in the World War*, vol. 2, pp. 57–58, 61–64.

7. Ryūkichi Kihara, *Hawaii Nihonjinshi*, pp. 618–619.

8. Kuykendall, *Hawaii in the World War*, vol. 2, pp. 328–329, 339–341, 344.

9. Ibid., pp. 337–340.

10. Ibid., pp. 373, 374, 376, 378.

11. Ibid., pp. 335–336, 341.

12. Ibid., pp. 343, 348, 362.

13. Ibid., pp. 324–325; Wakukawa, *History of Japanese People in Hawaii*, pp. 208, 209; Sōga, *Gojūnen no Hawaii Kaiko*, p. 304.

14. Kuykendall, *Hawaii in the World War*, vol. 2, pp. 136, 137, 140; Wakukawa, *History of Japanese People in Hawaii*, p. 273; Sōga, *Gojūnen no Hawaii Kaiko*, p. 300; Kawazoe, *Imin Hyakunen no Nenrin*, p. 273.

15. Sōga, *Gojūnen no Hawaii Kaiko*, pp. 302–303; Kuykendall, *Hawaii in the World War*, pp. 101–104; interviews and personal knowledge of this author during World War II.

16. Wakukawa, *History of Japanese People in Hawaii*, pp. 312–317.

Chapter 13

1. Yasutarō Sōga, *Gojūnen no Hawaii Kaiko*, pp. 538–539.

2. Reverend Okumura told his experiences to me when I was the general secretary of the YWCA in Nagoya, Japan.

3. Hugh Byas, *Government by Assassination*, pp. 119–127. The seventeen officers of the Japanese army responsible for the 226 Incident were punished in the same year, 1936. *Saishin Sekai Nempyō, Shintei-han*, p. 387.

4. Sōga, *Gojūnen no Hawaii Kaiko*, p. 559.

5. Ibid., pp. 534–535.

6. *Nippu Jiji*, October 1939; also personal accounts by Chinese in Hawaii about their families and relatives in China.

7. Sōga, *Gojūnen no Hawaii Kaiko*, pp. 561, 562.

8. Ibid., p. 560.

9. Ibid., p. 596–597.

10. Ibid., pp. 652–654.

11. *Hawaii Nihonjin Iminshi*, pp. 113, 114.

12. Robert L. Shivers, *Cooperation of Racial Groups in Hawaii during the War*, p. 2.

13. Ibid., pp. 2, 4.

14. Ibid., pp. 2–3; priests of Buddhist and Shinto temples, principals of Japanese language schools, publishers and editors of Japanese vernacular papers, officials of the Japanese Chamber of Commerce and the Japanese banks, successful businessmen and community leaders—all were detained throughout the war

years, not because of proven disloyalty to the United States but because they were leaders of the Issei community.

15. Ibid., pp. 5, 6.
16. Ibid., p. 6.
17. Ibid., pp. 6–7.
18. Ibid., pp. 7–8.
19. Ibid., pp. 4–5.
20. Ibid., p. 5.

Chapter 14

1. Gwenfread Allen, *Hawaii's War Years: 1941–1945,* pp. 2–5, 9, 33, 34, 149; also my personal observations.
2. Ibid., p. 143.
3. Robert L. Shivers, *Cooperation of Racial Groups in Hawaii during the War,* p. 5.
4. Allen, *Hawaii's War Years,* pp. 141, 142.
5. My personal observations and visits to families of internees.
6. Personal observations on December 7, 1941.
7. Keihō [Yasutarō] Sōga, *Tessaku Seikatsu* [Life behind the barbed-wire fence], pp. 1–2, 3–5. Keihō was Sōga's pen name.
8. Ted T. Tsukiyama, "Varsity Victory Volunteers, Pearl Harbor Tragedy and Triumph," *Honolulu Star-Bulletin,* December 7, 1978.
9. Interview, 1977.
10. Allen, *Hawaii's War Years,* pp. 39, 133, 143. The only person convicted of espionage in Hawaii was Otto Kuehn, a German, who came to Hawaii several years before the Pearl Harbor attack. He worked for the Japanese Consul General. He developed an elaborate signal system, but it was never used. The military commission sentenced him to death, but the United States Attorney General reduced his sentence to 50 years of imprisonment, the maximum penalty for peacetime espionage. Later he was deported to Germany. Yasutaro Soga, one of the Japanese detainees at the Immigration Service building, noted that Kuehn was confined in a solitary cell and his wife and daughter were in a separate room. (Tessaku Seikatsu, p. 41)
11. Shivers, *Cooperation of Racial Groups,* p. 3.
12. Allen, *Hawaii's War Years,* p. 138.
13. Sōga, *Tessaku Seikatsu,* pp. 16, 17.
14. *Letter to All Principals and Teachers,* January 10, 1942. Miscellaneous Circular no. 669, Department of Public Instruction, Territory of Hawaii, Honolulu.
15. Ibid., January 12, 1942.
16. Interview with a former language school principal who returned from internment on the U.S. mainland after the war. Very similar sentiments were expressed by the returned internees who had sons in the army.
17. Interview with the wife of an interned language school principal, 1942.
18. Interview, 1942.

19. Shivers, *Cooperation of Racial Groups,* p. 10.

20. Ibid., p. 9. The key members of the Morale Section were Hung Wai Ching, Shigeo Yoshida, and Charles Loomis.

21. Ibid., pp. 9, 10.

22. *Report of the Emergency Service Committee,* p. 2.

23. Ibid., p. 6.

24. From conversations with Issei whom I visited in January 1942. I received permission from Military Intelligence to visit Japanese families in the Japanese neighborhoods.

25. Carey McWilliams, *Prejudice: Japanese Americans, Symbol of Racial Intolerance,* pp. 144, 145.

26. Tsukiyama, "Varsity Victory Volunteers."

27. Ibid.

28. Ibid.

29. Ibid.

30. Allen, *Hawaii's War Years,* pp. 266, 267.

31. Ibid., pp. 271, 272.

32. Ibid., pp. 267–268.

33. Ibid., pp. 268–269.

34. Ibid., p. 272.

35. Comments of Issei women participants in the International Institute of the Honolulu YWCA service clubs.

36. Allen, *Hawaii's War Years,* p. 272.

37. Ibid., p. 264.

38. Ibid.; participant observation; *Final Report of Women's War Service Association,* June 30, 1946, p. 5.

39. Interview, 1947.

40. Interviews with the doctor and with his household service couple, 1946.

Chapter 15

1. Interview, 1945.

2. Interview, 1945.

3. Interview, 1945.

4. Interview, 1945.

5. Interview, 1945.

6. Interviews with ex-Katta-gumi leaders, 1946–1947.

7. Interview with staff of Foreign Funds Control, 1946. The Foreign Funds Control was a wartime federal agency that controlled the assets of enemy aliens. Evidently, the issuing of licenses to new organizations was part of its duties.

8. Participant observation, 1946.

9. This pamphlet indicated that the writer of the article was a former ambassador to Italy.

10. The Imperial Rescript of Education was promulgated on October 30, 1890. The *Colorado Times* mentioned Premier Koiso's broadcast on the anniversary of the Imperial Rescript on Education on October 30, 1944. Therefore, this article must have been written shortly after that.

11. A copy of this pamphlet was in my possession at the time.

12. Participant observation, 1946.

13. Interviews with all the Buddhist priests who returned from internment on the mainland, 1946.

14. Participant observation, 1946.

15. Interviews, 1947.

16. Gwenfread Allen, *Hawaii's War Years: 1941–1945*, pp. 195, 196. There were 320 Japanese prisoners of war on Oahu at the end of the war. They were repatriated in December 1946.

17. Interviews with Katta-gumi leaders, 1947.

18. Ibid.

19. Ibid.

20. *Hawaii Herald (Hawaii Hochi)*, December 7, 1950; *Hawaii Times*, June 3, 1950; *Hawaii Times*, May 26, 1951. The relief goods were shipped in August 1947 by two of the Katta-gumi groups, the Palama Kōsei-kai and the Honolulu Tōbu Dōshi-kai, for some four thousand wounded Japanese soldiers in ten national hospitals in prefectures such as Tokyo, Kanagawa, Niigata, Shizuoka, and Fukuoka. The combined members of these two groups was 471. Later, joined by other former Katta-gumi groups such as Kalihi Hakkō-kai, Hawaii Dōshi-kai, Waipahu Sekisei-kai, Waianae Nihonjin Dōshi-kai, and Palolo Kannon (not all of whom were Katta-gumi), they raised over $4,000 for the work of *Yūai Juji-kai* for its work toward the rehabilitation of wounded Japanese soldiers. They also began to solicit donations to help Japanese soldiers in nine other hospitals in Hiroshima and Yamaguchi prefectures. The *Hawaii Times* of May 26, 1951, reported more ambitious fundraising of $10,000 by March 1952. Along with their request for donations, Palama Kōsei-kai and Honolulu Tōbu Dōshi-kai published the following public statement:

> Due to misconceptions about our groups, we are unable to get cooperation from some of the Japanese population. Therefore, we take this opportunity to explain in order to clear up the misconception. It is true that in the past some of our members did not believe the defeat of Japan. But now we recognize Japan's defeat without any reservations. We are trying to overcome the hardships that resulted from the war so that Japan will again be able to join the international community. We deeply regret the troubles we caused in many places of the Japanese community in the past and we plead for your generous and wise understanding of our intentions.

21. Interviews with plantation laborers, 1947.

22. Interview, 1947.

23. Interview, 1947.

24. Kenpū Kawazoe, *Ishoku no Hana Hiraku*, pp. 462–463.

25. *Nippu Jiji Golden Jubilee Edition*, February 1935.

Bibliography

Adams, Romanzo. *The Japanese in Hawaii*. New York: The National Committee on American Japanese Relations, 1924.

———. *The Peoples of Hawaii*. Honolulu: American Council, Institute of Pacific Relations, 1935.

Allen, Gwenfread. *Hawaii's War Years: 1941–1945*. Honolulu: University of Hawaii Press, 1949.

Board of Immigration Reports 1878–99.

Byas, Hugh. *Government by Assassination*. New York: Knopt, 1942.

Chōshōin Ibunsho (Collection of Writings of Chōshōin, the late Bishop Yemyō Imamura). Honolulu: Hawaii Hongwanji Mission, 1937.

Dean, Arthur L., "A Memorial: Dr. Romanzo Adams," *Social Process in Hawaii*, Vol. 3.

88th Anniversary: 1888–1976. Harris United Methodist Church. Honolulu, Hawaii, 1976.

Embree, John F. *Acculturation among the Japanese of Kona, Hawaii*. Memoirs of the American Anthropological Association, American Anthropological Association. Mensha, Wisconsin, 1941.

Final Report of Women's War Service Association. Honolulu, 1946.

The Friend. Honolulu, Hawaii, June, 1913.

Fujii, Seidō Hidegorō. *Shin Hawaii* (New Hawaii). Tokyo: Bunkensha, 1902.

Fukushima Isseiki (The Century of Fukushima). Fukushima City, Japan: Fukushima Minyū Shinbunsha, 1976.

Furuya, Suikei Kumaji. *Imin no Rakugaki* (An Immigrant's Scribbling). Honolulu: Hawaii Times, 1968.

———. *Haisho Tenten* (Exile from place to place), Honolulu: Hawaii Times, 1964.

Golden Jubilee of the Government Contract Japanese Immigration to Hawaii: 1885–1935. Honolulu: Nippu Jiji, 1935.

Hawaiian Japanese Annual & Directory, 1928, 1934–35, 39–40, Honolulu: Nippu Jiji Co. Ltd.

Hawaii Herald (Hawaii Hochi). December 7, 1950.

Hawaii Pacific Press. June and July, 1980.

Hawaii Times. June 3, 1950; May 26, 1951.

Hawaii Nihonjin Iminshi: Hawaii Kanyaku Imin 75-nen Kinen (A History of Hawaii's Japanese Immigration: Commemoration of the 75th Anniversary of Government Contract Immigration). Honolulu: United Japanese Society of Hawaii, 1964.

A History of Japanese in Hawaii. Honolulu: United Japanese Society of Hawaii, 1971.

Historical Highlights, Dole-Hawaii. Honolulu: Castle & Cook, Inc., 1977.

Kanetake, Choki. *Mokuyo Gosankai Rokujugo-shunen Ko-Moroi Soryoji Tsuito Kinenshi* (Book commemorating the 65th anniversary of the Thursday Luncheon Club in memory of the late Consul General Moroi, its Founder).

Katsunuma, Tomizō. *Kansho no Shiborikasu* (Dregs of Sugar Canes). Honolulu: Katsunuma Kinen Publishing Society, 1924.

Kawazoe, Kenpū Zenichi. *Imin Hyakunen no Nenrin* (Annual Rings of One Hundred Years of Immigration). Honolulu: Imin Hyakunen no Nenrin Publishing Society, 1968.

———. *Ishoku no Hana Hiraku* (Blossoming of Transplanted Trees). Honolulu: Ishoku no Hana Hiraku Publishing Society, 1960.

Kihara, Ryūkichi. *Hawaii Nihonjinshi* (A History of Japanese in Hawaii). Tokyo: Benseisha, 1935.

Kimura, Yukiko, "A Sociological Note on the Preservation of the Portuguese Folk Dance," *Social Process in Hawaii,* Vol. 19, 1955.

———. "Sociological Significance of Japanese Language School Campaign in Hawaii," *Social Process in Hawaii,* 1956.

Ko Okazaki Nihei-Oh Tsuitō Kinenshi (The Memorial Booklet Honoring the late Venerable Nihei Okazaki). Fukushima City, Japan: Fikushima Hawaii-kai, 1952.

Kuykendall, Ralph S. *The Earliest Japanese Labor Immigration to Hawaii.* Honolulu: University of Hawaii, 1935.

———. *The Hawaiian Kingdom 1778–1854: Foundation and Transformation, Vol. 1.* Honolulu: University of Hawaii Press, 1938.

———. *The Hawaiian Kingdom 1854–1874, Twenty Critical Years, Vol. 2.* Honolulu: University of Hawaii Press, 1953.

———. *The Hawaiian Kingdom 1874–1893, Vol. 3.* Honolulu: University of Hawaii Press, 1967.

———. *Hawaii in the World War, Vol. 2.* Honolulu: The Historical Commission, 1928.

Loomis, Albertine. *To All People.* The Hawaii Conference of the United Church of Christ, Honolulu, Hawaii, 1970.

McWilliams, Carey. *Prejudice: Japanese Americans, Symbol of Racial Intolerance.* Boston: Little, Brown and Company, 1945.

Mizu no Maki of Seimei no Jissō (Vol. Water of Reality of Life, the Bible of Seichō no Ie). Tokyo: Kyobunsha, 1933.

Nihon Rekishi Daijiten (Encyclopedia of Japanese History) Vol. 12. Tokyo: Kawado Shobō, 1958.

Ōkubo, Kiyoshi. *Hawaii tō Nihonjin Iminshi* (A History of Japanese Immigrants on the Island of Hawaii). Hilo: *Hilo Times,* 1972.

Ōtani, Matsujiro. *Waga Hito to Narishi Ashiato: Hachijūnen no Kaiko* (My Memoir of 80 Years of My Footsteps). Honolulu: M. Otani Company, Ltd., 1971.

The Rainbow: A History of the Honolulu Japanese Chamber of Commerce. Honolulu: Honolulu Japanese Chamber of Commerce, 1970.

Reports of the Bureau of Immigration for Year Ending December 31, 1898.

Reports of the Commissioner of Labor on Hawaii 1900–1905.

Report of the Emergency Service Committee, Honolulu: Emergency Service Committee, 1944.

Sakihara, Mitsugu. *Gajimaru no Tsudoi: Stories of the Okinawan Immigrants in Hawaii.* Honolulu: Gajimaru-kai, 1980.

Saishin Sekai Nempyō, Shintei-han (Newest World Chronological Tables, Revised Edition). Tokyo: Sanseido, 1959.

Shivers, Robert L. *Cooperation of Racial Groups in Hawaii During the War.* Honolulu: Territorial Emergency Service Committee, 1946.

Sōga, Keihō Yasutarō. *Gojūnen no Hawaii Kaiko* (My Memoir of Fifty Years in Hawaii). Honolulu: Gojunen no Hawaii Kaiko Publishing Society, 1953.

———. *Tessaku Seikatsu* (Life Behind Barbed-Wire Fence). Honolulu: *Hawaii Times,* 1955.

The Story of Pineapple in Hawaii. (pamphlet) The Pineapple Growers' Association of Hawaii.

Takahashi, Kanji. *Fukushima Iminshi: Hawaii Kikansha no Maki* (A History of Overseas Emigration of Fukushimans: Vol. on Returned Former Emigrants to Hawaii). Fukushima City, Japan: Fukushima Hawaii-kai, 1958.

Tsukiyama, Ted T. "Varsity Victory Volunteers, Pearl Harbor Tragedy and Triumph." *Honolulu Star-Bulletin,* December 7, 1978.

Tuna: Hawaii's Harvest of the Sea. (brochure) Hawaiian Tuna Packers, Honolulu, Hawaii.

Wakukawa, Ernest K. *A History of the Japanese People in Hawaii.* Honolulu: Toyo Shoin, 1938.

Wakukawa, Seiyei. "Hawaii Okinawa Kenjin Shishō" (Excerpts from the History of the Okinawa Kenjin in Hawaii). *Okinawa, Hawaii Special Edition.* Tokyo: Okinawasha, March, 1951.

———. *The Life and Times of Kyūzō Tōyama.* Honolulu: Tōyama Kyūzō Memorial Committee, 1955.

Watanabe, Yakichi. *Hawaii Zaijū Fukushima Kenjin Ryakureki Shashinchō* (Album of Pictures and Personal Records of Fukushimans in Hawaii). Maui, Hawaii, 1955.

Yamamoto, Tsuneichi (editor). *Life of Kinzaburo Makino.* Honolulu: Committee for Publication of Kinzaburo Makino's Biography, 1977.

Index

281

About the Author

Yukiko Kimura was born in Yokohama, Japan, and graduated from the Ferris Presbyterian Mission College. She held various YWCA positions in Japan, Australia, and New Zealand. She came to the United States in 1935 for graduate study at Oberlin College, where she received an M.A. in religious education. She worked for the International Institute of the Honolulu YWCA from 1938 to 1944, responsible for the work among the Japanese. She earned an M.A. in sociology from the University of Hawaii. After receiving her Ph.D. from the University of Chicago in 1952, Kimura returned to Honolulu and worked at the Romanzo Adams Social Research Laboratory at the University of Hawaii until her retirement.

Production Notes

This book was designed by Roger Eggers.
Composition and paging were done on the
Quadex Composing System and typesetting
on the Compugraphic 8400 by the design
and production staff of University of
Hawaii Press.

The text typeface is Sabon and the
display typeface is Galliard.

Offset presswork and binding were done by
Vail-Ballou Press, Inc. Text paper is
Glatfelter Offset Vellum, basis 50.